THRIVE

ARIANNA HUFFINGTON

THRIVE

The Third Metric to Redefining
Success and Creating a Happier Life

2 4 6 8 10 9 7 5 3 1

First published in the United States in 2014 by Harmony Books,
An imprint of the Crown Publishing Group, a division of Random House LLC

First published in the United Kingdom in 2014 by WH Allen,
an imprint of Ebury Publishing
A Random House Group Company

Addresses for companies within The Random House Group Limited can
be found at: www.randomhouse.co.uk/offices.htm

The Random House Group Limited Reg. No. 954009

A CIP catalogue record for this book
is available from the British Library

The Random House Group Limited supports the Forest Stewardship
Council® (FSC®), the leading international forest-certification organisation.
Our books carrying the FSC label are printed on FSC®-certified paper.
FSC is the only forest-certification scheme supported by the leading
environmental organisations, including Greenpeace.
Our paper procurement policy can be found at:
www.randomhouse.co.uk/environment

Printed and bound by Clays Ltd, St Ives plc

Hardback ISBN: 9780753555408
Trade Paperback ISBN: 9780753555415

To buy books by your favourite authors and register for offers, visit:
www.randomhouse.co.uk

For my mother, Elli,
who embodied wisdom, wonder, and giving, and made
writing this book a homecoming

Contents

Thrive

Introduction

O N   T H E   morning of April 6, 2007, I was lying on the floor of my home office in a pool of blood. On my way down, my head had hit the corner of my desk, cutting my eye and breaking my cheekbone. I had collapsed from exhaustion and lack of sleep. In the wake of my collapse, I found myself going from doctor to doctor, from brain MRI to CAT scan to echocardiogram, to find out if there was any underlying medical problem beyond exhaustion. There wasn't, but doctors' waiting rooms, it turns out, were good places for me to ask myself a lot of questions about the kind of life I was living.

We founded *The Huffington Post* in 2005, and two years in we were growing at an incredible pace. I was on the cover of magazines and had been chosen by *Time* as one of the world's 100 Most Influential People. But after my fall, I had to ask myself, Was this what success looked like? Was this the life I wanted? I was working eighteen hours a day, seven days a week, trying to build a business, expand our coverage, and bring in investors. But my life, I realized, was out of control. In terms of the traditional measures of success, which focus on money and power, I was very successful. But I was not living a successful life by any sane definition of success. I knew something had to radically change. I could not go on that way.

This was a classic wake-up call. Looking back on my life, I had other times when I should have woken up but didn't. This time I really did and made many changes in the way I live my life, including adopting daily practices to keep me on track—and out of doctors' waiting rooms. The result is a more fulfilling life, one that gives me breathing spaces and a deeper perspective.

This book was conceived as I tried to pull together all the insights I had gleaned about my work and life during the weeks I spent writing the commencement speech I was to give to the class of 2013 at Smith College. With two daughters in college, I take commencement speeches very seriously. It's such a special moment for the graduating class—a pause, a kind of parenthesis in time following four (or five, or six) years of nonstop learning and growing just before the start of an adult life spent moving forward and putting all of that knowledge into action. It's a unique marker in their lives—and for fifteen minutes or so I have the graduates' undivided attention. The challenge is to say something equal to the occasion, something that will be useful during a charged time of new beginnings.

"Commencement speakers," I told the women graduates, "are traditionally expected to tell the graduating class how to go out there and climb the ladder of success. But I want to ask you instead to redefine success. Because the world you are headed into desperately needs it. And because you are up to the challenge. Your education at Smith has made it unequivocally clear that you are entitled to take your place in the world wherever you want that place to be. You can work in any field, and you can make it to the top of any field. But what I urge you to do is not just take your place at the top of the world, but to change the world."

The moving response to the speech made me realize how widespread is the longing among so many of us to redefine success and what it means to lead "the good life."

"What is a good life?" has been a question asked by philosophers going back to the ancient Greeks. But somewhere along the line we abandoned the question and shifted our attention to how much money we can make, how big a house we can buy, and how high we can climb up the career ladder. Those are legitimate questions, particularly at a time when women are still attempting to gain an equal seat at the table. But as I painfully discovered, they are far from the only questions that matter in creating a successful life.

Over time our society's notion of success has been reduced to money and power. In fact, at this point, success, money, and power have practically become synonymous in the minds of many.

This idea of success can work—or at least appear to work—in the short term. But over the long term, money and power by themselves are like a two-legged stool—you can balance on them for a while, but eventually you're going to topple over. And more and more people—very successful people—are toppling over.

So what I pointed out to the Smith College graduates was that the way we've defined success is not enough. And it's no longer sustainable: It's no longer sustainable for human beings or for societies. To live the lives we truly want and deserve, and not just the lives we settle for, we need a Third Metric, a third measure of success that goes beyond the two metrics of money and power, and consists of four pillars: well-being, wisdom, wonder, and giving. These four pillars make up the four sections of this book.

First, well-being: If we don't redefine what success is, the price we pay in terms of our health and well-being will continue to rise, as I found out in my own life. As my eyes opened, I saw that this new phase in my life was very much in tune with the zeitgeist, the spirit of our times. Every conversation I had seemed to eventually come around to the same dilemmas we are all facing—the stress of over-busyness, overworking, overconnecting on social media, and underconnecting with ourselves and with one another. The space, the gaps, the pauses, the silence—those things that allow us to regenerate and recharge—had all but disappeared in my own life and in the lives of so many I knew.

It seemed to me that the people who were genuinely thriving in their lives were the ones who had made room for well-being, wisdom, wonder, and giving. Hence the "Third Metric" was born—the third leg of the stool in living a successful life. What started with redefining my own life path and priorities led me to see an awakening that is taking place globally. We are entering a new era. How we measure success is changing.

And it's changing not a moment too soon—especially for women, since a growing body of data shows that the price of the current false promise of success is already higher for women than it is for men. Women in stressful jobs have a nearly 40 percent increased risk of heart disease, and a

60 percent greater risk of diabetes. In the past thirty years, as women have made substantial strides in the workplace, self-reported levels of stress have gone up 18 percent.

Those who have just started out in the workforce—and those who haven't even yet begun—are already feeling the effects. According to the American Psychological Association, the millennial generation is at the top of the chart for stress levels—more so than baby boomers and "matures," as the study dubbed those over sixty-seven.

The Western workplace culture—exported to many other parts of the world—is practically fueled by stress, sleep deprivation, and burnout. I had come face-to-face—or, I should say, face-to-floor—with the problem when I collapsed. Even as stress undermines our health, the sleep deprivation so many of us experience in striving to get ahead at work is profoundly—and negatively—affecting our creativity, our productivity, and our decision making. The *Exxon Valdez* wreck, the explosion of the *Challenger* space shuttle, and the nuclear accidents at Chernobyl and Three Mile Island all were at least partially caused by a lack of sleep.

And in the winter of 2013, the deadly Metro-North derailment caused whilst William Rockefeller, the engineer was at the controls, focused national attention on the dangers of sleep deprivation throughout the transportation industry. The investigation into the crash is ongoing at the time of writing but a union official stated that Rockefeller "nodded off" at the controls and "zoned out" before the accident, and Rockefeller's lawyer describes the engineer as having gone into a "daze" whilst driving the commuter train. As John Paul Wright, an engineer for one of the country's largest freight rail operators, put it, "The biggest issue with railroad workers is fatigue, not pay. We are paid very well. But we sacrifice our bodies and minds to work the long hours it takes to make the money, not to mention the high divorce rate, self-medicating, and stress."

Over 30 percent of people in the United States and the United Kingdom are not getting enough sleep. And it's not just decision making and cognitive functions that take a hit. Even traits that we associate with our core personality and values are affected by too little sleep. According to a study from the Walter Reed Army Institute of Research, sleep deprivation reduces our emotional intelligence, self-regard, assertiveness, sense of independence, empathy toward others, the quality of our interpersonal relationships, positive thinking, and impulse control. In fact, the only thing the study found that gets better with sleep deprivation is "magical thinking" and reliance on superstition. So if you're interested in fortune-telling, go ahead and burn the midnight oil. For the rest of us, we need to redefine what we value, and change workplace culture so that working till all hours and walking around exhausted become stigmatized instead of lauded.

In the new definition of success, building and looking after our financial capital is not enough. We need to do everything we can to protect and nurture our human capital. My mother was an expert at that. I still remember, when I was twelve years old, a very successful Greek businessman coming over to our home for dinner. He looked rundown and exhausted. But when we sat down to dinner, he told us how well things were going for him. He was thrilled about a contract he had just won to build a new museum. My mother was not impressed. "I don't care how well your business is doing," she told him bluntly, "you're not taking care of you. Your business might have a great bottom line, but you are your most important capital. There are only so many withdrawals you can make from your health bank account, but you just keep on withdrawing. You could go bankrupt if you don't make some deposits soon." And indeed, not long after that, the man had to be rushed to the hospital for an emergency angioplasty.

When we include our own well-being in our definition of success, another thing that changes is our relationship with time. There is even a term now for our stressed-out sense that there's never enough time for what we want to do—"time famine." Every time we look at our watches it seems to be later than we think. I personally have always had a very strained relationship with time. Dr. Seuss summed it up beautifully: "How did it get so late so soon?" he wrote. "It's night before it's afternoon. December is here before it's June. My goodness how the time has flewn. How did it get so late so soon?"

Sound familiar?

And when we're living a life of perpetual time famine, we rob ourselves of our ability to experience another key element of the Third Metric: wonder, our sense of delight in the mysteries of the universe, as well as the everyday occurrences and small miracles that fill our lives.

Another of my mother's gifts was to be in a constant state of wonder at the world around her. Whether she was washing dishes or feeding seagulls at the beach or reprimanding overworking businessmen, she maintained her sense of wonder at life. And whenever I'd complain or was upset about something in my own life, my mother had the same advice: "Darling, just change the channel. You are in control of the clicker. Don't replay the bad, scary movie."

Well-being, wonder. Both of these are key to creating the Third Metric. And then there is the third indispensable W in redefining success: wisdom.

Wherever we look around the world, we see smart leaders—in politics, in business, in media—making terrible decisions. What they're lacking is not IQ, but wisdom. Which is no surprise; it has never been harder to tap into our inner wisdom, because in order to do so, we have to disconnect from all our omnipresent devices—our gadgets, our screens, our social media—and reconnect with ourselves.

To be honest, it's not something that comes naturally to me. The last time my mother got angry with me before she died was when she saw me reading my email and talking to my children at the same time. "I abhor multitasking," she said, in a Greek accent that puts mine to shame. In other words, being connected in a shallow way to the entire world can prevent us from being deeply connected to those closest to us—including ourselves. And that is where wisdom is found.

I'm convinced of two fundamental truths about human beings. The first is that we all have within us a centered place of wisdom, harmony, and strength. This is a truth that all the world's philosophies and religions—whether Christianity, Islam, Judaism, or Buddhism—acknowledge in one form or another: "The kingdom of God is within you." Or as Archimedes said, "Give me a place to stand, and I will move the world."

The second truth is that we're all going to veer away from that place again and again and again. That's the nature of life. In fact, we may be off course more often than we are on course.

The question is how quickly can we get back to that centered place of wisdom, harmony, and strength. It's in this sacred place that life is transformed from struggle to grace, and we are suddenly filled with trust, whatever our obstacles, challenges, or disappointments. As Steve Jobs said in his now legendary commencement address at Stanford, "You can't connect the dots looking forward; you can only connect them looking backwards. So you have to trust that the dots will somehow connect in your future. You have to trust in something—your gut, destiny, life, karma, whatever. This approach has never let me down, and it has made all the difference in my life."

There is a purpose to our lives, even if it is sometimes hidden from us, and even if the biggest turning points and heartbreaks only make sense as we look back, rather than as we are experiencing them. So we might as well live life as if—as the poet Rumi put it—everything is rigged in our favor.

But our ability to regularly get back to this place of wisdom—like so many other abilities—depends on how much we practice and how important we make it in our lives. And burnout makes it much harder to tap into our wisdom. In an op-ed in *The New York Times*, Erin Callan, former chief financial officer of Lehman Brothers, who left the firm a few months before it went bankrupt, wrote about the lessons she learned about experiencing burnout: "Work always came first, before my family, friends and marriage—which ended just a few years later."

Looking back, she realized how counterproductive overworking was. "I now believe that I could have made it to a similar place with at least some better version of a personal life," she wrote. In fact, working to the point of burnout wasn't just bad for her personally. It was also, we now know, bad for Lehman Brothers, which no longer exists. After all, the function of leadership is to be able to see the iceberg before it hits the *Titanic*. And when you're burned out and exhausted, it's much harder to see clearly the dangers—or opportunities—ahead. And that's the connection we need to start making if we want to accelerate changing the way we live and work.

Well-being, wisdom, and wonder. The last element to the Third Metric of success is the willingness to give of ourselves, prompted by our empathy and compassion.

America's Founding Fathers thought enough of the idea of the pursuit of happiness to enshrine it in the Declaration of Independence. But their notion of this "unalienable right" did not mean the pursuit of more ways for us to be entertained. Rather, it was the happiness that comes from feeling good by doing good. It was the happiness that comes from being a productive part of a community and contributing to its greater good.

There is plenty of scientific data that shows unequivocally that empathy and service increase our own well-being. That's how the elements of the Third Metric of success become part of a virtuous cycle.

If you are lucky, you have a "final straw" moment before it's too late. For me, it was collapsing from exhaustion in 2007. For *New York Times* food writer Mark Bittman, it was obsessively checking his email via his in-seat phone on a transatlantic flight, leading him to confess, "My name is Mark, and I'm a techno-addict." For Carl Honoré, author of *In Praise of Slowness: How a Worldwide Movement Is Challenging the Cult of Speed*, it was contemplating "one-minute bedtime stories" for his two-year-old son to save time. For Aetna CEO Mark Bertolini, it was a skiing accident that left him with a broken neck and eventually led him to the rejuvenating practices of yoga and meditation. For HopeLab president Pat Christen, it was the alarming realization that, due to her dependence on technology, "I had stopped looking in my children's eyes." For Anna Holmes, the founder of the site Jezebel, it was the realization that the deal she had made with herself came at a very high price: "I realized, 'Okay, if I work at 110 percent, I get good results. If I work a little harder, I'll get even more out of it.' The caveat of this success, however, had personal repercussions: I never relaxed. . . . I was increasingly stressed. . . . Not only was I posting once every ten minutes for twelve hours straight, but I also worked for the two and a half hours before we started posting and late into the night to prepare for the next day." She finally decided to leave Jezebel. "It took over a year to decompress . . . a year until I was focusing more on myself than on what was happening on the Internet."

Since my own final straw moment, I have become an evangelist for the need to disconnect from our always-connected lives and reconnect with ourselves. It has guided the editorial philosophy behind *HuffPost*'s twenty-six Lifestyle sections in the United States, in which we promote the ways that we can take care of ourselves and lead balanced, centered lives while making a positive difference in the world. As *HuffPost* is spreading around the world, we're incorporating this editorial priority into all our international editions—in Canada, the United Kingdom, France, Italy, Spain, Germany, as well as in Japan, Brazil, and South Korea.

I remember it as if it were yesterday: I was twenty-three years old and I was on a promotional tour for my first book, *The Female Woman*, which had become an unexpected international bestseller. I was sitting in my room in some anonymous European hotel. The room could have been a beautifully arranged still life. There were yellow roses on the desk, Swiss chocolates by my bed, and French champagne on ice. The only noise was the crackling of the ice as it slowly melted into water. The voice in my head was much louder. "Is that all there is?" Like a broken record, the question famously posed by Peggy Lee (for those old enough to remember) kept repeating itself in my brain, robbing me of the joy I had expected to find in my success. "Is that really all there is?" If this is "living," then what is life? Can the goal of life really be just about money and recognition? From a part of myself, deep inside me—from the part of me that is my mother's daughter—came a resounding "No!" It is an answer that turned me gradually but firmly away from lucrative offers to speak and write again and again on the subject of "the female woman." It started me instead on the first step of a long journey.

My journey from that first moment of recognition that I didn't want to live my life within the boundaries of what our culture defined as success was hardly a straight line. At times it was more like a spiral, with a lot of downturns when I found myself caught up in the very whirlwind that I knew would not lead to the life I most wanted.

That's how strong is the pull of the first two metrics, even for someone as blessed as I was to have a mother who lived a Third Metric life before I knew what the Third Metric was. That's why this book is a kind of a homecoming for me.

When I first lived in New York in the eighties, I found myself at lunches and dinners with people who had achieved the first two metrics of success—money and power—but who were still looking for something more. Lacking a line of royalty in America, we have elevated to princely realms the biggest champions of money and power. Since one gains today's throne not by fortune of birth but by the visible markers of success, we dream of the means by which we might be crowned. Or perhaps it's the constant expectation, drummed into us from childhood, that no matter how humble our origins we, too, can achieve the American dream. And the American dream, which has been exported all over the world, is currently defined as the acquisition of things: houses, cars, boats, jets, and other grown-up toys.

But I believe the second decade of this new century is already very different. There are, of course, still millions of people who equate success with money and power—who are determined to never get off that treadmill despite the cost in terms of their well-being, relationships, and happiness. There are still millions desperately looking for the next promotion, the next million-dollar payday that they believe will satisfy their longing to feel better about themselves, or silence their dissatisfaction. But both in the West and in emerging economies, there are more people every day who recognize that these are all dead ends—that they are chasing a broken dream. That we cannot find the answer in our current definition of success alone because—as Gertrude Stein once said of Oakland—"There is no there there."

More and more scientific studies and more and more health statistics are showing that the way we've been leading our lives—what we prioritize and what we value—is not working. And growing numbers of women—and men—are refusing to join the list of casualties. Instead, they are re-evaluating their lives, looking to thrive rather than merely succeed based on how the world measures success.

The latest science proves that increased stress and burnout have huge consequences for both our personal health and our health care system. Researchers at Carnegie Mellon found that from 1983 to 2009, there was between a 10 and 30 percent increase in stress levels across all demographic categories. Higher levels of stress can lead to higher instances of diabetes, heart disease, and obesity. According to the Centers for Disease Control and Prevention, fully three-quarters of American health care spending goes toward treating such chronic conditions. The Benson-Henry Institute for Mind Body Medicine at Massachusetts General Hospital estimates that 60 to 90 percent of doctor visits are to treat stress-related conditions. While in the United Kingdom, stress has emerged in recent years as the top cause of illness across the nation. As Tim Straughan, the chief executive of the Health and Social Care Information Centre explained, "It might be assumed that stress and anxiety are conditions that result in a journey to a general practitioner's consulting room rather than a hospital ward. However, our figures suggest thousands of cases a year arise where patients suffering from stress or anxiety become hospitalised in England."

The stress we experience impacts our children, too. Indeed, the effects of stress on children—even in utero— were emphasized in the journal of the American Academy of Pediatrics. As Nicholas Kristof put it in *The New York Times*: "Cues of a hostile or indifferent environment flood an infant, or even a fetus, with stress hormones like cortisol in ways that can disrupt the body's metabolism or the architecture of the brain. The upshot is that children are sometimes permanently undermined. Even many years later, as adults, they are more likely to suffer heart disease, obesity, diabetes and other physical ailments. They are also more likely to struggle in school, have short tempers and tangle with the law."

One reason we give for allowing stress to build in our lives is that we don't have time to take care of ourselves. We're too busy chasing a phantom of the successful life. The difference between what such success looks like and what truly makes us thrive isn't always clear as we're living our lives. But it becomes much more obvious in the rearview mirror. Have you noticed that when we die, our eulogies celebrate our lives very differently from the way society defines success?

Eulogies are, in fact, very Third Metric. But while it's not hard to live a life that includes the Third Metric, it's very easy not to. It's easy to let ourselves get consumed by our work. It's easy to allow professional obligations to overwhelm us, and to forget the things and the people that truly sustain us. It's easy to let technology wrap us in a perpetu-ally harried, stressed-out existence. It's easy, in effect, to miss the real point of our lives even as we're living them. Until we're no longer alive. A eulogy is often the first for-mal marking down of what our lives were about—the foun-dational document of our legacy. It is how people remember us and how we live on in the minds and hearts of others. And it is very telling what we don't hear in eulogies. We almost never hear things like:

"The crowning achievement of his life was when he made senior vice president."

Or:

"He increased market share for his company multiple times during his tenure."

Or:

"She never stopped working. She ate lunch at her desk. Every day."

Or:

"He never made it to his kid's Little League games be-cause he always had to go over those figures one more time."

Or:

"While she didn't have any real friends, she had six hun-dred Facebook friends, and she dealt with every email in her in-box every night."

Or:

"His PowerPoint slides were always meticulously pre-pared."

Our eulogies are always about the other stuff: what we gave, how we connected, how much we meant to our fam-ily and friends, small kindnesses, lifelong passions, and the things that made us laugh.

So why do we spend so much of our limited time on this earth focusing on all the things our eulogy will never cover?

"Eulogies aren't résumés," David Brooks wrote. "They describe the person's care, wisdom, truthfulness and courage. They describe the million little moral judgments that emanate from that inner region."

And yet we spend so much time and effort and energy on those résumé entries—entries that lose all significance as soon as our heart stops beating. Even for those who die with amazing *Wikipedia* entries, whose lives were synonymous with accomplishment and achievement, their eulogies focus mostly on what they did when they weren't achieving and succeeding. They aren't bound by our current, broken definition of success. Look at Steve Jobs, a man whose life, at least as the public saw it, was about creating things— things that were, yes, amazing and game changing. But when his sister, Mona Simpson, rose to honor him at his memorial service, that's not what she focused on.

Yes, she talked about his work and his work ethic. But mostly she raised these as manifestations of his passions. "Steve worked at what he loved," she said. What really moved him was love. "Love was his supreme virtue," she said, "his god of gods.

"When [his son] Reed was born, he began gushing and never stopped. He was a physical dad, with each of his children. He fretted over Lisa's boyfriends and Erin's travel and skirt lengths and Eve's safety around the horses she adored."

And then she added this touching image: "None of us who attended Reed's graduation party will ever forget the scene of Reed and Steve slow dancing."

His sister made abundantly clear in her eulogy that Steve Jobs was a lot more than just the guy who invented the iPhone. He was a brother and a husband and a father who knew the true value of what technology can so easily distract us from. Even if you build an iconic product, one that lives on in our lives, what is foremost in the minds of the people you care about most are the memories you built in their lives.

In her 1951 novel *Memoirs of Hadrian*, Marguerite Yourcenar has the Roman emperor meditating on his death: "It seems to me as I write this hardly important to have been emperor." Thomas Jefferson's epitaph describes him as "author of the Declaration of American Independence . . . and father of the University of Virginia." There is no mention of his presidency.

The old adage that we should live every day as if it were our last usually means that we shouldn't wait until death is imminent to begin prioritizing the things that really matter. Anyone with a smartphone and a full email in-box knows that it's easy to be busy while not being aware that we're actually living.

A life that embraces the Third Metric is one lived in a way that's mindful of our eventual eulogy. "I'm always relieved when someone is delivering a eulogy and I realize I'm listening to it," joked George Carlin. We may not be able to witness our own eulogy, but we're actually writing it all the time, every day. The question is how much we're giving the eulogizer to work with.

In the summer of 2013, an obituary of a Seattle woman

named Jane Lotter, who died of cancer at sixty, went viral. The author of the obit was Lotter herself.

"One of the few advantages of dying from Grade 3, Stage IIIC endometrial cancer, recurrent and metastasized to the liver and abdomen," she wrote, "is that you have time to write your own obituary." After giving a lovely and lively account of her life, she showed that she lived with the true definition of success in mind. "My beloved Bob, Tessa, and Riley," she wrote. "My beloved friends and family. How precious you all have been to me. Knowing and loving each one of you was the success story of my life."

Whether you believe in an afterlife—as I do—or not, by being fully present in your life and in the lives of those you love, you're not just writing your own eulogy; you're creating a very real version of your afterlife. It's an invaluable lesson—one that has much more credence while we have the good fortune of being healthy and having the energy and freedom to create a life of purpose and meaning. The good news is that each and every one of us still has time to live up to the best version of our eulogy.

This book is designed to help us move from knowing what to do to actually doing it. As I know all too well, this is no simple matter. Changing deeply ingrained habits is especially difficult. And when many of these habits are the product of deeply ingrained cultural norms, it is even harder. This is the challenge we face in redefining success. This is the challenge we face in making Third Metric principles part of our daily lives. This book is about the lessons I've learned and my efforts to embody the Third Metric principles—a process I plan to be engaged in for the rest of my life. It also brings together the latest data, academic research, and scientific findings (some of them tucked away in endnotes), which I hope will convince even the most skeptical reader that the current way we lead our lives is not working and that there are scientifically proven ways we can live our lives differently—ways that will have an immediate and measurable impact on our health and happiness. And, finally, because I want it to be as practical as possible, I have also included many daily practices, tools, and techniques that are easy to incorporate into our lives. These three threads are pulled together by one overarching goal: to reconnect with ourselves, our loved ones, and our community—in a word, to thrive.

Well-Being

For a long time it had seemed to me that life was about to begin—real life. But there was always some obstacle in the way. Something to be got through first, some unfinished business, time still to be served, a debt to be paid. Then life would begin. At last it dawned on me that these obstacles were my life.

—Fr. Alfred D'Souza

A New Blueprint: Time to Renovate
the Architecture of Our Lives

NOTHING SUCCEEDS like excess, we are told. If a little of something is good, more must be better. So working eighty hours a week must be better than working forty. And being plugged in 24/7 is assumed to be a standard requirement of every job worth having today—which means that getting by on less sleep and constant multitasking is an express elevator to the top in today's work world. Right?

The time has come to reexamine these assumptions. When we do, it becomes clear that the price we are paying for this way of thinking and living is far too high and unsustainable. The architecture of how we live our lives is badly in need of renovation and repair. What we really value is out of sync with how we live our lives. And the need is urgent for some new blueprints to reconcile the two. In Plato's *Apology*, Socrates defines his life's mission as awakening the Athenians to the supreme importance of attending to their souls. His timeless plea that we connect to ourselves remains the only way for any of us to truly thrive.

Too many of us leave our lives—and, in fact, our souls—behind when we go to work. This is the guiding truth of the Well-Being section and, indeed, of this entire book. Growing up in Athens, I remember being taught in my classics class that, as Socrates said, "the unexamined life is not worth living." Philosophy for the Greeks was not an academic exercise. It was a way of life—a daily practice in the art of living. My mother never went to college, but she would still preside over long sessions in our small kitchen in Athens discussing the principles and teachings of Greek philosophy to help guide my sister, Agapi, and me in our decisions and our choices.

Our current notion of success, in which we drive ourselves into the ground, if not the grave—in which working to the point of exhaustion and burnout is considered a badge of honor—was put in place by men, in a workplace culture dominated by men. But it's a model of success that's not working for women, and, really, it's not working for men, either. If we're going to redefine what success means, if we are going to include a Third Metric to success, beyond money and power, it's going to be women who will lead the way—and men, freed of the notion that the only road to success includes taking the Heart Attack Highway to Stress City, will gratefully join both at work and at home.

This is our third women's revolution. The first women's revolution was led by the suffragettes more than a hundred years ago, when courageous women such as Susan B. Anthony, Emmeline Pankhurst, and Elizabeth Cady Stanton fought to get women the right to vote. The second was led by Betty Friedan and Gloria Steinem, who fought—and Gloria continues to fight—to expand the role of women in our society and give them full access to the rooms and corridors of power where decisions are made.

This second revolution is still very much in progress, as

it needs to be. But we simply can't wait any longer for the third revolution to get under way.

That's because women are paying an even higher price than men for their participation in a work culture fueled by stress, sleep deprivation, and burnout. That is one reason why so many talented women, with impressive degrees working in high-powered jobs, end up abandoning their careers when they can afford to. Let me count the ways in which these personal costs are unsustainable: As mentioned in the introduction—but it is so important it bears repeating—women in highly stressful jobs have a nearly 40 percent increased risk of heart disease and heart attacks compared with their less-stressed colleagues, and a 60 percent greater risk for type 2 diabetes (a link that does not exist for men, by the way). Women who have heart attacks are almost twice as likely as men to die within a year of the attack, and women in high-stress jobs are more likely to become alcoholics than women in low-stress jobs. Stress and pressure from high-powered careers can also be a factor in the resurgence of eating disorders in women ages thirty-five to sixty.

Most of the time, the discussion about the challenges of women at the top centers around the difficulty of navigating a career and children—of "having it all." It's time we recognize that, as the workplace is currently structured, a lot of women don't want to get to the top and stay there because they don't want to pay the price—in terms of their health, their well-being, and their happiness. When women do leave high-powered jobs, the debate is largely taken over by the binary stay-at-home-mom versus the independent career woman question. But, in fact, when women at the top—or near enough—opt out, it's not just because of the kids, even though that's sometimes what takes the place of the job they've left. And the full reasons why they're leaving also have implications for men.

Caroline Turner, author of *Difference Works: Improving Retention, Productivity, and Profitability Through Inclusion*, was one of those women at the top. After successfully climbing the corporate ladder, she decided to get off. And it wasn't because of her children, who were grown. "I lacked the passion it took to keep it up," she writes. Once she left, she realized she had new colleagues of a sort. "I began to notice how much company I had as a former successful woman executive," she writes. "I began to reflect on what really caused me to leave."

What she found was research that showed that, yes, child care and elder care were cited most often as the reasons women left. But after those, the motivation most often given was lack of engagement or enjoyment in the job. And, of course, none of the three reasons are exclusive. "If a woman doesn't really like her job, she may be less willing or able to juggle work and family responsibilities," Turner writes. "If she is fully engaged in her work, the juggling act may be worthwhile."

So what often looks from the outside like a simple choice to quit and take care of the children can actually be more complicated. Children are a formidable option—time spent with them can be meaningful and engaging. And if the career alternative ceases to be meaningful or engaging, some women who are able to will take the former. In fact, 43 percent of women who have children will quit their jobs at some point. Around three-quarters of them will return to the workforce, but only 40 percent will go back to working full-time. As Turner writes, for women to be engaged in the workplace, they need to feel valued. And the way many workplaces are set up, masculine ways of succeeding—fueled by stress and burnout—are often accorded more value. Take Wall Street, for example, where Roseann Palmieri worked for twenty-five years, becoming a managing director at Merrill Lynch. Suddenly, in 2010, she came to a realization: "I'm at the table. I've made it. I've networked, I've clawed, I've said 'yes,' I've said 'no,' I've put in all this time and effort and I was underwhelmed. What I was getting back was not acceptable to me."

You are not your bank account, or your ambitiousness. You're not the cold clay lump with a big belly you leave behind when you die. You're not your collection of walking personality disorders. You are spirit, you are love.

—ANNE LAMOTT

Likewise, after getting a master's in education at Harvard and an MBA at Wharton, Paulette Light had a successful career in management consulting. Ten weeks after her daughter was born, she was back at work. "I was an exhausted, nervous wreck," she writes. Her company tried to be flexible to keep her, telling her to "just get the job done" however she could. But "that was the problem," she writes. "Getting the job done was all about giving everything to the job."

So she quit, and had three more children. But leaving the business world did not mean leaving behind achievement and accomplishment. Far from it. In the time since, she's started a preschool, cofounded a synagogue, and launched an Internet start-up, momstamp.com, focused on making moms' lives easier. She's also been surveying the work landscape for ways in which the doors to the business world could be more two-way and allow for the talents and skills of those who have chosen alternative paths to be put to use. A healthy economy isn't just about the efficient allocation of capital, but of talent, as well. As more and more people—both men and women—begin to choose not to work themselves into the ground, it's important that humane pathways back to the workforce be created so their skills are not lost.

One idea is to expand the project-based world—where businesses simply give a skilled worker a project and a deadline. "If you want high-achieving mothers back in the workforce," Light writes, "don't give us an office and a work week filled with facetime, give us something to get done and tell us when you need it by."

And it's not just women with children who are looking for an alternative. After graduating from college, Kate Sheehan quickly worked her way up in communications and by twenty-seven was a speechwriter for the CEO of a large finance company. But seven years of twelve-hour days later, she began to have second thoughts about where she was going. It wasn't the answers that were changing for her, but the questions. "It's not 'What do I want to do?', it's 'What kind of life do I want to have?'" she says. Her answer made her realize she had to make some changes.

I do not try to dance better than anyone else. I only try to dance better than myself.

—MIKHAIL BARYSHNIKOV

So she moved to Cape Cod and started a communications consulting business. "There was something about being on Cape Cod—I was inspired by the people around me, in this beautiful geography, who were making it work," she says. "I started to think, 'I could make a more independent path work for me as well.' I felt inspired by the natural surroundings, by being close to the ocean where I grew up. Emotionally, mentally and physically, I had more space to create.

"There are a lot of women doing what I'm doing," she says, "but they're doing it 15, 20 years later. I don't want to be someone who, 15 years from now, has horrible health problems and who hasn't created a life that feels really meaningful to me."

According to a *ForbesWoman* survey, an amazing 84 percent of working women say that staying at home to raise kids is a financial luxury they aspire to. This says just as much about the fulfillment we're getting from our work as it does about our love of our no-doubt-adorable children.

Burnout: Our Civilization's Disease

Belgian philosopher Pascal Chabot calls burnout "civilization's disease." It's certainly symptomatic of our modern age. "It is not only an individual disorder that affects some who are ill-suited to the system, or too committed, or who don't know how to put limits to their professional lives," he writes. "It is also a disorder that, like a mirror, reflects some excessive values of our society."

Marie Asberg, professor at the Karolinska Institutet in Stockholm, describes burnout as an "exhaustion funnel" we slip down as we give up things we don't think are important. "Often, the very first things we give up are those that nourish us the most but seem 'optional,'" write Mark Williams and Danny Penman in *Mindfulness: An Eight-Week Plan for Finding Peace in a Frantic World*. "The result is that we are increasingly left with only work or other stressors that often deplete our resources, and nothing to replenish or nourish us—and exhaustion is the result."

If I were called upon to state in a few words the essence of everything I was trying to say both as a novelist and as a preacher, it would be something like this: Listen to your life. See it for the fathomless mystery that it is. In the boredom and pain of it, no less than in the excitement and gladness: touch, taste, smell your way to the holy and hidden heart of it, because in the last analysis, all moments are key moments, and life itself is grace.

—FREDERICK BUECHNER

Another result of our current toxic definition of success is an epidemic of addiction. More than twenty-two million people in the United States are using illegal drugs, more than twelve million are using prescription painkillers without a medical reason, and almost nine million need prescription sleep aids to go to sleep. And the percentage of adults taking antidepressants has gone up 400 percent since 1988.

Burnout, stress, and depression have become worldwide epidemics. And as we found out when we held a Third Metric conference in London in the summer of 2013, and then one in Munich in the fall, the need to redefine success is a global need. In the United Kingdom, prescriptions for antidepressants have gone up 495 percent since 1991. In Europe, from 1995 to 2009, the use of antidepressants went up by nearly 20 percent per year. And the health consequences of stress are increasingly documented around the world. According to a Danish study, women who described work-related pressures as "a little too high" faced a 25 percent increased risk of heart disease. As June Davison, a nurse at the British Heart Foundation, cautioned, "Feeling under pressure at work means stressed employees may pick up some unhealthy bad habits and add to their risk of developing heart problems."

In Germany, more than 40 percent of workers say that their jobs have become more stressful in the past two years. Germany lost fifty-nine million workdays to psychological illness in 2011, up over 80 percent in fifteen years. When she was the German Labour Minister, Ursula von der Leyen, now Germany's defense minister, estimated that burnout is costing the country up to ten billion euros per year. "Nothing is more expensive than sending a good worker into retirement in their mid-forties because they're burned out," she said. "These cases are no longer just the exception. It's a trend that we have to do something about."

In China, according to a 2012 survey, 75 percent of Chinese workers said their stress levels have risen in the previous year (versus a global average of 48 percent).

According to a Harvard Medical School study, an astounding 96 percent of leaders said they felt burned out. In fact, one of the legal defenses offered by Steve Cohen, CEO of SAC Capital, the hedge fund that was indicted in 2013 and agreed to a record $1.2 billion fine, was that he missed a warning about insider trading because of the one thousand emails he gets every day. There is a price to pay for that kind of daily deluge. After less than a year as CEO of Lloyds Banking Group, António Horta-Osório took a two-month leave in 2011. Lloyds's chairman Sir Winfried Bischoff blamed "overwork, lack of sleep." Upon his return, Horta-Osório said, "With the benefit of hindsight I should have gone a bit slower." And in October 2013, Hector Sants, head of compliance at Barclays, took a leave of absence. A month later he quit his job entirely, after being diagnosed with exhaustion and stress.

The word "stress" was first used in its modern sense in 1936 by physician Hans Selye. It means "the body's non-specific response to an external demand," as immunologist Esther Sternberg put it in her book *Healing Spaces*:

> The ancient Romans used a word with a similar meaning—*stringere*, "to squeeze tight," "graze," "touch," or "injure." When the word entered the English language in the fourteenth century, it continued to refer to physical hardships of the environment. By the nineteenth century, the word had begun to take on a meaning combining the environment's physical

effects with the body's responses to them. Then, in 1934, physiologist Walter B. Cannon showed that animals produce adrenaline in response to such stressors. This was indeed the first proof that the physical environment could trigger a bodily response. Selye took the concept one step further, showing that many other hormones were produced in response to stress, and that these could have lasting physical consequences on the body.

What produces stress in our bodies is deeply subjective. It's as if stress is always floating around looking for something—or someone—to land on. And it often lands on completely trivial and insignificant things. We only realize how trivial and insignificant they are—and unworthy of our attention, let alone our stress over them—when something truly significant intrudes upon our routine: the loss of a loved one, sickness, a health scare.

The greatest weapon against stress is our ability to choose one thought over another.

—WILLIAM JAMES

I remember when we had just moved to Washington. I was completely preoccupied with decorating our new home, getting our two young children into new schools, responding to my editor's queries on a manuscript I had just sent in, and organizing a birthday dinner. In the middle of all this, I drove to Georgetown hospital for a routine physical exam. When I arrived at the hospital I moved mindlessly through my exam, silently processing my to-do list while a nurse took my blood pressure. The doctor was in, then out, then in again. At some point it occurred to me that she was speaking with unusual seriousness. I think she caught my attention with the word "lump." It needed to "come out as soon as possible."

One of the problems with my philosophy of assuming the best until told the worst is that when I had first noticed the lump at home I assumed it was just a harmless cyst. It had happened before. No problem. But now the doctor was using words such as "biopsy" and "surgery," and telling me the lump would not "aspirate"—that she could get no fluid from it and wanted to get it out right away. I felt myself beginning to black out, and I asked if I could lie on the examination table while she explained what this meant. As if through a thick fog, I heard the doctor talking about how long it takes to "get lab results after surgery" and that she always likes her patients to come to her office to review the results and discuss alternatives in person. In an instant, deadlines were disappearing and priorities recalculated.

A week after my surgery we got the results. The lump was benign. It had been a long week full of "what-ifs," a week that brought home one great truth about life: the ease with which the big crises can wipe out the small ones that seemed so critical just a moment before. All of our small anxieties and trivial preoccupations evaporate with the sudden recognition of what really matters. We are reminded of the impermanence of much that we assume is forever and the value of so much we take for granted.

Again and again, all around the world, it often takes a

personal health crisis to get us to pay attention. That moment came for the former president of Google China, Lee Kai-Fu, in the fall of 2013 when he was diagnosed with cancer. Lee told his fifty million followers on Sina Weibo (a Chinese social media network) that he had decided to change his life: "I naively used to compete with others to see who could sleep less. I made 'fighting to the death' a personal motto. . . . It's only now, when I'm suddenly faced with possibly losing 30 years of life, that I've been able to calm down and reconsider. That sort of persistence may have been a mistake." His new plan: "Sleep enough, adjust my diet and start exercising again."

And every day, the world will drag you by the hand, yelling, "This is important! And this is important! And this is important! You need to worry about this! And this! And this!"

And each day, it's up to you to yank your hand back, put it on your heart and say, "No. This is what's important."

—Iain Thomas

Healthy Employees, Healthy Bottom Lines

Looking at the Western workplace today, we see two very different and competing worlds. In one world, we see a clear manifestation of the burnout disorder: a business culture single-mindedly obsessed with quarterly earnings reports, maximizing short-term profits, and beating growth expectations. In the other world, we see an increasing recognition of the effects workplace stress can have on the well-being of employees—and on a company's bottom line.

There is growing evidence that the long-term health of a company's bottom line and the health of its employees are, in fact, very much aligned, and that when we treat them as separate, we pay a heavy price, both personally and collectively. Individually, we compromise our health and happiness. For businesses, the costs will be exacted in dollars and cents, talent retention, and diminished productivity. But the reverse is also true—what's good for us as individuals is also good for businesses and for countries. And sick care is a lot more expensive than real health care.

The World Economic Forum, held in Davos, Switzerland, each year and typically associated with finding solutions to the big economic problems facing us, is a kind of weather vane for ideas being embraced by political and business leaders around the world. In 2013 and even more so in 2014, it was clear from the multiple sessions devoted to mindful leadership, meditation, neuroscientific findings, and even "rethinking living," that the powers that be are beginning to accept the connection between our ability to deal with the crises that surround us and the way we live our lives and care for our bodies, minds, and spirit. The plenary session I moderated in January 2014 was entitled "Health Is Wealth," referencing the health of individuals, companies, and countries alike.

Studies show that U.S. employers spend 200 to 300 percent more on the indirect costs of health care, in the form of absenteeism, sick days, and lower productivity, than they do on actual health care payments. In the United Kingdom, stress results in 105 million lost workdays each year. No wonder Harvard Business School professor Michael Porter recommends that companies "mount an aggressive approach to wellness, prevention, screening and active management of chronic conditions." The voice of sanity is getting louder in our burned-out world, challenging the conventional wisdom that during hard times you cut employees' health care benefits.

Howard Schultz, the CEO of Starbucks, faced such pressure from investors during Starbucks' less profitable years. But he did not give in. At age seven, Schultz had watched his father get fired from his job as a driver for a diaper delivery service after slipping on a sheet of ice at work, breaking his hip and ankle. His father was sent home without health care coverage, workers' compensation, or severance. During Starbucks' earlier years, Schultz was adamant about expanding health care coverage to include part-timers who worked as little as twenty hours a week, unheard of in the late 1980s. Two decades later, during the company's toughest financial period, Schultz stood fast, refusing to cut those benefits despite the urging of investors. Schultz sees the benefits plan "not as a generous optional benefit but as a core strategy. Treat people like family, and they will be loyal and give their all." It's this principle that led to the creation of BeanStock, the company's employee stock option plan, which turned Starbucks employees into partners.

Too many companies don't yet realize the benefits of focusing on wellness. "The lack of attention to employee needs helps explain why the United States spends more on healthcare than other countries but gets worse outcomes," says Jeffrey Pfeffer, professor at Stanford's Graduate School of Business. "We have no mandatory vacation or sick day requirements, and we do have chronic layoffs, overwork, and stress. Working in many organizations is simply hazardous to your health. . . . I hope businesses will wake up to the fact that if they don't do well by their employees, chances are they're not doing well, period."

One company that did wake up to the importance of employee health was Safeway. The supermarket chain's former CEO Steve Burd recounts that in 2005 Safeway's health care bill hit $1 billion and was going up by $100 million a year. "What we discovered was that 70 percent of health care costs are driven by people's behaviors," he says. "Now as a business guy, I thought if we could influence the behavior of our 200,000-person workforce, we could have a material effect on health care costs."

So Safeway offered incentives for employees to lose weight and control their blood pressure and cholesterol levels. It established a baseline health insurance premium with behavior-based discounts. As Burd explained, "If you are a confirmed non-smoker, we give you a discount. If you have cholesterol under control, a discount. Blood pressure under control, a discount. And so behavior becomes a form of currency for people to accomplish their lifestyle changes." And it was a huge success. "You allow and encourage your employees to become healthier, they become more productive, your company becomes more competitive," Burd says. "I can't think of a single negative in doing this. Making money and doing good in the world are not mutually exclusive."

Esther Sternberg explains that "healing is a verb; the

body is constantly repairing itself. That's what life is. You know, a rock just sits there and it eventually gets into sand or mud or something as the elements affect it. But a living being is constantly repairing itself against all of these different insults at a very molecular level, at a cellular level, at an emotional level. So disease happens when the repair process is not keeping up with the damage process."

Right now in the majority of our companies and the majority of our lives, the repair process is not keeping up with the damage process. But there are many different paths to well-being, and in the next few sections we will explore some of them.

Meditation: It's Not Just for Enlightenment Anymore

One of the best—and most easily available—ways we can become healthier and happier is through mindfulness and meditation. Every element of well-being is enhanced by the practice of meditation and, indeed, studies have shown that mindfulness and meditation have a measurable positive impact on the other three pillars of the Third Metric—wisdom, wonder, and giving.

When I first heard about mindfulness, I was confused. My mind was already full enough, I thought—I needed to empty it, not focus on it. My conception of the mind was sort of like the household junk drawer—just keep cramming things in and hope it doesn't jam. Then I read Jon Kabat-Zinn's writings on mindfulness and it all made sense. "In Asian languages," he wrote, "the word for 'mind' and the word for 'heart' are the same word. So when we hear the word 'mindfulness,' we have to inwardly also hear 'heartfulness' in order to grasp it even as a concept, and especially as a way of being." In other words, mindfulness is not just about our minds but our whole beings. When we are all mind, things can get rigid. When we are all heart, things can get chaotic. Both lead to stress. But when they work together, the heart leading through empathy, the mind guiding us with focus and attention, we become a harmonious human being. Through mindfulness, I found a practice that helped bring me fully present and in the moment, even in the most hectic of circumstances.

What was the very best moment of your day? . . . Often, it's a moment when you're waiting for someone, or you're driving somewhere, or maybe you're just walking diagonally across a parking lot and you're admiring the oil stains and the dribbled tar patterns. One time it was when I was driving past a certain house that was screaming with sunlitness on its white clapboards, and then I plunged through tree shadows that splashed and splayed over the windshield.

—NICHOLSON BAKER

Mark Williams and Danny Penman give a variety of quick and easy ways to practice mindfulness, including what they call "habit breaking." Each day for a week you choose a habit such as brushing your teeth, drinking your morning coffee, or taking a shower, and simply pay attention to what's happening while you do it. It's really not so much habit breaking as habit unmaking—it's taking something we've placed on autopilot and putting it back on the list of things we pay attention to. "The idea," they write, "is not to make you feel different, but simply to allow a few more moments in the day when you are 'awake.' . . . If you notice your mind wandering while you do this, simply notice where it went, then gently escort it back to the present moment."

I love the image of gently escorting my mind back to the present moment—without any negative judgment that it wandered. It will, no doubt, be a familiar process for anybody who has parented or babysat a toddler, which is not a bad comparison for our modern multitasking minds. As for meditation, it has long been an important part of my life. My mother had actually taught my younger sister, Agapi, and me how to meditate when I was thirteen years old. But although I've known its benefits since my teens, finding time for meditation was always a challenge because I was under the impression that I had to "do" meditation. And I didn't have time for another burdensome thing to "do." Fortunately, a friend pointed out one day that we don't "do" meditation; meditation "does" us. That opened the door for me. The only thing to "do" in meditation is nothing. Even writing that I don't have to "do" one more thing makes me relax.

You wander from room to room
Hunting for the diamond necklace
That is already around your neck

—RUMI

I've found that meditation can actually be done in very short windows of time, even while on the move. We think of ourselves as breathing, but, in reality, we are being breathed. At any time we choose, we can take a moment to bring our attention to the rising and falling of our breath without our conscious interference. I know when I have "connected" because I usually take a spontaneous deep breath, or release a deep sigh. So, in a sense, the engine of mindfulness is always going. To reap the benefits of it, all we have to do is become present and pay attention.

Our breath also has a sacredness about it. Sometimes when I'm giving a talk, I'll first ask everyone in the room to focus on the rising and falling of their breath for ten seconds. It's amazing how the room, which moments before hummed with chaotic energy, will suddenly be filled with a stillness, an attentiveness, a sacredness. It's something quite palpable.

There are many forms of meditation, but whichever form you choose, it's important to remember that its benefits are only a breath away. And the only price we pay is a few moments of our attention.

My sister, Agapi, has always been a natural on all matters spiritual, and has been my guide throughout our lives, sending books and people my way, nudging my spiritual explorations, calling to wake me up at a hotel in Kalamazoo, Michigan, at five in the morning so I could have time to meditate before another grueling book-tour day began.

When I was growing up, meditation was seen as a cure for just about everything. My mother had convinced us that if we meditated, we would be able to do our homework faster and improve our grades. We knew that meditation made us more peaceful and less upset when things didn't go our way, but we also realized that it made us happier. And now, science has provided evidence to back this all up. If anything, my mother was underselling the benefits of meditation. Science has caught up to ancient wisdom, and the results are overwhelming and unambiguous.

What study after study shows is that meditation and mindfulness training profoundly affect every aspect of our lives—our bodies, our minds, our physical health, and our emotional and spiritual well-being. It's not quite the fountain of youth, but it's pretty close. When you consider all the benefits of meditation—and more are being found every day—it's not an exaggeration to call meditation a miracle drug.

First, let's look at physical health. It's hard to overstate what meditation can do for us here, and the medical uses for it are just beginning to be explored. "Science—the same reductionistic science that is used to evaluate various drugs and medical procedures—has proven that your mind can heal your body," Herbert Benson and William Proctor write in their book *Relaxation Revolution*. Indeed, the authors recommend that mind-body science be considered as the third primary treatment option in medicine, right along with surgery and drugs. They write how meditation can impact nausea, diabetes, asthma, skin reactions, ulcers, cough, congestive heart failure, dizziness, postoperative swelling, and anxiety: "Because all health conditions have some stress component." The authors conclude, "It is no overstatement to say that virtually every single health problem and disease can be improved with a mind-body approach."

It's the Swiss army knife of medical tools, for conditions

both small and large. A study funded by the National Institutes of Health showed a 23 percent decrease in mortality in people who meditated versus those who did not, a 30 percent decrease in death due to cardiovascular problems, and a significant decrease in cancer mortality. "This effect is equivalent to discovering an entirely new class of drugs (but without the inevitable side effects)," observe Mark Williams and Danny Penman. Another study found that meditation increased levels of antibodies to the flu vaccine, and the practice was also found to decrease the severity and length of colds, while researchers at Wake Forest University found that meditation lowered pain intensity.

How does it do all this? It's not about just distracting us from pain and stress; it literally changes us at the genetic level. Researchers at Massachusetts General Hospital, Beth Israel Deaconess Medical Center, and Harvard Medical School found that the relaxation response—the state of calm produced by meditation, yoga, and breathing exercises—actually switched on genes that are related to augmenting our immune system, reducing inflammation, and fighting a range of conditions from arthritis to high blood pressure to diabetes. So with all these results, it's no surprise that, according to another study, meditation correlates to reduced yearly medical costs.

It also physically changes our brains. One study found that meditation can actually increase the thickness of the prefrontal cortex region of the brain and slow the thinning that occurs there as we age, impacting cognitive functions such as sensory and emotional processing. Dr. Richard Davidson, professor of psychiatry at the University of Wisconsin and a leading scholar on the impact of contemplative practices on the brain, used magnetic resonance imaging machines (MRIs) to study the brain activity of Tibetan monks. The studies, as Davidson put it, have illuminated for the first time the "further reaches of human plasticity and transformation." He calls meditation mental training: "What we found is that the trained mind, or brain, is physically different from the untrained one." And when our brain is changed, so is the way in which we experience the world. "Meditation is not just blissing out under a mango tree," says French Buddhist monk and molecular geneticist Matthieu Ricard. "It completely changes your brain and therefore changes what you are."

And this automatically changes how you respond to what is happening in your life, your level of stress, and your ability to tap into your wisdom when making decisions. "You don't learn to sail in stormy seas," Ricard says. "You go to a secluded place, not to avoid the world, but to avoid distractions until you build your strength and you can deal with anything. You don't box Muhammad Ali on day one."

And the building of your strength, equanimity, and wisdom is actually very tangible and measurable, which is how Matthieu Ricard earned the moniker "the happiest man in the world." After placing more than 250 sensors on Ricard's skull, Richard Davidson found that Ricard exhibited gamma wave levels (high-frequency brain waves) "never before reported in the neuroscience literature," indicative of an atypically high capacity for happiness and reduced tendency toward negative thoughts and feelings. As Ricard explains, "Pleasure depends very much on circumstances . . . and also it's something that basically doesn't radiate to others. . . .

Happiness is a way of being that gives you the resources to deal with the ups and downs of life, that pervades all the emotional states including sadness."

People look for retreats for themselves, in the country, by the coast, or in the hills . . . There is nowhere that a person can find a more peaceful and trouble-free retreat than in his own mind. . . . So constantly give yourself this retreat, and renew yourself.

—MARCUS AURELIUS

Meditation can also have profound effects on a host of other psychological conditions. Researchers at UCLA found that mindfulness and meditation helped lower feelings of loneliness among the elderly, while researchers from the University of Michigan documented that military veterans experienced lowered levels of post-traumatic stress disorder after mindfulness training. Meditation has also been found to reduce depression among pregnant women and teens. And it's not just about reducing negative emotions; it's also about boosting positive ones. A study led by University of North Carolina professor Barbara L. Fredrickson found that meditation increased "positive emotions, including love, joy, gratitude, contentment, hope, pride, interest, amusement"; it also resulted in "increases in a variety of personal resources, including mindful attention, self-acceptance, positive relations with others, and good physical health." A study of patients with a history of depression at the University of Cambridge found that mindfulness-based cognitive therapy lowered the risk of depression relapse in participants who had experienced three or more episodes from 78 to 36 percent.

Meditation may be a wonder drug, but it does need to be regularly refilled. To get all these benefits, we need to make it a part of our everyday lives. Happiness and well-being are not just magical traits that some are blessed with and others not. Richard Davidson has come to view "happiness not as a trait but as a skill, like tennis. . . . If you want to be a good tennis player, you can't just pick up a racket—you have to practice," he said. "We can actually practice to enhance our well-being. Every strand of scientific evidence points in that direction. It's no different than learning to play the violin or play golf. When you practice, you get better at it." And trust me, it's much easier than mastering the violin or becoming a golf pro. Davidson found "remarkable results with practitioners who did fifty thousand rounds of meditation, but also with three weeks of twenty minutes a day, which, of course, is more applicable to our modern times."

While meditation may be a solitary activity that involves a certain inward focus, it also increases our ability to connect with others, actually making us more compassionate. Scientists from Harvard and Northeastern Universities found that meditation "made people willing to act virtuous—to help another who was suffering—even in the face of a norm not to do so."

And meditation boosts our creativity. "Ideas are like fish," wrote director and longtime meditator David Lynch in his book *Catching the Big Fish*. "If you want to catch little fish, you can stay in the shallow water. But if you want to catch the big fish, you've got to go deeper. Down deep, the fish are more powerful and more pure. They're huge and abstract. And they're very beautiful."

Steve Jobs, a lifelong practitioner of meditation, affirmed the connection between meditation and creativity: "If you just sit and observe, you will see how restless your mind is. If you try to calm it, it only makes it worse, but over time it does calm, and when it does, there's room to hear more subtle things—that's when your intuition starts to blossom and you start to see things more clearly and be in the present more. Your mind just slows down, and you see a tremendous expanse in the moment. You see so much more than you could see before."

Meditation can help us not only focus, but also refocus after being distracted—which is an increasingly common peril of our technology-besieged lives. Giuseppe Pagnoni, a neuroscientist at Emory University, found that, after an interruption, the minds of participants who meditated were able to return to what they had been focusing on faster than nonmeditators. "The regular practice of meditation may enhance the capacity to limit the influence of distracting thoughts," he said. This is especially valuable for those who feel like their days have become a noisy, beeping, blinking obstacle course of distracting thoughts.

No wonder mindfulness and meditation are being increasingly adopted by corporations and institutions throughout the world. The Bank of England has offered meditation sessions for its staff as well as the option to enroll in a self-funded six-week meditation course. And in the military, while the United States Marine Corps is experimenting with a Mind Fitness Training program, the David Lynch Foundation's Operation Warrior Wellness has helped bring meditation to veterans and armed service personnel and their families, leading to a substantial decrease in PTSD and depression symptoms.

No longer is meditation seen as some sort of New Age escape from the world. It's increasingly seen for what it is: a practice that helps us be in the world in a way that is more productive, more engaged, healthier, and less stressful. The list of public figures "outing" themselves as meditators is growing longer every day. It includes Ford chairman Bill Ford, LinkedIn CEO Jeff Weiner, Aetna CEO Mark Bertolini, Salesforce CEO Marc Benioff, Twitter cofounder Evan Williams, ABC host George Stephanopoulos, *New York Times* columnist and CNBC anchor Andrew Ross Sorkin, Jerry Seinfeld, Kenneth Branagh, Oprah Winfrey, whose twenty-one-day Meditation Experience program with Deepak Chopra has had nearly two million participants in more than two hundred countries, and Rupert Murdoch, who, in April 2013, tweeted: "Trying to learn transcendental meditation. Everyone recommends, not that easy to get started, but said to improve everything!" As Bob Roth, the executive director of the David Lynch Foundation, who has taught meditation to many corporate leaders, recently told me, "I've been doing this for forty years and in the past year there has been a dramatic change in the perception of meditation."

Lena Dunham, the creator and star of *Girls*, has been meditating since she was nine years old when she was diagnosed with an obsessive-compulsive disorder. She jokes that she comes "from a line of neurotic Jewish women who need Transcendental Meditation more than anyone," and describes how calming meditation is when it feels like her world is "spinning quickly" around her: "Meditation gathers me up for the day and makes me feel organized and happy and capable of facing the challenges of the world, both internal and external."

Padmasree Warrior, the chief technology officer of Cisco, calls meditation "a reboot for your brain and your soul." She meditates every night and spends her Saturdays doing a digital detox. Warrior drew on her meditation practice to manage twenty-two thousand employees in her previous role as Cisco's head of engineering.

It's hard to think of anything else that is simultaneously so simple and so powerful. It's a vital tool not just for us as individuals, but collectively, as well. "Vanquishing infectious disease has left us living with chronic diseases of lifestyle and aging," says Matthieu Ricard, "leading to the possibility that healthcare can focus on increasing human flourishing by putting the person's well-being—body, mind and spirit—at the center, empowering them for optimal life."

For those who still think of meditation and mindfulness as exotic imports, it's important to recognize that our Western traditions of prayer and contemplation, and the Stoic philosophy of ancient Greece and Rome, fulfill the same purpose as the Eastern practice of meditation. According to Taoist philosophy, "Rest is prior to motion and stillness prior to action." And every Christian tradition incorporates some equivalent form of mindfulness.

In the sixth century, Saint Benedict established the tradition of Lectio Divina ("divine reading"), a four-part practice of reading, meditation, prayer, and contemplation.

The Quakers built their belief system almost entirely around what are, in effect, the principles of mindfulness.

Believing that the light of God is in everyone, Quakers structure their services, called "meetings," around silence. There is no leader or minister, and members usually arrange themselves in a circle, facing one another, to emphasize the collective spirit and lack of hierarchy. Meetings, which are open to everybody of any faith, begin with silence, which continues until someone feels moved to speak. But the silence isn't interstitial or an intermission—it's the main show. It allows all those present to access their own inner light, and be nourished by the collective silence of the group.

"If pressed to say what they are actually doing in a meeting for worship," wrote Richard Allen, professor at the University of South Wales, "many Quakers would probably say that they are waiting—waiting in their utmost hearts for the touch of something beyond their everyday selves. Some would call it 'listening to the quiet voice of God'—without trying to define the word."

In the 1970s, Basil Pennington, a Trappist monk, developed a practice called the "centering prayer." It entails four steps:

1. Sit comfortably with your eyes closed, relax, and quiet yourself. Be in love and faith to God.

2. Choose a sacred word that best supports your sincere intention to be in the Lord's presence and open to His divine action within you (for example, "Jesus," "Lord," "God," "Savior," "Abba," "Divine," "Shalom," "Spirit," "Love").

3. Let that word be gently present as your symbol of your sincere intention to be in the Lord's presence and open to His divine action within you.

4. Whenever you become aware of anything (thoughts, feelings, perceptions, images, associations), simply return to your sacred word, your anchor.

It's remarkable how similar the pathways that connect us with our own being are: the symbols and the mantras differ, but the essence and the truth remain through the ages and across many different continents, religions, and psychological practices.

Catholicism includes the rosary, a prayer devoted to Mary, but also a practice about contemplation deepening through ritualistic repetition. Prayer beads are used as a method of releasing the mind by giving the fingers a physical focus.

Prayer beads are also used in many other traditions, including Buddhism, Hinduism, and Islam, in which they're used to recite the ninety-nine names of Allah as part of the Tasbih of Fatima prayer. As the Prophet Muhammad himself said, "One hour's meditation on the work of the Creator is better than seventy years of prayer."

Sufism, a mystical tradition of Sunni Islam, emphasizes inner enlightenment and love as the pathways to ultimate truth. It also gave birth to the whirling dervishes, who perform a ritual dance as an offering, a meditation, and an expression of the love of the divine.

Judaism also has a long mystical tradition that emphasizes inner wisdom and enlightenment. The twelfth-century Kabbalah talks about using meditative practices to "descend to the end of the world," and thus transcend our external selves and deepen our engagement with the divine.

Torah coach Frumma Rosenberg-Gottlieb wrote about leaving her farm in the mountains of Colorado and moving to New York to study the Torah (while also demonstrating that heightened spirituality doesn't always involve moving from the big city to the mountains). "As I became more sophisticated in my understanding of Torah," she writes, "I realized that mindfulness and a peaceful, balanced soul is indeed an objective in Jewish life, and that the tools for attaining it are subtly woven into the tapestry of Torah knowledge. I learned, for example, that the Hebrew word 'shalom' implies not just peace, but also completion, perfection, wholeness. We bless one another with peace; our daily prayers culminate in a request for peace." She also notes that meditation in Judaism goes way back, all the way to Abraham's son Isaac, who, as Genesis 24 tells us, "went out to meditate in the field toward evening" as he awaited his bride-to-be, Rebecca.

So no matter what tradition you follow—or if you follow no tradition—there is some form of meditation and mindfulness that can be integrated into your life.

And if you want to enjoy the benefits of mindfulness but don't want to start with meditation, prayer, or contemplation, just go fly-fishing. In fact, I have friends who have said to me, "My meditation is running," or "skydiving" or "gardening." But can you create that state of mind at will without having to put on your running shoes, open your parachute, get out your trowel, or cast your fishing rod in the water? The point is to find some regular activity that trains your mind to be still, fully present, and connected with yourself. Just do it regularly and integrate the benefits into your everyday life. And, of course, throw the fish back—mindfulness shouldn't be about coming home with a trophy to mount above the fireplace.

In her forthcoming book, *Mindful London*, Tessa Watt, a mindfulness teacher and consultant, writes about incorporating mindful reminders into our city lives. Here are three of my favorites, which we can adopt wherever we find ourselves—whether in a frantic metropolis or an idyllic village: "Use the famous British queue—at the bus stop, post office, or shop—as a chance to slow down and practice mindfulness. Instead of letting the frequent wailing of sirens irritate us, we could use the sound to remind us to take a pause and notice the moment. At the traffic crossing, instead of being impatient for the green man, appreciate how the red man gives us a chance to stop, breathe and look around."

Have patience with all things, but chiefly have patience with yourself. Do not lose courage by considering your own imperfections, but instantly set about remedying them; every day begin the task anew.

—FRANCIS DE SALES

Why Gazelles Are My Role Models

At *The Huffington Post*, since the news never stops, and there is the temptation for editors, reporters, and engineers to try to match the twenty-four-hour news cycle, we do a lot to prevent burnout. First, we make it very clear that no one is expected to check work email and respond after hours or over the weekend (unless, of course, these are their working hours). Everyone has at least three weeks of vacation time, which they are highly encouraged to take. And I have implored HuffPosters—without much success, I must admit—to eat lunch away from their desks.

We also have two nap rooms in our newsroom, which are now full most of the time, even though they were met with skepticism and reluctance when we installed them in the spring of 2011. Many were afraid their colleagues might think they were shirking their duties by taking a nap. We've made it very clear, however, that walking around drained and exhausted is what should be looked down on— not taking a break to rest and recharge. In our New York offices we host meditation, breathing, and yoga classes throughout the week, while our new D.C. offices have dedicated meditation, yoga, and nap rooms. And the benefits of standing and walking as opposed to sitting all day long, which I describe later in the chapter, led us to provide a standing desk to anyone who requests it. We also have a gym and take part in the Virgin Pulse wellness program, where employees can earn up to $500 a year by engaging in healthy practices. And to facilitate such healthy practices, we have refrigerators stocked with healthy snacks, including yogurt, hummus, fruit, and baby carrots—although I've noticed that the bulk of the baby carrots remain unclaimed and look rather forlorn by the end of the week. This is not just good for those who work at *HuffPost*; it's good for *HuffPost*.

At Facebook, COO Sheryl Sandberg has said publicly that she leaves the office at 5:30 to have dinner with her two young children and she encourages others to find schedules that work for them so they can get the time with their families—or just the time for themselves—that they need.

The relationship between overwork and a loss of productivity is consistent regardless of nationality or culture. According to 2012 numbers from the Organization for Economic Cooperation and Development (OECD), among European countries, Greece was number one in hours worked, Hungary was second, and Poland third. Their productivity rankings, however, were eighteenth, twenty-fourth, and twenty-fifth (dead last). Working the fewest hours were the Dutch, Germans, and Norwegians, who came in at fifth, seventh, and second in productivity.

Increasingly, companies are realizing that their employees' health is one of the most important predictors of the company's health, as well. In those all-important Wall Street conference calls, business analysts, in addition to asking about sales reports, market share, and earnings, should be quizzing CEOs about their employees' stress levels.

One of the most popular classes Google offers employees is known as SIY, which is an acronym for "Search Inside Yourself." The class was started by Chade-Meng Tan, an engineer and Google employee number 107. Tan went on to write a book about his principles, *Search Inside Yourself*.

The course is divided into three parts: attention training, self-knowledge, and building useful mental habits. Richard Fernandez, the cofounder of Wisdom Labs who took Tan's course when he was at Google, explained its value: "I'm definitely much more resilient as a leader. . . . It's almost an emotional and mental bank account. I've now got much more of a buffer there."

But the trend goes far beyond Silicon Valley. Janice Marturano set up a popular mindfulness program at General Mills when she served as its deputy general counsel, with a meditation room in every building of the campus. She has since founded the Institute for Mindful Leadership. "Mindfulness is about training our minds to be more focused, to see with clarity, to have spaciousness for creativity and to feel connected," she says. "That compassion to ourselves, to everyone around us—our colleagues, customers—that's what the training of mindfulness is really about. . . . There is no work-life balance. We have one life. What's most important is that you be awake for it." And it works. Eighty percent of senior executives from General Mills and a dozen other Fortune 500 companies who participated in her mindfulness leadership trainings said they felt the mindfulness program had improved their ability to make better decisions.

"The main business case for meditation is that if you're fully present on the job, you will be more effective as a leader," says Bill George, a Harvard Business School professor and the former CEO of medical devices company Medtronic. "You will make better decisions."

One of the primary obstacles keeping many businesses from adopting more sane and sustainable metrics of success is the stubborn—and dangerously wrongheaded—myth that there is a trade-off between high performance at work and taking care of ourselves. This couldn't be less true.

And soon, the companies that still believe this will be in the minority. Right now, about 35 percent of large and midsize U.S. employers offer some sort of stress-reduction program, including Target, Apple, Nike, and Procter & Gamble. And those that do are starting to be recognized for their efforts, especially by employees. Glassdoor.com, the social jobs and careers community, releases an annual list of the top twenty-five companies for work-life balance: "Companies that make sincere efforts to recognize employees' lives outside of the office," said Glassdoor's Rusty Rueff, "will often see the payoff when it comes to recruiting and retaining top talent."

In 2013, among *Fortune*'s "100 Best Companies to Work For," several stood out for their commitment to well-being. Salesforce.com, which offers free yoga, a $100 benefit for wellness, and forty-eight hours of paid time to volunteer, came in at number nineteen. At number four was the Boston Consulting Group, which flags employees working too many long weeks with a "red zone report" and allows new hires to delay starting for six months and receive $10,000 when they volunteer to work for a nonprofit.

At Promega, a biotech company in Wisconsin, employees have access to on-site yoga classes, fitness centers, healthy meals, offices filled with natural light, and "third spaces"—community areas that are neither work nor home, such as cafés and lounges. "You create a culture of wellness," Promega's chief medical officer, Ashley G. Anderson, Jr., said. "If you create a culture in which vibrant physicality is an admired thing, you've achieved a lot. A healthy workforce is a productive workforce."

The Minneapolis staffing company Salo has enlisted the bestselling author Dan Buettner for help. Buettner is an expert in "Blue Zones," regions of the world with the highest life expectancy, including Okinawa, Japan; Nicoya, Costa Rica; and Ikaria, Greece, where people are a thousand percent more likely to live to one hundred than in the United States. Now Buettner is helping make Salo the first certified Blue Zone workplace. With meditation rooms, adjustable-height desks, cooking lessons, and "purpose workshops" to help employees follow their nonwork passions, the effort is yielding results—for both employees and the company. "There's a culture and developing reputation at Salo as a place that puts the well-being of its employees and partners in front of just profits," Buettner said. "We're already seeing well-being and life expectancy increase with the employees there. . . . It pays off we believe in higher worker engagement, lower healthcare costs, higher productivity and lower absenteeism."

At the nearly one-hundred-year-old supermarket chain Wegmans, Danny Wegman, grandson of the founder, has recognized the benefit of encouraging his forty-five thousand employees to get healthier. The company now offers on-site yoga and Zumba classes, nutritional counseling, and high blood pressure screenings.

At Aetna, the third-largest health insurance provider in the United States, CEO Mark Bertolini discovered the health benefits of meditation, yoga, and acupuncture while recovering from a horrible ski accident that left him with a broken neck. He proceeded to make them available to his forty-nine thousand employees and brought in Duke University to conduct a study on the cost savings. The results? A 7 percent drop in health care costs in 2012 and sixty-nine minutes of additional productivity per day for those employees who participated in Aetna's wellness programs. And doing yoga one hour each week reduced stress among employees by one-third. Ray Dalio, the founder of Bridgewater, one of the largest hedge funds in the world, who has been meditating for more than thirty-five years and considers it "the single most important reason" for his success, pays for half of his employees' meditation classes and picks up the entire bill if they commit to it for more than six months.

No one in our time finds it surprising if a man gives careful daily attention to his body, but people would be outraged if he gave the same attention to his soul.

—ALEKSANDR SOLZHENITSYN

LinkedIn CEO Jeff Weiner coined the term "managing compassionately." He wrote that the objective to "expand the world's collective wisdom and compassion . . . has influenced every aspect of my work. . . . Compassion can and should be taught, not only throughout a child's K–12 curriculum, but in higher education and corporate learning and development programs as well." Managing compassionately includes practicing and expecting transparent communications, and practicing walking in someone else's shoes:

When strongly disagreeing with another, most of us have a tendency to see things solely through our own world view. . . . In these circumstances, it can be constructive to take a minute to understand why the other person has reached the conclusion that they have. For instance, what in their background has led them to take that position? . . . Are they fearful of a particular outcome that may not be obvious at surface level? Asking yourself these questions, and more importantly, asking the other person these questions, can take what would otherwise be a challenging situation and transform it into a coachable moment and truly collaborative experience.

John Mackey, the CEO of Whole Foods, summed up his vision of compassionate management at *HuffPost*'s first Third Metric conference in the summer of 2013: "We must bring love out of the corporate closet." And Third Metric wellness practices extend far beyond yoga and meditation. Farhad Chowdhury, CEO of the software development company Fifth Tribe, connects with colleagues during four-mile hikes. As Gregory Berns, author of *Iconoclast: A Neuroscientist Reveals How to Think Differently*, writes, insight and discovery are most accessible to us when we break up our routine. "Only when the brain is confronted with stimuli that it has not encountered before does it start to reorganize perception. The surest way to provoke the imagination, then, is to seek out environments you have no experience with." Nobel Prize–winning chemist Kary Mullis, he notes, landed on the principle of polymerase chain reaction, or PCR, not in a lab but on a Northern California highway.

What matters is that we find a way—any way—to recharge and renew ourselves. My screensaver is a picture of gazelles: They are my role models. They run and flee when there is a danger—a leopard or a lion approaching—but as soon as the danger passes, they stop and go back to grazing peacefully without a care in the world. But human beings cannot distinguish between real dangers and imagined ones. As Mark Williams explains, "The brain's alarm signals start to be triggered not only by the current scare, but by past threats and future worries. . . . So when we humans bring to mind other threats and losses, as well as the current scenario, our bodies' fight-or-flight systems do not switch off when the danger is past. Unlike the gazelles, we don't stop running." This is modern man's predicament, perfectly summed up by Montaigne: "There were many terrible things in my life, but most of them never happened." We need to liberate ourselves from the tyranny of our fight-or-flight mechanism. And yet much of our life has actually been structured so that we live in an almost permanent state of fight-or-flight—here comes another dozen emails calling out for a response; must stay up late to finish the project; I'll just use these four minutes of downtime to return six more calls. Under our current definition of success, a chronic state of fight-or-flight is a feature, not a bug.

Overconnectivity: The Snake in Our Digital Garden of Eden

Unfortunately the ever-increasing creep of technology—into our lives, our families, our bedrooms, our brains—makes it much harder to renew ourselves. The average smartphone user checks his or her device every six and a half minutes. That works out to around 150 times a day. Our brains are naturally wired to connect, so it's not easy to turn away from these kinds of stimuli.

But the connection that comes from technology is often an unfulfilling, ersatz version of connection. Its siren call (or beep, or blinking light) can crowd out the time and energy we have for real human connection. Worse, there is evidence that it can begin to actually rewire our brains to make us less adept at real human connection.

David Roberts, a writer for the environmental online magazine *Grist*, saw this happening in his own life. "I am burnt the f— out," he wrote in a memorable good-bye-to-the-Internet-and-his-job-for-a-year letter. So he decided to do something about it:

> I enjoy sharing zingers with Twitter all day; I enjoy writing long, wonky posts at night. But the lifestyle has its drawbacks. I don't get enough sleep, ever. I don't have any hobbies. I'm always at work. . . . I'm never disconnected. It's doing things to my brain. I think in tweets now. My hands start twitching if I'm away from my phone for more than 30 seconds. I can't even take a pee now without getting "bored." I know I'm not the only one tweeting in the bathroom. . . . The online

world, which I struggle to remember represents only a tiny, unrepresentative slice of the American public, has become my world. I spend more time there than in the real world.

He is not alone. A 2012 McKinsey Global Institute study found that the average knowledge economy employee spends 28 percent of his or her time dealing with email—more than eleven hours a week. According to SaneBox, which makes email-filtering software, it takes us sixty-seven seconds to recover from each email that lands in our in-boxes. "At some point," says SaneBox's Dmitri Leonov, "we have to understand this process is hurting us."

Our relationship with email has become increasingly one-sided. We try to empty our in-boxes, bailing like people in a leaky lifeboat, but more and more of it keeps pouring in. How we deal with our email has become a big part of our techno-stress. And it's not just the never-ending e-deluge of emails we never get to—the growing pile that just sits there, judging us all day—but even the ones we do get to, the replied-to emails that we think should be making us feel good. Linda Stone worked on emerging technologies at both Apple and Microsoft in the 1980s and '90s. In 1997, she coined the term "continuous partial attention" to describe the state of always being partly tuned into everything while never being completely tuned in to anything. Now it feels like a good three-word description of modern life. Ten years later Stone noticed something peculiar happening when she read her email: She would hold her breath for short bursts of time. So she dubbed it "email apnea." She also conducted a study to see if others experience the same thing. The results? Eighty percent of those she examined were found to have periods of "email apnea."

It might sound trivial, but it's not. Disrupting your body's breathing pattern can knock your body's balance of oxygen, nitric oxide, and carbon dioxide out of whack, which can, in turn, play a part in exacerbating stress-related conditions.

The simplest tool for avoiding email apnea? To observe your breathing as you deal with your emails—to pull yourself out of automatic pilot. And remember, as *Financial Times* columnist Tim Harford puts it, "Email is your servant. Corner-office people have secretaries to prevent them from being interrupted. . . . Email will do all this for you too." His advice: Turn off all notifications; you should control when you want information, not the reverse.

The problem is that with smartphones, email is no longer confined to the office. It comes with us—to the gym, to dinner, to bed. But there are more and more ingenious ways to fight back. Like the "phone stacking" game when friends meet for dinner—they put their phones in a stack in the middle of the table and the first one who checks his device before the bill comes has to pick up the check. Kimberly Brooks, *HuffPost*'s founding arts editor, plays another game at dinner—the "don't take a picture of your meal" game. "Unless you're an on-call doctor or food professional," she says, "pulling out your cell phone during a meal with family, co-workers, friends, and especially kids, at home or a restaurant, pierces the sanctity of mealtime or, as I like to think of it, the invisible-ceremonial-dome-under-which-humankind-forges-civilization." She wants to add inappropriate phone-checking to the standard list of etiquette no-nos: "I seriously look forward to the day when the widely accepted practice of having phones anywhere near meals, never mind taking pictures, is looked upon as repugnant as picking one's nose, scratching one's balls, or chainsmoking in public."

The editor of *Scene* magazine Peter Davis recounted a dinner party in which the host offered to check the guests' smartphones at the door. Perhaps smartphones at a party should be treated like coats, usually taken to a back room or otherwise stowed away until guests are ready to leave—a signal, like taking off your coat, that you're happy to be here and you're going to stay awhile.

Leslie Perlow, professor at Harvard Business School, introduced something called predictable time off (PTO), in which you take a planned night off—no email, no work, no smartphone. At one company that tried it, the Boston Consulting Group, productivity went up, and it's now a company-wide program. And after noticing that engineers at a software company were tired and harried from working all-nighters and weekends, Perlow came up with "quiet time," set periods in which employees agree to let one another work unfettered.

Given that we multitask now for most of our days, if not our lives, unfettered work and play—unitasking—is something that has to be scheduled.

A study by researchers from the University of California, Irvine, and the U.S. Army found that avoiding your inbox—taking an "email vacation"—reduces stress and allows you to focus more. It can have an even bigger effect when an entire company decides to take an email vacation. That's what Shayne Hughes, CEO of Learning as Leadership, decided to do in 2013, sending out an announcement that "all internal e-mail is forbidden for the next week." Employees were skeptical, but he says the results were unequivocal. "Our high-octane, stay-on-top-of-whatever-is-happening-via-e-mail mentality disappeared," he wrote in *Forbes*. "In its place we experienced a more focused and productive energy. . . . The decrease in stress from one day to the next was palpable. So was our increase in productivity." The experience, he concluded, "reconnected us with the neglected power of human interaction." Volkswagen has a special policy for employees who are provided with a smartphone and aren't part of management: The phone is programmed to switch off work emails automatically from 6 p.m. to 7 a.m. so that the employees can take care of themselves and their families without feeling they have to stay plugged in to work. FullContact, a Denver software company, gives employees a $7,500 bonus if they follow three rules: "1. You have to go on vacation, or you don't get the money. 2. You must disconnect. 3. You can't work while on vacation."

Paradoxically, one of the biggest growth sectors for tools to help us deal with technology is . . . technology. The first stages of the Internet were about data and more data. But now we have plenty of data—indeed, we're drowning in it—and all the distraction we could ever hope for. Technology has been very good at giving us what we want, but not always what we need. So now, many in the tech world have realized there's a growth opportunity for applications and tools that help us focus and filter all that data and distraction. I have collected some of my favorites in Appendix A at the end of the book.

The good news, as immunologist Esther Sternberg explained, is that "you don't need to go offline—I mean, offline, off your brain's line—for very long to reset things. . . . if you feel your stress level mounting, you just turn away and look at the trees and listen to the birds and be quiet for a few moments. You can bring it down."

Going offline can often become harder and harder as you advance up the career ladder. Increased power also brings with it the danger of losing the very qualities that are most essential to leadership. One study found that increased power lowers an executive's ability to be empathic. Another study on leadership and perspective found that power makes us "prone to dismiss" or misunderstand others' viewpoints. And relying increasingly on non-empathy-building electronic communications would only seem to exacerbate these tendencies. So any tool that can increase our self-awareness and ability to listen and be in the moment is invaluable.

Secure Your Own Mask First

Meditation, yoga, mindfulness, napping, and deep breathing once upon a time might have been thought of as New Agey, alternative, and part of a counterculture. But in the past few years we've reached a tipping point as more and more people realize that stress-reduction and mindfulness aren't only about harmonic convergence and universal love—they're also about increased well-being and better performance.

Indeed not only is there no trade-off between living a well-rounded life and high performance, performance is actually improved when our life becomes more balanced. As Sheryl Sandberg told me, "I found that when I cut my office hours dramatically once I had kids, I was not just working less, but I was more productive. Having children forced me to treat every minute of my time as precious—did I really need that meeting? Was that trip essential? And not only did I get more productive, but everyone around me did too as I cut out meetings that weren't essential for them also."

In 2008 and then again in 2012, *The Huffington Post* decided to demonstrate that a balanced life is possible even during the most compulsively hectic days on the political calendar. During the 2008 Democratic National Convention in Denver, we offered harried conventioneers—including delegates and members of the media—a chance to unplug and recharge at the *HuffPost* Oasis, where we offered yoga classes, Thai massages, hand massages, minifacials, healthy snacks and refreshments, music, and comfortable seating for lounging and unwinding.

The response was overwhelming. In fact, many hardened reporters told us that they had a difficult time tearing themselves away and returning to the convention, and we also had plenty tell us that taking time to recharge allowed them to cover the convention with more energy and come through the grueling week without being completely burned out. So in 2012, we did it again, on a larger scale, bringing our Oasis to both the Republican convention in

Tampa and the Democratic convention in Charlotte. The connection between being able to unplug and recharge and to think more deeply and productively about critical issues, such as poverty, education, the environment, and the jobs crisis, may not be immediately obvious. But the better people are at taking care of themselves, the more effective they'll be in taking care of others, including their families, their coworkers, their communities, and their fellow citizens. When you're on an airplane you're told to "secure your own mask first before helping others," even your own child. After all, it's not easy to help somebody else breathe easier if you're fighting for air yourself. As Aleksandr Solzhenitsyn asked in his novel *In the First Circle*: "If you wanted to put the world to rights, who should you begin with: yourself or others?"

Of course, the idea of taking time out of our busy lives to rest dates back to the Ten Commandments, when God commanded the Israelites to "Remember the Sabbath day, to keep it holy. Six days you shall labor, and do all your work, but the seventh day is a Sabbath to the Lord your God. On it you shall not do any work. . . . For in six days the Lord made heaven and earth, the sea, and all that is in them, and rested on the seventh day. Therefore the Lord blessed the Sabbath day and made it holy." For observant Jews, the time from sundown on Friday to sundown on Saturday is a time for introspection, spending time with family and friends, and doing anything but working—a biblical mandate to unplug and recharge. And Shabbat ends with the ceremony of *Havdalah*—separation—in which participants thank God for distinguishing "light and darkness" and "the seventh day of rest and the six days of labor."

For women with jobs and careers, taking care of themselves becomes even harder if they become mothers. In our current corporate culture, having children is often seen as a major barrier to career advancement. There are certainly challenges in juggling family and career, and there are many badly needed institutional reforms that would make it less challenging. But for me, having children was the best possible antidote to my workaholic "always on" tendencies. It gave me perspective and the ability to be more detached from the inevitable ups and downs of work life. Of course, you don't need to have children to have a healthy sense of priorities, but for me, they did make it easier. Just knowing I was going to see my daughters at the end of the day put my whole workday in a different light. Even a simple phone call from one of my daughters during the day, I found, was a reminder of what is really important in my life. And that is true to this day, now that my daughters are in their twenties. I'm far less likely to get stressed over a setback. And by the way, have you ever experienced a day without setbacks? Perhaps one day a brilliant scientist—undoubtedly a scientist with a big family—will come up with a name for this effect. But whatever it is, it has had a big impact on things like my confidence, mood, and enthusiasm, all of which are huge assets in the workplace.

Here, too, the science has caught up. According to a 2009 study from Brigham Young University, having a family has a measurable impact on our health, including on our blood pressure. Attaching blood pressure monitors to nearly two hundred husbands and wives, researchers noticed that couples with children had significantly lower blood pressure than those without kids. The effect was even more pronounced among women.

This is not to say that companies don't urgently need to address the structural impediments that make having children and a successful career so much harder. For far too many people—women especially—there is too little support in place to help balance career and family—which is crucial if we are truly going to redefine success for everyone. Flexible time, telecommuting, project-based work, and a company culture that does not expect employees to be wired and responsive 24/7 need to become the norm if we are to make our workplaces truly sustainable.

Our current toxic definition of success and our addiction to our devices is having a particularly negative impact on the next generation. "Generation Y," otherwise known as the millennials, could be given a third, more alarming, name: "generation stress." A study commissioned by the American Psychological Association asked participants to rank their stress level. Millennials marched at the front of the stress parade.

Moreover, the findings were dismally consistent across almost every question. Nearly 40 percent of millennials said their stress had increased over the past year, compared to 33 percent for baby boomers and 29 percent for older Americans. Over half of millennials said that stress had kept them awake at night during the past month, compared to 37 percent for baby boomers and 25 percent for older Americans. And only 29 percent of millennials say they're getting enough sleep.

In the United Kingdom, according to a study by Oxford

professor Russell Foster, more than half of British teenagers may be sleep deprived: "Here we have a classic example where sleep could enhance enormously the quality of life and, indeed, the educational performance of our young people. Yet they're given no instruction about the importance of sleep and sleep is a victim to the many other demands that are being made of them."

Higher levels of stress put millennials at higher risk downstream for all sorts of destructive consequences. Stress, as we've seen, is a huge contributing factor in heart disease, diabetes, and obesity. And already, 19 percent of millennials have been diagnosed with depression, compared to 12 percent of baby boomers and 11 percent of older Americans.

Not surprisingly, one of the biggest causes of stress among younger Americans is work. Seventy-six percent of millennials report work as a significant stressor (compared to 62 percent of baby boomers and 39 percent of older Americans). Among the challenges facing millennials is the growing number of them who graduate college with massive student debt and find themselves entering a weak job market. So millennials more than any other generation are casualties of the stress built into our economy—either overworking and hooked on technology, or unable to find work and struggling to pay the bills and survive.

Of course, many of these are problems that require political action and economic reform. But whatever end of the spectrum one finds oneself, mindfulness, meditation, and assorted tools and practices not only help strengthen our resilience and ingenuity in the face of adversity, they also lead to greater performance in the workplace.

And, yes, I realize there is a paradox in using the idea of enhanced performance as a selling point for practices that would help us redefine success. What we are talking about, after all, is what's ultimately important in our lives. In other words, meditation, yoga, getting enough sleep, renewing ourselves, and giving back make us better at our jobs at the same time that they make us aware that our jobs don't define who we are.

Whatever your entry point is—take it. Right now you may just want to be better at your job, or help your company become more successful, and that's the reason you start meditating, or practicing mindfulness, or sleeping more. But along the way you will likely also gain some added perspective on what matters in your life. Writing in *The New York Times* about the Third Metric conference we held in June 2013, Anand Giridharadas pointed out that "there is risk in this approach. . . . To make the case for greater attention to well-being in terms of its effect on work performance may be to win the battle and lose the war. The victor remains the idea that what is good for work is good for us."

I believe we can win both the battle and the war. Paying greater attention to our well-being—for whatever reason— connects us with parts of ourselves that now lie dormant and makes it more likely that there will no longer be any split between being successful at work and thriving in life.

Sleep Your Way to the Top

The most basic shift we can make in redefining success in our lives has to do with our strained relationship to sleep. As Dr. Michael Roizen, chief wellness officer of the Cleveland Clinic, put it, "Sleep is the most underrated health habit." Most of us fail to make good use of such an invaluable part of our lives. In fact, we deliberately do just the opposite. We think, mistakenly, that success is the result of the amount of time we put in at work, instead of the quality of time we put in. Sleep, or how little of it we need, has become a symbol of our prowess. We make a fetish of not getting enough sleep, and we boast about how little sleep we get. I once had dinner with a man who bragged to me that he'd gotten only four hours of sleep the night before. I resisted the temptation to tell him that the dinner would have been a lot more interesting if he had gotten five.

There's practically no element of our lives that's not improved by getting adequate sleep. And there is no element of life that's not diminished by a lack of sleep. Including our leaders' decisions. Bill Clinton, who used to famously get only five hours of sleep a night, admitted, "Every important mistake I've made in my life, I've made because I was too tired." And in 2013, when the European Union was working on a plan to bail out Cyprus, an agreement was reached during the wee hours of the night that was described by one commentator as "impressively stupid." The financial journalist Felix Salmon describes the decision as "born of an unholy combination of procrastination, blackmail, and sleep-deprived gamesmanship." The role of sleep deprivation in international negotiations would make an excellent doctoral dissertation (just don't pull any all-nighters to finish it).

Our creativity, ingenuity, confidence, leadership, and decision making can all be enhanced simply by getting enough sleep. "Sleep deprivation negatively impacts our mood, our ability to focus, and our ability to access higher-level cognitive functions: the combination of these factors is what we generally refer to as mental performance," say Drs. Stuart Quan and Russell Sanna, from Harvard Medical School's Division of Sleep Medicine. I have been such a sleep evangelist for the past five years that I was asked to join its executive council—a role that has provided me with a great education in the latest sleep research, and that has, in turn, further reinforced my sleep evangelism!

A study at Duke University has found that poor sleep is associated with higher stress levels and a greater risk of heart disease and diabetes. They also found that these risks are greater in women than in men. Till Roenneberg, a professor at Ludwig-Maximilians University in Munich, who is an expert on sleep cycles, coined the term "social jetlag" to explain the discrepancy between what our body clocks need and what our social clocks demand. Of course, plain old jet lag can also play havoc with our body clocks—so, as someone who travels a lot across multiple time zones, I am ruthless in enforcing my anti-jetlag rules. While airborne, I drink as much water as possible, strictly avoid sugar and alcohol, move around the plane as much as space and security restrictions will allow, and, above all, sleep as long as I can with the help of my meditation music playlist (and by putting away portable electronic devices—even when they're allowed).

Like meditation, our sleep patterns can have a physical effect on our brain. A study conducted at Harvard Medical School found that people who got more sleep than the bare minimum they needed increased the volume of gray matter in their brains, which is linked to improved psychological health.

A 2013 study on mice showed that during sleep the brain clears out harmful waste proteins that build up between its cells—a process that may reduce the risk of Alzheimer's. "It's like a dishwasher," said one of the study's authors, Maiken Nedergaard, a professor of neurosurgery at the University of Rochester. Professor Nedergaard made an analogy to a house party: "You can either entertain the guests or clean up the house, but you can't really do both at the same time. . . . The brain only has limited energy at its disposal and it appears that it must choose between two different functional states—awake and aware or asleep and cleaning up." Far too many of us have been doing too much entertaining and not enough cleaning up.

As the Great British Sleep Survey found, poor sleepers are seven times more likely to feel helpless and five times more likely to feel alone. These are consequences that can impact everything from our relationships and our ability to focus to our health. Our sleep deficit has significant economic costs, as well. A 2011 Harvard Medical School study found that insomnia was significantly associated with lost work performance, and when projected onto the entire U.S. workforce, the study estimates that the lost performance due to insomnia costs businesses more than $63 billion per year.

More and more scientific studies speak to the irrefutable benefits of sleep. A study published in *Science* even calculated that for the sleep deprived, an extra hour of sleep can do more for their daily happiness than a $60,000 raise. In fact, a number of studies have failed to find a consistent connection between extra money and happiness—as large increases of real income in the developed world over the past half century have not correlated with increases in reported happiness. University of Southern California economics professor Richard Easterlin conducted a study that analyzed the correlation between income and reported well-being, and found that in Japan, well-being levels remained constant between 1958 and 1987, despite a 500 percent increase in real income!

But what do we do if, despite our best intentions, we're not getting the seven or eight hours a night of sleep we need? Researchers have found that even short naps can help us course correct. Throughout history, famous nappers have included Leonardo da Vinci, Thomas Edison, Eleanor Roosevelt, Winston Churchill, and John F. Kennedy. Charlie Rose, a famous napper of our time, told me that he is now taking up to three naps a day: "I have a nap after we finish our CBS morning show, a nap before I tape my own show, and a nap before I go out in the evening. I don't like the feeling of going through my day tired!" According to David Randall, author of *Dreamland: Adventures in the Strange Science of Sleep*, a short nap "primes our brains to function at a higher level, letting us come up with better ideas, find solutions to puzzles more quickly, identify patterns faster and recall information more accurately."

Of course, getting more sleep is easier said than done—believe me, I know! This is especially true in a culture that's wired and connected 24/7. And more and more science is proving that glowing screens and sleep are natural enemies. Researchers at Rensselaer Polytechnic Institute recently published a study showing that the light from computer screens obstructs the body's production of melatonin, which helps govern our internal body clock and regulates our sleep cycle. Technology allows us to be so hyperconnected with the outside world that we can lose connection to our inner world.

We desperately need to purge our lives of the poison of what Anne-Marie Slaughter called "time macho." She describes it as our "relentless competition to work harder, stay later, pull more all-nighters, travel around the world and bill the extra hours that the international date line affords you."

In January 2010, I convinced Cindi Leive, editor in chief of *Glamour* magazine, to join me in a New Year's resolution that we believed would improve the lives of women everywhere in the world: to get more sleep. To us, sleep was a feminist issue. You see, of all the sleep-deprived Americans, women are the most fatigued. Working moms get the least sleep, with 59 percent of respondents to a national survey reporting sleep deprivation, and 50 percent saying they get six hours of sleep or less. Cindi admitted that between her work, her two young children, and her TV addiction, she was averaging just over five hours a night.

"Women are significantly more sleep-deprived than men," confirms Dr. Michael Breus, author of *Beauty Sleep*. "They have so many commitments, and sleep starts to get low on the totem pole. They may know that sleep should be a priority, but then, you know, they've just got to get that last thing done. And that's when it starts to get bad." Cheating your body out of the R & R it needs can make you more prone to illness, stress, traffic accidents, and weight gain. (Dr. Breus swears that sleeping will actually do more to take off weight than exercise!)

But there's more to sleep deprivation than physical problems. Rob yourself of sleep and you'll find you do not function at your personal best. This is true of work decisions, relationship challenges, or any life situation that requires judgment, emotional equilibrium, problem solving, and creativity. "Everything you do, you'll do better with a good night's sleep," says Dr. Breus. Yet we constantly push ourselves to get by on less until we often don't even know what "peak performance" feels like anymore.

There's a reason why sleep deprivation is classified as a form of torture and is a common strategy employed by religious cults. They force prospective members to stay awake for extended periods to reduce their subjects' decision-making ability and make them more open to persuasion. So the choice is ours. Do we want to be empowered women and men taking charge of our lives? Or do we want to drag ourselves around like zombies?

Back to our New Year's resolution. For a month, Cindi and I committed to getting a full night's sleep—in Cindi's case seven and a half hours of sleep, in mine eight (arrived at through trial and error as the number of hours it takes for each of us to be at our most creative and effective).

Getting a good night's sleep, of course, is an easier resolution to make than to keep. We had to tune out a host of temptations—from Jon Stewart to our email in-boxes. And most of all, we had to ignore the workaholic wisdom that says we're lazy for not living up to the example set by notoriously self-professed undersleepers.

Of course, the truth is just the opposite: Each of us is much more likely to be a professional powerhouse if we're not asleep at the wheel. The problem is that women too often feel that they don't "belong" in the boys' club atmosphere that still dominates many workplaces. So they attempt to overcompensate by working harder and longer than the guy next to them. Hard work helps women fit in and gain a measure of security. And it can work, at least initially. So they begin to do it more and more and more often, making long hours part of their professional lifestyle. But it's a Pyrrhic victory: The workaholism leads to lack of sleep, which, in turn, leads to not being at our best. Too many of us are fueled by the fear that getting the proper amount of sleep means we must not be passionate enough about our work and our life.

By sleeping more we, in fact, become more competent and in control of our lives. It gives new meaning to the old canard of women sleeping our way to the top. Women have already broken glass ceilings in Congress, space travel, sports, business, and the media—imagine what we can do when we're all fully awake.

Having a buddy certainly made our efforts to get more sleep much easier and more fun. I remember Cindi emailing me on day three: "I got seven and a half last night but it was *very stressful* to get myself to bed on time! I was rushing around like I was trying to make a train!" She helped me identify that same feeling in myself. One night, I was discussing a potential *HuffPost* headline with our founding editor Roy Sekoff at 10:30 p.m. and I started getting nervous that I was going to miss the train. So Roy and I sped up our brainstorming so we could get the new headline up on the site without me missing my sleep deadline (it felt as if we were defusing a bomb in an action movie). Most important, as we were hanging up, I was able to laugh at myself—always a great stress buster.

And I discovered a number of great sleep aids: for starters, the yummy pink silk pajamas Cindi sent me as a gift. Just putting them on made me feel ready for bed—so much more than the cotton T-shirts I usually wear at night. Those pajamas were unmistakably "going-to-bed clothes," not to be confused with "going-to-the-gym clothes." Too many of us have ignored the distinction between what you wear during the day and what you wear to bed. Slipping on the PJs was a signal to my body: Time to shut down!

An even more important signal that it's time to shut down is turning off our devices: I made sure I had my iPhone and my BlackBerrys (yes, I have more than one!) charging far, far away from my bed, to help me avoid the middle-of-the-night temptation to check the latest news or latest emails.

And Cindi came up with a new trick to use if she was having trouble falling asleep: "Counting backward from 300 by threes—it works like magic and you never get below 250." On the few occasions when I feel too wired to sleep, my panacea is a hot bath with my favorite bath salts.

On day four of our "sleep rehab" I actually woke up without an alarm. I looked around anxiously to see what was wrong, wondering what emergency my body had summoned my attention for. It took me a minute or two to realize that the reason I was wide awake was because . . . I didn't need to sleep anymore. Imagine that.

Professor Roenneberg explains that although 80 percent of the world uses an alarm clock to wake up on workdays, discovering how much sleep we truly need is fairly simple: "We sometimes overeat, but we generally cannot oversleep. When we wake up unprompted, feeling refreshed, we have slept enough."

He goes on: "With the widespread use of electric light, our body clocks have shifted later while the workday has essentially remained the same. We fall asleep according to our (late) body clock, and are awakened early for work by the alarm clock. We therefore suffer from chronic sleep deprivation." It's like we're going deeper and deeper into debt, and we're never going to get out.

One of the benefits of getting enough sleep was starting my day feeling like one of those horrible "rise and shine" people you normally want to throttle when you are among the sleep-deprived majority. I hit the ground running, minus the morning mental fog.

Many of us know that regular exercise helps us sleep better, but what I discovered is that it's a two-way street: Regular sleep also helps us exercise better. It's a truth that I felt, quite literally, in my bones, and that has been borne out by science. According to a recent study in the *Journal of Clinical Sleep Medicine* by researchers from Northwestern, after a bad night's sleep, participants reported having shorter exercise sessions.

When I hit the workout machines as part of my morning exercise routine, I was lifting heavier weights, punching the treadmill button to go faster, and giving it a higher incline than usual. If someone who knows my usual exercise routine saw me during these workouts, I'd probably be asked to submit to mandatory drug testing. But the only performance-enhancing stimulant I was on was a couple of eight-hour nights of sleep. This is one reason why, as Dr. Breus points out, getting more sleep can lead to weight loss.

And my energy lasted throughout the day. I have a group of friends with whom I hike. It's our tradition that whoever is feeling the most energized that day has to talk on the way up the hill we climb. The rest talk on the way down. Let's just say I'm pretty well-known as a consistent downhill talker. But on my last hike I was talking nonstop on the way up—mostly haranguing my hiking partners to get more sleep.

I also took another cue from Cindi, who devised a plan to treat her bedtime like an appointment—with the same urgency and importance that we give all our work-related appointments. It is, in effect, a meeting you've scheduled with yourself. She calculates what time she needs to be up, counts back seven and a half hours (that's her goal) and whatever time that is becomes her appointment. If you have Type A tendencies (guilty!), and feel satisfaction by meeting deadlines and appointments, it's a brilliant way to use your compulsion more productively.

Too many of us think of our sleep as the flexible item in our schedule that can be endlessly moved around to accommodate our fixed and top priority of work. But like a flight or train, our sleep should be thought of as the fixed point in our day, and everything else should be adjusted as needed so we don't miss it.

And to help keep her appointment, Cindi utilized Dr. Breus's suggestion to set an alarm to go off—in your bedroom—when it's time to *go* to bed. "You'll be forced to enter your bedroom to turn the damn thing off—which at least gets you into the right room at the right time," she told me.

Going public about your decision to get more sleep can be one way to make that commitment stick. You'll be surrounded, as I found out, by sympathetic friends who have been wanting to do the same thing and who will help you stick to your sleep goals. In my case, because I blogged about my sleep commitment on *The Huffington Post*, I started having complete strangers come up to me at events, glancing at their watches and wondering how much longer I planned to stay and whether I was going to be able to get my eight hours. I felt like a kid out on a school night—with dozens of babysitters all anxious to help me keep my commitment.

One result of getting more—and better—sleep has been an increase in the intensity of my dreams. I'm not sure if my dreams are actually more intense, vivid, and interesting, or if they only seem that way because I'm not waking up longing to sleep more. Whatever the reason, I suddenly find myself in possession of a rich and compelling dream life.

Reconnecting with my dreams has been like reuniting with an old flame. I've always been fascinated by dreams. On a trip to Luxor in Egypt, I visited the "sleep chambers" at the Luxor Temple where the high priests and priestesses retired after they had prepared, through prayer and meditation, to receive in their sleep divine guidance and inspiration. In stark contrast to our modern habit of drugging ourselves senseless, hoping to "crash" for a few hours before having to face another frantic day, the ancient Egyptians went to sleep expectantly. This spiritual preparation for sleep allowed them to bring back remnants of their dreams and notes from their night's travels.

Even before my trip to Egypt, I had long been captivated by Carl Jung's emphasis on dreams and archetypes. His autobiographical *Memories, Dreams, Reflections* is one of my favorite books. It helped me explore the possibility that the world of dreams, far from shutting us off from what we consider "the real world," actually opens us up to another reality—a timeless place that allows us to listen to our souls.

Following that trip to Egypt, and for many years after, I used to write down my dreams in a journal. I filled notebook after notebook. But then life—especially motherhood—intervened. And between nursing a newborn, comforting a crying baby, or holding a feverish toddler—to say nothing of trying to continue to write books and newspaper columns—time evaporated into the night, and sleep became aspirational, more of a survival tactic and less of a way to connect to the sacred and the divine.

Night and sleep soon became all about transitions: Head hitting the pillow only when the schedule allowed. Waking up already late, already on the run. Life became a cycle of crash and rush, crash and rush. It was a cycle I eventually became used to. It seemed normal.

Then came my "reawakening"—my reacquaintance with sleep, when I made sleep a priority. When I did so, I also gave myself permission to remember my dreams. A side benefit of remembering your dreams is that it is a great opportunity to connect even more deeply with the people closest to you. My younger daughter and I now regularly exchange our dreams.

One of her recurring dreams is a good metaphor for what a good night's sleep allows us to do. She imagines herself as a living "Stop" sign, forcing people to come to a complete stop before moving on with their lives.

Dr. Breus explains why dreaming is so important. "Dreaming (most often in REM sleep) helps consolidate your memories. So what might that mean for you? You will begin to see an improvement in your overall memory and your ability to organize your thoughts, and maybe getting things done."

Beyond the practical benefits of remembering your dreams, there are the deeper, spiritual reasons, summed up by Rumi: "There is a basket of fresh bread on your head, and yet you go door to door asking for crusts. Knock on your inner door. No other." Remembering our dreams is a way to knock on our inner door and find deeper insights and self-awareness.

The sleep experts I have consulted with have provided me a number of additional sleep tips. Here are some of the ones I found the most useful:

- Get a new pillow. And a new pillowcase.
- Make your bedroom darker and keep it cool.
- Practice deep breathing before bed.
- Take a warm bath before bed.
- Exercise or at least walk every day.
- Banish all LCD screens (laptops, tablets, smart-phones, TV) at night.
- Cut down on coffee after 2 p.m. and avoid alcohol right before bedtime to give the body time to me-tabolize it.

And during the day, to prevent stress from building up—which makes it harder to fall asleep at night—every few hours take sixty seconds of recovery time the way top tennis players introduce tiny slots of recovery rituals into their game. All you have to do is stop what you are doing, and simply bring your awareness to the palms of your hands or the soles of your feet, or both. Let it stay there for a minute, and feel all tension leaving your body, drifting away from you through your hands and feet.

Four years after our Sleep Challenge, Cindi and I launched an Unplugging Challenge—and this time we were joined by Mika Brzezinski, who, in addition to cohosting *Morning Joe*, is also my cohost for our series of Third Metric conferences. For the last week of December, we all pledged to swear off TV, social media, and email so we could truly connect with our loved ones and with ourselves.

"Try unplugging," wrote Mika of her initial response to shutting off her devices, "when, for the last decade, you have eaten, slept, showered, and exercised with your iPhone in hand. 'Obsessed' is not the word. 'Addicted' doesn't sum it up either. 'Tethered'? 'On permanent phone-IV'? 'Permanently attached'? Closer." Her unplugged week was spent on vacation with her family—including her phone-addicted teenage daughters. She vividly described what those first moments of phantom phone pain were like: "When I put the phone down, I felt weird, incomplete, like I wasn't wearing a bra or something. At times during the beginning of the vacation, I actually held the phone even though it was off. It was like weaning: The turned-off phone was my binky." But she was amply rewarded for following through. "I got so much out of unplugging," she wrote. "Complete conversations with my dad and mom. A fun swim with my niece. Running with Carlie. Running with Jim and Carlie. Walking with Emilie. Connecting. I even watched the sun go down without stopping to check my binky." Her conclusion: "I highly recommend unplugging! For your health. For your relationships. For your life!"

As for Cindi, she also went through a shaky withdrawal, but the week taught her several lessons. For instance, as she wrote, "When you're not on your phone, you instantly notice: everyone else is. Like, literally everyone. We returned from vacation slightly less informed but slightly more blissed out, and more likely to stay Zen in annoying situations because of the little digital detox." She also decided to carry some of those lessons forward: "I'm vowing to stay off email for most of my evenings, to keep my phone in my bag, not my hand, more often this year. Anyone with me?" I urge you to join her!

Lessons from the Sports Page: The Ultimate Performance-Enhancing Drugs

The fundamental flaw at the heart of our misguided definition of success is the belief that overworking is the route to high performance and exceptional results. One easy way to see the folly of this belief is to look at the world of sports, where performance is objectively quantified and measurable. The sports world, the source of many metaphors in the business world—"home run," "slam dunk," "dropping the ball," "heavy hitters," "step up to the plate," and so forth—is, in fact, way ahead of the business world in its thinking about productivity and burnout.

Top athletes are all about results. And because sports are endlessly quantifiable, it's often very easy to measure just what does and doesn't work. The tough, hard-hitting world of elite sports is increasingly embracing meditation, yoga, mindfulness, enough sleep, and napping precisely because athletes and coaches realize that they work. And for the shrinking pool of doubters, there is perhaps no better way to see the tangible effects of mindfulness and stress-reduction tools on performance than in the world of sports.

One of the most interesting—and widely cited—studies came out of Stanford. Over ten years ago, Cheri Mah, a researcher at the Stanford Sleep Disorders Clinic, was looking into the impact of sleep on the brain. Several of the subjects in her research were on the Stanford swim team. They revealed to Mah that during the portions of the test when they were asked to get more sleep they swam better and set personal bests. So Mah set out to see how strong the connection was between increased sleep and increased performance.

Some early studies—using swimmers, football players, and tennis players—had pointed to a strong connection. So Mah ran a bigger study, which, as ESPN's Peter Keating writes, "jolted the world of sports analytics by essentially showing that you can get safe, legal HGH [human growth hormone] just by shutting off the lights."

Over three seasons, Mah had eleven Stanford basketball players keep a normal schedule for a few weeks and then, for five to seven weeks, had them take naps, eat carefully, and try to get ten hours of sleep a night. All eleven players saw improvements in their performance. Three-point shooting went up 9.2 percent. Free throws were up 9 percent. Not only did on-court performance improve, but players said their moods were lifted and that they generally felt less fatigued. "What these findings suggest is that these athletes were operating at a sub-optimal level," Mah said. "They'd accumulated a sleep debt. . . . It's not that they couldn't function—they were doing fine—but that they might not have been at their full potential."

And all over the sports world, new practices are being introduced:

- In 2005, the U.S. Olympic Committee, in consultation with sleep expert Mark Rosekind, upgraded the rooms at its Colorado Springs training center. The renovation consisted of better mattresses, blackout curtains, and encouragement for the athletes to aim for nine or ten hours of sleep. And many have taken the advice to heart. "Sleep is huge in my sport," says Olympic marathoner Ryan Hall. "Recovery is the limiting factor, not my ability to run hard. I typically sleep about eight to nine hours a night but then I make sure to schedule 90 minute 'business meetings'—aka naps—into my day for an afternoon rest."

- The Dallas Mavericks partnered with Fatigue Science from Vancouver to monitor players' sleep and compare it with their on-court performance using a wristband device. Fatigue Science founder Pat Byrne explained the logic: "If a player is sleeping six hours a night and says, 'I feel fine,' we can actually say, 'We can make your reaction time better if you're sleeping eight hours.' We can prove it to you, we can show you."

• Los Angeles Lakers superstar Kobe Bryant will often linger at the team hotel before a game to get more sleep. He's also done meditation—a practice brought in by former coach Phil Jackson. Jackson also taught the concept of "one breath, one mind" to his players and had them engage in exercises such as a day of silence. "I approached it with mindfulness," he told Oprah. "As much as we pump iron and we run to build our strength up, we need to build our mental strength up . . . so we can focus . . . so we can be in concert with one another."

• When Michael Jordan was the star of the Chicago Bulls, the team worked with meditation teacher George Mumford. "When we are in the moment and absorbed with the activity, we play our best," Mumford explained. "That happens once in a while, but it happens more often if we learn how to be more mindful." And a video of four-time NBA MVP LeBron James meditating during a timeout became a hit on YouTube.

• Former Miami Dolphins running back Ricky Williams used to meditate before every game, and later ended up teaching a class on meditation at Nova Southeastern University in Florida. "This is my passion," he said. "I think a lot of people are so used to being stressed, they don't realize they're stressed. And I was one of those people."

• Tennis great Ivan Lendl used mental exercises to deepen his concentration. He would schedule downtime for relaxing and recharging often by taking naps.

Since Lendl became Andy Murray's coach in 2012, the four-time grand slam runner-up won the U.S. Open in 2012 and Wimbledon in 2013. Charlie Rose, in an interview with Murray, described what it's like watching Murray and other great pro players: "You see the ball coming off the racket . . . it almost looks like slow motion."

What a great image to hold in mind: a performer at the top of his game—rested, recharged, and focused; time slowing down, the ball moving in slow motion, allowing him to make the best decision and execute it. I have found that mindfulness and stress-reduction techniques do the exact same thing for the rest of us. In a rushed, harried, stressed-out state, the onslaught of what we have to do can go by in a jumbled blur. But rested and focused, what's coming next appears to slow down, allowing us to manage it with calm and confidence.

As Tony Schwartz, founder of the Energy Project, says, with exercise, it's during rest and downtime that muscle growth occurs. To achieve peak physical fitness, we push ourselves hard in short bursts of high intensity, and then we rest and recover. And that's exactly how we should live our lives for overall performance and well-being.

"The same rhythmic movement serves us well all day long, but instead we live mostly linear, sedentary lives," Schwartz writes. "We go from email to email, and meeting to meeting, almost never getting much movement, and rarely taking time to recover mentally and emotionally. . . .

The most effective way to operate at work is like a sprinter, working with single-minded focus for periods of no longer than 90 minutes, and then taking a break. That way when you're working, you're really working, and when you're recovering, you're truly refueling the tank."

As with elite athletes who put in the necessary preparation—both mentally and physically—you'll see a tangible difference in your work performance. In a study last year at the University of Washington, computer scientist David Levy had a group of human resources managers go through an eight-week mindfulness and meditation course. He then gave them some challenging office tasks, involving email, instant messages, and word processing. Members of the group who had gone through the training could concentrate for longer stretches of time, were less distracted, and, most important, had lower stress levels. "Meditation is a lot like doing reps at a gym," Levy said. "It strengthens your attention muscle."

We don't have to have a four-foot vertical leap to be like Michael Jordan and perform at our best. All we need is the commitment to get enough sleep, take time to recharge our mental and emotional batteries, put away our phones and laptops and tablets regularly, and try to introduce some stress-reduction tools into our lives. Mindfulness, yoga, prayer, meditation, and contemplation aren't just tools reserved for retreats over long weekends anymore—they are the ultimate everyday performance enhancers.

Walk This Way

When I was living in Los Angeles, I discovered that I came up with many of my best ideas while I was hiking. And whenever I could, I would schedule hikes instead of sit-down meetings, with both my friends and *HuffPost* editors.

Silicon Valley executive Nilofer Merchant calls this the "walk the talk" method. If you've got to talk to someone in person, why not do it while walking? "What I love is that you're literally facing your problem or situation together when you walk side by side with someone," she said. "I love that people can't be checking e-mail or Twitter during walking meetings. You're awake to what's happening around you, your senses are heightened and you walk away with something office meetings rarely give you—a sense of joy."

How many times have you experienced a sense of joy in a stale conference room while half listening to an endless PowerPoint presentation? Between our minds and our legs, *one* of them is going to wander. Sit still and our minds want to ramble. Get up and start walking, and our minds can slow down and be more focused.

One of my favorite phrases is *solvitur ambulando*—"It is solved by walking." It refers to the fourth-century-BC Greek philosopher Diogenes's response to the question of whether motion is real. To answer, he got up and walked. As it turns out, there are many problems for which walking is the solution. In our culture of overwork, burnout, and exhaustion, how do we tap into our creativity, our wisdom, our capacity for wonder? *Solvitur ambulando.*

A lot of the planning for *The Huffington Post* was done on hikes. Our first investor, Laurie David, decided to invest after I pitched her the idea on a hike. Our founding arts editor, Kimberly Brooks, pitched me the idea of an arts section on a hike. Walking was also really important when I went into labor. Indeed, doctors are discovering that keeping women in bed for hours while they're in labor is one of the worst ways to facilitate the baby coming through the birth canal. Even though I was scheduled to give birth at the UCLA Medical Center, I spent most of my labor walking with my midwife around the grounds of the nearby hotel where we were staying. By some strange coincidence, that was the day that the sale of the hotel to new Japanese owners had been announced. So my strolls—around the grounds, past the herb garden, across the grass, and back to the lobby—were punctuated by the stares of worried disbelief from tourists, Japanese cameramen, and a couple of local television crews, as well as by my occasional sharp contraction–induced gasps and my midwife's confident words of support.

When the midwife estimated I was within an hour of delivering, we piled into the car—by then my mother and sister had joined us—and off we went to the hospital. Thirty minutes later Christina was born.

For as long as I can remember, walking has frequently led to solutions to whatever preoccupied me. When I was growing up in Greece, my favorite poem was "Ithaka" by the Greek poet Constantine Cavafy. My sister, Agapi, and I had memorized the poem long before we could actually understand what it meant. It opens:

As you set out for Ithaka,
hope the voyage is a long one,
full of adventure, full of discovery.

Over the years, I came to realize that a journey that is full of adventure and discovery doesn't have to involve planes and cars and passports. The benefits of a journey are available simply by walking. Now that I live in Manhattan, I walk all the time, both to get from place to place and to catch up with friends instead of having breakfast or lunch meetings.

There are many accounts throughout history on the virtues of walking. Thomas Jefferson claimed the purpose of walking was to clear the mind of thoughts. "The object of walking is to relax the mind," he wrote. "You should therefore not permit yourself even to think while you walk. But divert your attention by the objects surrounding you." For Ernest Hemingway, walking was a way of developing his best thoughts while mulling a problem. "I would walk along the quais when I had finished work or when I was trying to think something out," he wrote in *A Moveable Feast*. "It was easier to think if I was walking and doing something or seeing people doing something that they understood." Nietzsche went even further and proclaimed that "only thoughts conceived while walking have any value"! For Henry David Thoreau, walking wasn't just a means to an end; it was the end itself: "The walking of which I speak has nothing in it akin to taking exercise . . . but is itself the enterprise and adventure of the day."

Scientific studies increasingly show the psychological benefits of walking and other forms of exercise. "It's become clear that this is a good intervention, particularly for mild to moderate depression," said Jasper Smits, a psychologist at Southern Methodist University. The results are so clear-cut that Smits and a colleague have written a guidebook for mental health professionals with advice on how to actually prescribe exercise for patients. And, surprise, there is no page-long list of dangerous side effects accompanying this prescription. In the United Kingdom, in a series of studies at the University of Essex, researchers found that 94 percent of those who took part—walking, running, cycling, gardening—saw mental health benefits.

Psychologist Laurel Lippert Fox has taken the idea one step further and conducts walking sessions with her patients. As she says, "It's so much more dynamic than sitting in your Eames chair."

Walking as a tool for dealing with depression is no small thing when you consider that, according to the World Health Organization, more than 350 million people worldwide suffer from depression.

Research has shown similar benefits from simply being outdoors and surrounded by nature, which has "implications not only for city planning but also for indoor design and architecture," according to Richard Ryan of the University of Rochester Medical Center. He coauthored a study showing that spending time in natural settings makes us more generous and more community oriented. Another study, this one by Dutch researchers, shows that those who live within one kilometer of a park or wooded area suffer lower rates of depression and anxiety than those who don't. But even if we don't live surrounded by trees and greenery, we can always take a walk through them.

"As health-care costs spiral out of control, it behooves us to think about our green space in terms of preventive health care," said Dr. Kathryn Kotrla of the Texas A&M College of Medicine. "This highlights very clearly that our Western notion of body-mind duality is entirely false. The study shows that we are a whole organism, and when we get healthy that means our body and our mind get healthy."

On the flip side, it turns out that sitting is as bad for us as walking is good for us. According to an American Cancer Society study, people with a sitting job are more likely to develop cardiovascular disease than those with standing jobs. This is not a new discovery. A 1950s study of people in similar lines of work showed London bus drivers had a higher incidence of death from cardiovascular disease than bus conductors, and government clerks had a higher incidence than postal workers.

The benefits of getting up and walking—of moving—go beyond our bodies. A study led by University of Illinois researchers shows that walking three times a week for forty minutes at one's own natural pace helps combat the effects of aging and increases brain connectivity and cognitive performance. So it's not just ruminative, creative thinking that's enhanced by walking—our focused, get-things-done type of thinking is improved, as well. Perhaps in addition to walking meetings we should consider creating walking classrooms.

Though he didn't have the science to back up his beliefs about the benefits of walking, Henry David Thoreau was onto this truth long ago. "Methinks that the moment my legs begin to move, my thoughts begin to flow," he wrote. In her book *Wanderlust*, author Rebecca Solnit noted the connection between the act of walking and how we experience the world. "Walking shares with making and working that crucial element of engagement of the body and the mind with the world," she wrote, "of knowing the world through the body and the body through the world."

This touches on a concept critical in the Japanese aesthetic, including the traditional tea ceremony—the concept of Ma, which can be loosely translated as the essential space, or interval, or gap between things, and the importance of creating and fully experiencing such spaces. So whether we are just "taking a walk" without wanting to get anywhere in particular, or whether we are walking toward a destination, walking to connect two places, the space, the interval in between, can be important. It can, in fact, be the point.

Except for the point, the still point,
There would be no dance,
and there is only the dance.

—T. S. ELIOT

"Space is substance," as graphic designer Alan Fletcher put it. "Cézanne painted and modeled space. Giacometti sculpted by 'taking the fat off space.' Mallarmé conceived poems with absences as well as words. Ralph Richardson asserted that acting lay in pauses. . . . Isaac Stern described music as 'that little bit between each note—silences which give the form.'"

Walking is one of the ways we move through our world;

language and writing are how we articulate that experience. "Words inscribe a text in the same way that a walk inscribes space," writes British author Geoff Nicholson. "Writing is one way of making the world our own, and . . . walking is another."

To fully experience the world around us, we first have to be able to free ourselves from the distractions that are constantly begging for our attention. Even the supremely focused Thoreau struggled to stay in the moment: "I am alarmed when it happens that I have walked a mile into the woods bodily, without getting there in spirit. In my after-noon walk I would . . . forget all my morning occupations and my obligations to Society. But it sometimes happens that I cannot easily shake off the village. The thought of some work will run in my head and I am not where my body is—I am out of my senses. . . . What business have I in the woods, if I am thinking of something out of the woods?"

"Shake off the village"—what a perfect way of convey-ing a vitally important and universal human need. Since Thoreau's time, the village has grown exponentially bigger and become more intrusive and seemingly more intimate—giving us the semblance of human connection without any of the real benefits of that connection. Technology has en-abled the village to become exceptionally good at not allow-ing us to shake it off. With the advent of the smartphone, getting away from it all is no longer as easy as simply get-ting up and walking away. Increasingly, we don't even try to shake off the village. We surrender to a life of distractions, living, as Thoreau put it, much of our lives out of our senses.

We walk the city texting and talking and listening to music on our smartphones, disconnected from those around us and from ourselves. Journalist Wayne Curtis calls these hyperconnected individuals "the digital dead, shuffling slowly, their eyes affixed to a small screen in their hands." He cites a University of Washington study that focused on a single intersection in Seattle. The study found that one in three pedestrians was distracted while crossing the street, and in the vast majority of cases, they were distracted by either listening to music or typing or talking on a phone. And, not surprisingly, it took those who were texting almost 20 percent longer to cross the street. Another study found that those texting were 33 percent slower getting to a planned destination.

As *Guardian* columnist Oliver Burkeman wrote, "Smartphones have been ubiquitous for years, of course—but much more recently, there seems to have been a shift in social norms. For many people, the unwritten rules of sidewalk choreography now include this: If what I'm reading or watching on my phone is sufficiently interesting to me, it's entirely up to you to get out of my way, just as if I were very frail, or three years old, or blind. Or a lamppost." It can be a dangerous habit. In December 2013, a tourist in Melbourne fell off a pier and plunged into the sea while checking Facebook on her phone. She still had it in her hand when she was rescued. And she was one of the lucky ones. According to an Ohio State University study, in 2010 more than 1,500 pedestrians were admitted to emergency rooms as a result of accidents involving cell phones or other mobile devices.

In trying to lessen the hold of technology on our lives, we need all the help we can get. Some of us are able to switch our devices on and off, go cold turkey for periods of time, or go on periodic digital diets. But not all of us have that kind of willpower. Walking—without our devices, or with our devices turned off—is a start.

"I suspect the greatest mental benefits of walking are explained not by what it is, but by what it isn't," writes Burkeman. "When you go outside, you cease what you're doing, and stopping trying to achieve something is often key to achieving it."

Forcing our brains to process in a new environment can help us to engage more fully. Gregory Berns, author of *Iconoclast: A Neuroscientist Reveals How to Think Differently*, writes that our brain gains "new insights from people and new environments—any circumstance in which the brain has a hard time predicting what will come next."

So, please, walk. It makes us healthier, it enhances cognitive performance, from creativity to planning and scheduling, and it helps us to reconnect with our environment, ourselves, and those around us.

(Furry) Friends with (Different) Benefits

There are many different ways of inserting Third Metric values into our lives. Meditation, long walks, exercise, yoga, reconnecting with family and friends, and making sure to unplug, recharge, and get enough sleep—all will increase some aspect of our well-being and sense of fulfillment. Another way is by being close to animals. A purpose of life is to expand the boundaries of our love, to widen the circle of our concern, to open up rather than shut down, and to expand rather than contract. Every week brings more stories and science about the amazing ways in which pets can open our hearts and enhance our lives. Allen McConnell, professor of psychology at Miami University, writes in *Psychology Today* that it's well-known that our social network is important for our emotional well-being. But that network is not limited to people. According to research from McConnell's lab, pet owners have higher self-esteem, fewer feelings of loneliness, and are more physically fit and socially outgoing than people without pets.

In another study involving ninety-seven pet owners, some in the group were made to feel rejected socially (sounds like high school all over again). Afterward, some in the study were asked to write about their best friends, while others wrote about their pets. What the researchers found was that thinking about a pet provided the same power to recover from the negative feelings of rejection as thinking about a best friend.

Interestingly, the studies found no support for the idea that socially isolated people turn to pets as a kind of human replacement—an idea that led to the "crazy cat lady" cliché. To the contrary, McConnell writes, "owners seem to extend their general human social competencies to their pets as well." In other words, those with deep human relationships gain the greatest benefits from having a pet.

Like spouses and close friends, pets can become "included in the self," the core of our being that forms our perspective. As McConnell put it, "They become as much a part of the self as many family members," and end up having a powerful impact on our health and happiness.

But the benefits of pets go beyond the everyday. "Pets offer an unconditional love that can be very helpful to people with depression," said Ian Cook, psychiatrist and director of UCLA's Depression Research and Clinic Program. They also add a sense of responsibility, regular activity, a set routine, and reliable companionship, which can be an invaluable source of healing.

Studies have also found that pet owners have lower blood pressure, a reduced risk of heart disease, and lower levels of stress. All with no side effects, other than the occasional chewed furniture leg. Pets can also be a plus in the workplace. A 2012 study published in the *International Journal of Workplace Health Management* found that in the course of the workday, stress levels decreased for workers who brought in their dogs. "The differences in perceived stress between days the dog was present and absent were significant," said Randolph Barker, professor at Virginia Commonwealth University. "The employees as a whole had higher job satisfaction than industry norms." Barker also found that the good feelings didn't just occur in pet owners. Employees who didn't have a dog at work often asked those who did if they could take the dog out for a break. Having a dog in the office had a positive effect on the general atmosphere, counteracting stress and making everyone around happier. "Pet presence may serve as a low-cost wellness intervention readily available to many organizations," concluded Barker.

Today, only 17 percent of American businesses allow workers to bring their pets to the office. But that 17 percent includes some of the most innovative companies—Amazon, Zynga, Tumblr, and Google among them. Google takes it so seriously that its pet policy is written into its Code of Conduct: "Dog Policy: Google's affection for our canine friends is an integral facet of our corporate culture."

The role of animals, and especially dogs, as roving ambassadors of goodwill can be seen most clearly in their role as therapy dogs. After the tragic massacre in Newtown, Connecticut, in December 2012, therapy dogs from all over the country were brought in to help the community, and especially the children of Sandy Hook Elementary School. Six months later Newtown held a "Day of Thanks" to show its gratitude. Fifty dogs (and many more owners and residents) attended the gathering. One parent explained that her daughter had had a rough time after the shooting. "But when she talked about the dogs that she saw every day at school, she lit up."

Another young girl and a therapy dog developed an especially moving bond. At a Christmas party for Sandy Hook children just after the shooting, nine-year-old Emma Wishneski happened upon a therapy dog named Jeffrey, rescued from a New York City shelter and nicknamed the "Positively Peaceful Pit Bull." When Emma met Jeffrey, it was love at first sight, and the two were inseparable for the whole party. And since then they've had regular playdates. "It was still a really vulnerable time for her, and she just was comfortable sitting next to Jeffrey," Emma's mother said. "He's strong and I think she just feels safe." Since then Emma has begun to train her family's dog Jedi (also a rescue dog) as a therapy dog. "Emma has a smile that could light the world, and I feel like we used to see that smile a lot more, but it's definitely still there," her mother said. "When she's with Jeffrey she doesn't stop smiling."

Animals help us be better humans. Quite often, they show us how to be our best selves. Always in the moment, sticking their noses into everything (literally), they see a world that we take for granted, one we're usually just hurriedly passing through on our way to lives we never quite reach.

In her book *On Looking: Eleven Walks with Expert Eyes*, cognitive scientist Alexandra Horowitz writes about seeing the world through a variety of eyes. One set of eyes belongs to her dog, who inspired her to "see the spectacle of the ordinary."

While the term "pet owner" implies a hierarchy with humans on top in the relationship, in reality, as John Grogan, author of *Marley & Me*, put it, "A person can learn a lot from a dog, even a loopy one like ours. Marley taught me about living each day with unbridled exuberance and joy, about seizing the moment and following your heart. He taught me to appreciate the simple things—a walk in the woods, a fresh snowfall, a nap in a shaft of winter sunlight. And as he grew old and achy, he taught me about optimism in the face of adversity. Mostly, he taught me about friendship and selflessness and, above all else, unwavering loyalty."

Novelist Jonathan Carroll put it this way:

Dogs are minor angels, and I don't mean that facetiously. They love unconditionally, forgive immediately, are the truest of friends, willing to do anything that makes us happy, etcetera. If we attributed some of those qualities to a person we would say they are special. If they had ALL of them, we would call them angelic. But because it's "only" a dog, we dismiss them as sweet or funny but little more. However, when you think about it, what are the things that we most like in another human being? Many times those qualities are seen in our dogs every single day—we're just so used to them that we pay no attention.

Pets are the unrivaled masters of giving back. The pleasure they take in giving themselves to us is perhaps their greatest lesson. Like our animals, we are wired to connect, to reach out, to love. But unlike them, with us other things get in the way—jealousy, insecurity, irritation, anger. Pets help us constantly come back to what makes us human. They're a furry version of our best selves.

Beyond Economic Indicators: A True Happiness Index

Though it may be difficult to measure, the idea that happiness should be part of our national dialogue and purpose is not new. As I mentioned in the introduction, the "pursuit of happiness" is enshrined in the Declaration of Independence as one of the unalienable rights we are endowed with by our Creator. Efforts in various countries, including France, the United Kingdom and the United States, to measure the actual well-being of their citizens were the subject of a piece by *The Washington Post*'s Peter Whoriskey.

As he noted, the idea of a broader measure of a country's success beyond economic indicators was memorably articulated by Robert F. Kennedy in 1968:

Too much and too long, we seem to have surrendered personal excellence and community values in the mere accumulation of material things. Our gross national product . . . if we judge America by that . . . counts air pollution and cigarette advertising, and ambulances to clear our highways of carnage. . . . Yet the gross national product does not allow for the health of our children, the quality of their education, or the joy of their play. It does not include the beauty of our poetry or the strength of our marriages; the intelligence of our public debate or the integrity of our public officials. It measures neither our wit nor our courage; neither our wisdom nor our learning; neither our compassion nor our devotion to our country; it measures everything, in short, except that which makes life worthwhile.

In France in 2008, then-president Nicolas Sarkozy launched an initiative headed by economists and Nobel laureates Joseph Stiglitz and Amartya Sen "to shift emphasis from measuring economic production to measuring people's well-being."

David Cameron, now Great Britain's prime minister, made the same point at a Google Zeitgeist Europe conference in 2006. "It's time we admitted that there's more to life than money, and it's time we focused not just on GDP, but on GWB—general well-being. Well-being can't be measured by money or traded in markets. It's about the beauty of our surroundings, the quality of our culture and, above all, the strength of our relationships." Four years later, he announced that a national well-being survey would be conducted by the Office for National Statistics. "To those who say that all this sounds like a distraction from the serious business of government," he said, "I say finding out what will really improve lives and acting on it is the serious business of government."

The idea of measuring our well-being is gaining ground. The European Union runs a "European Quality of Life Survey." The Paris-headquartered Organization for Economic Cooperation and Development has a "Better Life Index"; it declared Australia the world's happiest industrialized country in 2011, 2012, and 2013. And the United Nations commissioned a "World Happiness Report," which found that Scandinavian countries were the happiest, and that the least happy countries were in Africa. The director of the Earth Institute at Columbia University, Jeffrey Sachs, who edits the UN report, said: "There is now a rising worldwide demand that policy be more closely aligned with what really matters to people as they themselves characterize their well-being." And in 2011, the National Academies convened a panel that includes Nobel laureate Daniel Kahneman to come up with a way to measure "subjective well-being."

In fact, the idea of measuring our well-being is so widespread that last year *The Economist* declared that "the happiness industry" was "one of the more surprising industries to have taken off during the current period of economic downturn."

I completely support any effort to show that we're more than just our marginal contribution to our bank accounts, the bottom line of our employers, or the gross national product of our countries. But to truly measure our state of happiness and well-being, it's important to look at the whole picture.

In the United Kingdom, for instance, the Office for National Statistics based its conclusions entirely on a survey in which they asked around 165,000 people over the age of sixteen a few questions about how satisfied they were with their lives on a scale of 0 to 10 (0 being "not at all" and 10 being "completely"). Based on this methodology, the Office for National Statistics found that happiness in the United Kingdom had climbed from 7.41 in April 2012 to 7.45 in March 2013. But is a .04 increase really a meaningful difference—one solid enough to conclude that happiness in Britain is on the rise—as some papers trumpeted?

Moreover, if you are unhappy, answering survey questions about how satisfied you are with your life might not be high on your to-do list—and indeed, about half of the people approached refused to participate. This is just one illustration of the danger of drawing too many conclusions from too little data.

It's pretty easy to find real data for the United Kingdom that completely contradict the results of the happiness index. In 2011, there were more than forty-five million prescriptions written for antidepressants, up 9 percent from the previous year, and the National Health Service spent more than £270 million on antidepressants, a 23 percent increase from 2010.

So while the idea behind conducting happiness surveys is worthwhile, it should be broadened to include as much data as possible. A more comprehensive happiness index would include not only data such as the use of antidepressants and sleeping pills but also alcoholism rates; suicide rates; the incidence of illnesses linked to stress, including diabetes and high blood pressure; health care spending for stress-related illnesses; the percentage of employers offering wellness programs and flexible work schedules; and the number of workdays lost to stress.

Nonetheless, it is significant that so many leaders finally recognize that the well-being of their citizens depends on more than just a country's quarterly growth rate (as important as that is), especially if this leads to policy changes—from job creation to family leave—that reduce stress and improve well-being.

At the personal level, there are three simple steps each one of us can take that can have dramatic effects on our well-being:

1. Unless you are one of the wise few who already gets all the rest you need, you have an opportunity to immediately improve your health, creativity, productivity, and sense of well-being. Start by getting just thirty minutes more sleep than you are getting now. The easiest way is to go to bed earlier, but you could also take a short nap during the day—or a combination of both.

2. Move your body: Walk, run, stretch, do yoga, dance. Just move. Anytime.

3. Introduce five minutes of meditation into your day. Eventually, you can build up to fifteen or twenty minutes a day (or more), but even just a few minutes will open the door to creating a new habit—and all the many proven benefits it brings.

And here are some simple steps to get you started meditating:

1. Choose a reasonably quiet place to begin your practice, and select a time when you will not be interrupted.

2. Relax your body. If you would like to close your eyes, do so. Allow yourself to take deep, comfortable breaths, gently noticing the rhythm of your inhalation and exhalation.

3. Let your breathing be full, bring your attention to the air coming in your nostrils, filling up your abdomen, and then releasing. Gently and without effort, observe your breath flowing in and out.

4. When thoughts come in, simply observe them and gently nudge your attention back to the breath. Meditation is not about stopping thoughts, but recognizing that we are more than our thoughts and our feelings. You can imagine the thoughts as clouds passing through the sky. If you find yourself judging your thoughts or feelings, simply bring yourself back to the awareness of the breath.

5. Some people find it helpful to have a special or sacred word or phrase that they use to bring their awareness back to the breath. Examples include "om," "hu," "peace," "thank you," "grace," "love," and "calm." You can think of that word each time you inhale, or use it as your reminder word if your mind starts to wander.

6. It is really important not to make your meditation practice one more thing you stress about. In fact, *reducing* stress is one of the major benefits of meditation together with increased intuition, creativity, compassion, and peace.

For more support and guidance, there are many meditation tools in Appendix B to help you start or deepen your practice.

Wisdom

The endless cycle of idea and action,
Endless invention, endless experiment,
Brings knowledge of motion, but not of stillness;
Knowledge of speech, but not of silence;
Knowledge of words, and ignorance of the Word. . . .
Where is the Life we have lost in living?
Where is the wisdom we have lost in knowledge?
Where is the knowledge we have lost in information?

—T. S. ELIOT

Life as a Classroom

ROWING UP in Athens, I was brought up on the classics and the Greek myths. They were taught to me not as ancient history, as my children learned them in their American classrooms, but as my personal roots and the source of my identity. Athena was the goddess of wisdom, and, for me, the idea of wisdom is forever identified with her—weaving together strength and vulnerability, creativity and nurturing, passion and discipline, pragmatism and intuition, intellect and imagination, claiming them all, the masculine and the feminine, as part of our essence and expression.

Today we need Athena's wisdom more than ever. She breathes soul and compassion—exactly what has been missing—into the traditionally masculine world of work and success. Her emergence, fully armed and independent, from Zeus's head, and her total ease in the practical world of men, whether on the battlefield or in the affairs of the city; her inventive creativity; her passion for law, justice, and politics—they all serve as a reminder that creation and action are as inherently natural to women as they are to men. Women don't need to leave behind the deeper parts of themselves in order to thrive in a male-dominated world. In fact, women—and men, too—need to reclaim these instinctual strengths if they are to tap into their inner wisdom and redefine success.

Wisdom is precisely what is missing when—like rats in the famous experiment conducted by B. F. Skinner more than fifty years ago—we press the same levers again and again even though there is no longer any real reward. By bringing deeper awareness into our everyday lives, wisdom frees us from the narrow reality we're trapped in—a reality consumed by the first two metrics of success, money and power, long after they have ceased to fulfill us. Indeed, we continue to pull the levers not only after their diminishing returns have been exhausted, but even after it's clear they're actually causing us harm in terms of our health, our peace of mind, and our relationships. Wisdom is about recognizing what we're really seeking: connection and love. But in order to find them, we need to drop our relentless pursuit of success as society defines it for something more genuine, more meaningful, and more fulfilling.

Icarus, the Greek mythological figure who flew too close to the sun until his wax wings melted, is a great distillation of the tragedy of modern man. Ignoring all warnings until it is too late, he plunges headlong to his death in the ocean below. As Christopher Booker, author of *The Seven Basic Plots*, puts it, "Puffed up by his power to fly, he falls into the state of hubris, the cosmic pride which is the essence of egocentricity. Hubris defies the supreme law of balance and proportion which governs everything in the universe, and the inter-relatedness of all its parts." Icarus defies physical laws and the wax on his wings burns up as a result, just as we have been defying our true nature and end up burning out.

When we reexamine what we really want, we realize that everything that happens in our lives—every misfortune, every slight, every loss, and also every joy, every surprise, every happy accident—is a teacher, and life is a giant classroom. That's the foundation of wisdom that spiritual teachers, poets, and philosophers throughout history have given expression to—from the Bible's "Not a single sparrow can fall to the ground without God knowing it" to Rilke's "Perhaps all the dragons of our life are princesses, who are only waiting to see us once beautiful and brave." My favorite expression of wisdom—one that I keep laminated in my wallet—is by Marcus Aurelius:

> True understanding is to see the events of life in this way: "You are here for my benefit, though rumor paints you otherwise." And everything is turned to one's advantage when he greets a situation like this: You are the very thing I was looking for. Truly whatever arises in life is the right material to bring about your growth and the growth of those around you. This, in a word, is art—and this art called "life" is a practice suitable to both men and gods. Everything contains some special purpose and a hidden blessing; what then could be strange or arduous when all of life is here to greet you like an old and faithful friend?

I had a dream many years ago that sums up this thought in a different way, one that has become a sustaining metaphor for me. I am on a train going home to God. (Bear with me!) It's a long journey, and everything that happens in my life is scenery along the way. Some of it is beautiful;

I want to linger over it awhile, perhaps hold on to it or even try to take it with me. Other parts of the journey are spent grinding through a barren, ugly countryside. Either way the train moves on. And pain comes whenever I cling to the scenery, beautiful or ugly, rather than accept that all the scenery is grist for the mill, containing, as Marcus Aurelius counseled us, some hidden purpose and a hidden blessing.

My family, of course, is on board with me. Beyond our families, we choose who is on the train with us, who we share our journey with. The people we invite on the train are those with whom we are prepared to be vulnerable and real, with whom there is no room for masks and games. They strengthen us when we falter and remind us of the journey's purpose when we become distracted by the scenery. And we do the same for them. Never let life's Iagos— flatterers, dissemblers—onto your train. We always get warnings from our heart and our intuition when they appear, but we are often too busy to notice. When you realize they've made it on board, make sure you usher them off the train; and as soon as you can, forgive them and forget them. There is nothing more draining than holding grudges.

Divorce, especially if you have children, is one of life's hardest classrooms and can be one of the biggest sources of stress in our personal lives. Michael, my ex-husband, and I were married for eleven years and have been divorced for sixteen. And though we no longer had a marriage to keep us together, we had something even more powerful and permanent—our daughters. And, spurred by our mutual devotion to them, we have made a huge effort to work through all the difficulties and be friends. This has included spending Christmas Day and both of our girls' birthdays together as a family every year. And, little by little, with a lot of hard work, we've grown closer and closer. I remember the first time we went as a family on a summer vacation after our divorce, and how healing it was to be able to let go of our grudges and focus instead on the fact that we have two daughters together—a bond that transcends all grievances we'd built up through the years. We spent a lot of time on that vacation, and on many others since, strolling down memory lane with our girls or taking fanciful forays into the future (we spent a lot of time one night debating the pros and cons of evening weddings and the names of yet-to-be-born—and, thankfully, yet-to-be-conceived—grandchildren).

Our marriage may have been over, but our relationship wasn't. And isn't. And, like any relationship, it requires work and care and attention. The surest sign that my ex and I had reached a better place was a newfound willingness on both our parts to not let our pet peeves get in the way of our having a good time. Even in the happiest of marriages, there are little things that each partner does that inevitably set the other one off. These annoyances are magnified tenfold when you are no longer together as a couple—which is why making an effort to avoid them is one of the secrets of a good divorce.

For instance, Michael was a pioneer in insisting on no digital devices on holidays when the family was together. So I have kept to a 100 percent BlackBerry ban during our times together.

For my part, I was always put off by the way he would openly fume if I was even one second late for something— even on vacation (I always thought not having to adhere to a strict timetable was one of the defining features of a vacation!). But gradually that changed. When I would roll in a few minutes late to dinner, he wouldn't glare.

While we did not survive as a couple, at least we've survived in the joint parenting of our daughters—and the children are usually the biggest casualties of a bad divorce.

"God," Isabella said one day during a recent vacation, "it's hard to remember you guys are divorced." For some reason, that made me very, very happy. It felt like I had reached the end of a long and arduous journey. And we were all the better for having made it. For the sake of our inner peace and happiness, as well as for the sake of all the many children whose parents get divorced every year, this is a journey well worth taking.

Resentment is like drinking poison and waiting for the other person to die.

—CARRIE FISHER

There is nothing that we need more today than having proportion restored to disproportion, and separating our everyday worries and preoccupations from what is truly important. An amazing array of seemingly incompatible people and activities can coexist in our lives with harmony and a sense of order when we find an unambiguous center in ourselves.

I felt that when I first went to India at the age of seventeen. I had gone to Visva-Bharati University, founded in Shantiniketan by Rabindranath Tagore, to study comparative religion. As part of my course, I visited the holy shrine of Benaras, where dead bodies floated by on the Ganges as part of a Hindu ritual of spiritual transition, and emaciated holy men knelt in prayer among goats and pigeons. Pilgrims, most in rags but one in a gold sari, listened to the nonstop buzz of gurus and hawkers. It was chaotic, to be sure, and yet, in the middle of the chaos, I felt an unfathomable peace. I knew then that my life was never going to be lived on a serene mountaintop, but I also knew that it was possible to find peace and wisdom in the middle of a bustling marketplace, that we can achieve that elusive combination between stillness and the stream of the world—that we can be in the world but not of the world.

The seventeenth-century French mathematician and philosopher Blaise Pascal said that "all of humanity's problems stem from man's inability to sit quietly in a room alone." When we have learned to sit quietly in a room alone, we can maintain that inner connection that allows life to proceed from the inside out, whether we are alone or in a crowd of screaming people. And we can remain in this state of being no matter how much we're doing. It seems so simple, and when I'm in that place I wonder why I ever leave it. But it takes tremendous commitment and dedication to hold to it and, when I slip out of it, to catch myself quickly—again and again and again, and without judgment.

At *HuffPost* we developed a course-correcting free smartphone app called GPS for the Soul. It provides tools to help us return to a state of calm and balance. I know it's something of a paradox to look to an app to help us reconnect to ourselves, but there's no reason not to use the technology we always have in our pockets or purses to help free us from technology. Think of it as spiritual training wheels. GPS for the Soul connects us to a personalized guide, with music, poetry, breathing exercises, and pictures of our loved ones, to help us destress and recenter. You can also access the guides of experts, other users, or your friends.

It always amazes me how quickly I am able to move back to that centered place, and how it gets even easier as the path back becomes more and more familiar. We all have within us the ability to move from struggle to grace, whatever the challenges we encounter. When I'm in that "bubble of grace," it doesn't mean that the everyday things that used to bother, irritate, and upset me disappear; they don't, but they no longer have the power to bother, irritate, or upset me. And when the really hard things come our way—death, sickness, loss—we are better able to deal with them instead of being overwhelmed by them.

I faced one such big test on March 4, 2012. That's the day I got the sort of call every parent dreads more than anything else: "Mommy, I can't breathe." It was Christina, my oldest daughter, in her senior year at Yale, two months away from graduating.

Looking back on that March day as I was frantically driving from New York to the emergency room in New Haven, and later when we left the emergency room with my sedated daughter crying in my arms, and later still over the hard weeks that followed, I focused on all that I was grateful for: that my daughter was alive, that she had a loving family that rallied around her, and that she wanted to get well. Christina had struggled with drugs before, but we had thought that was behind her. And never before had it gotten to this point.

Everything else I thought was important in my life fell away. Over the next year, until Christina decided to go public with her addiction, only our family, her closest friends, and my daughters' godmothers knew. I felt like it was her story and her life—and, therefore, her decision if and when to talk about it. I was proud of her when, thirteen months later, she decided to write about her struggle:

Writing this blog a year ago would have been impossible, because of the shame and the deep guilt I felt about being an addict. I have never been abused or neglected. I didn't grow up in an alcoholic home. I have been blessed with an unconditionally loving family and I have been given every opportunity to thrive. Why then? Why cause the people who love me so much pain? Why be seemingly intent on throwing it all away?

The honest answer is: I don't know. What I do know—and I have grappled with this over the past 13 months—is that addiction is a disease. It is progressive, it can be fatal and it can touch anyone.

My life as it is today was unthinkable thirteen months ago. Yes, I mean the particulars—I have a steady job and healthy, loving relationships—but more than that I've learned to be vulnerable. I've learned how to apologize and how to forgive. I've learned how much strength it takes to let go. If writing this can help one person feel a little less alone, if it encourages one person to ask for help, if it allows one person to know that no matter how hopeless it feels right now, it can get better, then that is enough.

"Here's what no one tells you about sobriety," Christina says. "Giving up drugs is easy compared to dealing with the emotions drugs protected you from." Learning to be vulnerable without shame and accepting our emotions without judgment becomes much easier when we realize that we are more than our emotions, our thoughts, our fears, and our personalities. And the stronger the realization, the easier it becomes to move from struggle to grace.

The harder we press on a violin string, the less we can feel it. The louder we play, the less we hear. . . . If I "try" to play, I fail; if I race, I trip. The only road to strength is vulnerability.

—STEPHEN NACHMANOVITCH

Moving from struggle to grace sums up, as well, the experience of childbirth—going from a body racked with pain to the miracle of birth all in a few hours (if you're lucky). For all our medical advances, that miracle has never been diminished over the millennia. The staggering reality that we mortals can actually accomplish the act of human creation leaves us changed forever. It's a miracle that we honor with a yearly celebration until we die.

Having longed to have children for years, I was over the moon when, at thirty-eight, I finally became a mother. A few hours after Christina's birth, I had another grace-filled experience that, as I've since discovered, an amazing number of women have also had. And as personal diaries from previous generations show, this is not just a modern phenomenon.

I lay in bed nestling Christina to me for hours. When I finally grew sleepy, we put her in the crib next to my bed. A few moments later, after everyone had left the room, I began trembling convulsively. I tried to calm myself with the same soothing words I had just offered to my baby: "It's all right . . . it's all right."

And then I stopped shaking. I had left my body and was suddenly looking down at myself, at Christina, at the tuberoses on the nightstand, at the entire room. I had no fear at all; I knew I would return. And I was awash in an enormous sense of well-being and strength. It was as if a curtain had been pulled back to give me a glimpse of the wholeness of birth, life, and death. Seeing them all at once, I could accept them all. For I don't know how long, I hovered in that state of almost tangible peace. Then I watched a nurse enter the room; as she touched me, she jolted me back into the hospital reality. I returned with a great sense of confidence and joy. The anxiety of taking Christina home had disappeared. I knew we would be fine.

In our daily lives, moving from struggle to grace requires practice and commitment. But it's in our hands. I've come to believe that living in a state of gratitude is the gateway to grace. Gratitude has always been for me one of the most powerful emotions. Grace and gratitude have the same Latin root, *gratus*. Whenever we find ourselves in a stop-the-world-I-want-to-get-off mindset, we can remember that there is another way and open ourselves to grace. And it often starts with taking a moment to be grateful for this day, for being alive, for anything. Christina found tremendous value during her recovery by doing a nightly list of all she was grateful for that day and sharing it with three friends, who, in turn, emailed her their gratitude lists. And she has continued this practice to this day. The Oxford clinical psychologist Mark Williams suggests the "ten finger gratitude exercise," in which once a day you list ten things you're grateful for and count them out on your fingers. Sometimes it won't be easy. But that's the point—"intentionally bringing into awareness the tiny, previously unnoticed elements of the day."

Gratitude exercises have been proven to have tangible benefits. According to a study by researchers from the University of Minnesota and the University of Florida, having participants write down a list of positive events at the close of a day—and why the events made them happy—lowered their self-reported stress levels and gave them a greater sense of calm at night.

I find that I'm not only grateful for all the blessings in my life, I'm also grateful for all that hasn't happened—for all those close shaves with "disaster" of some kind or another, all the bad things that almost happened but didn't. The distance between them happening and not happening is grace.

And then there are the disasters that *did* happen, that leave us broken and in pain. For me, such a moment was losing my first baby. I was thirty-six and ecstatic at the prospect of becoming a mother. But night after night, I had restless dreams. Night after night I could see that the baby—a boy—was growing within me, but his eyes would not open. Days became weeks, and weeks turned into months. Early one morning, barely awake myself, I asked out loud, "Why

won't they open?" I knew then what was only later confirmed by the doctors. The baby's eyes were not meant to
open; he died in my womb before he was born.

Women know that we do not carry our unborn babies
only in our wombs. We carry them in our dreams and in
our souls and in our every cell. Losing a baby brings up so
many unspoken fears: Will I ever be able to carry a baby to
term? Will I ever be able to become a mother? Everything
felt broken inside. As I lay awake during the many sleepless
nights that followed, I began to sift through the shards and
splinters, hoping to find reasons for my baby's stillbirth.

Staggering through a minefield of hard questions and
partial answers, I began to make my way toward healing.
Dreams of my baby gradually faded, but for a time it seemed
as if the grief itself would never lift. My mother had once
given me a quotation from Aeschylus that spoke directly
to these hours: "And even in our sleep, pain which cannot
forget falls drop by drop upon the heart, and in our own
despair, against our will, comes wisdom to us by the awful
grace of God." At some point, I accepted the pain falling
drop by drop and prayed for the wisdom to come.

I had known pain before. Relationships had broken, illnesses had come, death had taken people I loved. But I had
never known a pain like this. What I learned through it
is that we are not on this earth to accumulate victories, or
trophies, or experiences, or even to avoid failures, but to be
whittled and sandpapered down until what's left is who we
truly are. This is the only way we can find purpose in pain
and loss, and the only way to keep returning to gratitude
and grace.

I love saying grace—even silently—before meals and when I travel around the world, observing different traditions. When I was in Tokyo in 2013 for the launch of *HuffPost Japan* I loved learning to say *itadakimasu* before every meal. It simply means "I receive." When I was in Dharamsala, India, every meal started with a simple prayer.

Growing up in Greece, I was used to a simple blessing before each meal, sometimes a silent one, even though I wasn't brought up in a particularly religious household. "Grace isn't something that you go for, as much as it's something you allow," wrote John-Roger, the founder of the Movement of Spiritual Inner Awareness. "However you may not know grace is present, because you have conditioned the way you want it to come, for example, like thunder or lightning, with all the drama, rumbling, and pretense of that. In fact, grace comes in very naturally, like breathing."

On a day when the wind is perfect, the sail just needs to open and the world is full of beauty. Today is such a day.

—RUMI

Both monks and scientists have affirmed the importance of gratitude in our lives. "It is a glorious destiny to be a member of the human race," wrote Thomas Merton, a Trappist monk from Kentucky, "though it is a race dedicated to many absurdities and one which makes many terrible mistakes: yet, with all that, God Himself gloried in becoming a member of the human race. A member of the human race! To think that such a commonplace realization should suddenly seem like news that one holds the winning ticket in a cosmic sweepstake."

What the foremost researchers in the field of gratitude, Robert Emmons of the University of California, Davis, and Michael McCullough of the University of Miami, have established is that "a life oriented around gratefulness is the panacea for insatiable yearnings and life's ills. . . . At the cornerstone of gratitude is the notion of undeserved merit. The grateful person recognizes that he or she did nothing to deserve the gift or benefit; it was freely bestowed." Gratitude works its magic by serving as an antidote to negative emotions. It's like white blood cells for the soul, protecting us from cynicism, entitlement, anger, and resignation. It's summed up in a quote I love (attributed to Imam Al-Shafi'i, an eighth-century Muslim jurist): "My heart is at ease knowing that what was meant for me will never miss me, and that what misses me was never meant for me."

The Power of the Hunch: When Your Inner Voice Speaks, Shut Up and Listen

One big indicator of the absence of wisdom is our failure to heed warning signs. History is filled with examples. The consequences of ignoring warning signs came to life for me a few years ago when I was visiting Pompeii. Walking around the ancient city, I was reminded how its people were wiped out in AD 79 by a volcanic eruption.

There had been many warning signs, including a severe earthquake in AD 62, tremors over the ensuing years, springs and wells that dried up, dogs that ran away, and birds that no longer sang. And then the most obvious warning sign: columns of smoke belching out of Mount Vesuvius before the volcano blew its top, burying the city and its inhabitants under sixty feet of ash and volcanic rock.

The warning tremors had been dismissed as "not particularly alarming." The warning signs of impending catastrophes are all around us today, pointing out the gulf between what we know we should be doing—on climate change, on growing economic inequalities, on the failed war on drugs—and what we're choosing to do instead. And the source of this gulf is an absence of wisdom.

One big source of wisdom is intuition, our inner knowing. We've all experienced it: a hunch, an inkling, our inner voice telling us to do something or not to do something. We hear the message, and it feels right, even if we can't explain why. Or for those of us who are more visual, we see something. A flickering insight, sometimes gone by the time it has registered if we don't learn to pay attention to it—the smile on the face of a child seen from the window of our train rushing by a playground. Even when we're not at a fork in the road, wondering what to do and trying to hear that inner voice, our intuition is always there, always reading the situation, always trying to steer us the right way. But can we hear it? Are we paying attention? Are we living a life that keeps the pathway to our intuition unblocked? Feeding and nurturing our intuition, and living a life in which we can make use of its wisdom, is one key way to thrive, at work and in life.

Intuition, not intellect, is the "open sesame" of yourself.

—ALBERT EINSTEIN

There are some for whom the word "intuition" conjures the idea of hippy-dippy New Age thinking, or something to do with the paranormal. But, in fact, from the beginning of recorded history, we have had the recognition of a kind of wisdom that is not the product of logic and reason. Western culture is a monument to reason. It gave us the Enlightenment and the industrial revolution and the information age, and all that has followed. But it wasn't reason alone that gave us those triumphs, nor is it reason alone that gets us through the day.

The third-century philosopher Plotinus wrote that there are three kinds of knowledge: "opinion, science, illumination. The means or instrument of the first is sense, of the second, dialectic, of the third, intuition." The Internet has made the first two types of knowledge very easy to come by. But it has taken us further away from that illumination, or wisdom, that is essential to living a life that matters.

Science has confirmed how important intuition is in the way we make decisions. "It has long been realized," psychologists Martin Seligman and Michael Kahana wrote, "that many important decisions are not arrived at by linear reasoning, but by intuition."

They go on to describe intuition-based decision making as: "a) rapid, b) not conscious, c) used for decisions involving multiple dimensions, d) based on vast stores of prior experiences, e) characteristic of experts, f) not easily or accurately articulated afterwards, and g) often made with high confidence."

There's a reason why we feel that our intuition comes from deep inside—why it's referred to sometimes as a "gut instinct" or a "feeling in your bones." It's because it's part of the core of our internal wiring. In his book *Blink*, Malcolm Gladwell describes how that core, the adaptive unconscious, functions as "a kind of giant computer that quickly and quietly processes a lot of the data we need in order to keep functioning as human beings."

Indeed, the point of *Blink* was how the reading of a situation by our adaptive unconscious, or intuition, can actually be much more accurate than our conscious, well-thought-out take. Gladwell tells the story of a kouros, a statue from ancient Greece, acquired by the J. Paul Getty Museum in Los Angeles. A team of scientists, after many tests, vouched for its authenticity. But a few art historians, including Thomas Hoving, former director of the Metropolitan Museum of Art, instantly knew otherwise; Hoving felt an "intuitive repulsion" for the piece. "In the first two seconds of looking—in a single glance," writes Gladwell, "they were able to understand more about the essence of the statue than the team at the Getty was able to understand after fourteen months." Could they explain why they knew? Gladwell asks. "Not at all. But they knew." And they turned out to be right. It was a fake.

In his book *Sources of Power: How People Make Decisions*, Gary Klein tells the story of a group of firemen fighting a fire inside a one-story house, spraying water at the flames in the kitchen: "The lieutenant starts to feel as if something is not right. He doesn't have any clues; he just doesn't feel right about being in that house, so he orders his men out of the building—a perfectly standard building with nothing out of the ordinary." The commander later said that he couldn't explain what had led him to shout the warning, attributing it to a "sixth sense." It was a very good thing that he did because just after the men followed his order and left, the floor they'd been standing on collapsed. The fire, it turned out, had been centered right below them, in the basement, which he had no clue even existed.

Klein also recounts a story of experienced nurses in a neonatal intensive care unit who could tell when a premature baby had sepsis despite conflicting symptoms—a crucial thing to know, since an infection could be fatal if not immediately treated. Often the nurses would know even before the test results came up positive. When he asked them how they knew, they said: intuition. "They looked," Klein writes. "They knew. End of story." Their intuition, it turned out, was based on subtle clues that the nurses themselves would be hard put to articulate. But they drew the proper conclusion in an instant.

We all know we have access to intuition if we nourish it and listen to it. We know that our intuition can be more accurate than trying to bear down on a problem with cold, hard logic. And we know that the consequences of listening to—or not listening to—our intuition can be, literally, a matter of life or death. So why do we so often ignore or disregard that inner voice in our lives?

I'm certainly not immune. I think about how often in my life I have ignored those whisperings, how easy it is to dismiss them or brush them aside or get so busy and harried that I simply don't take the time to listen. And often it's because I haven't got a rational explanation for why I'm feeling the way I'm feeling. But, of course, that's precisely why we should pay attention. That is part of what wisdom, as opposed to logic or data, is all about.

Let's say you're walking home one night. You come upon a dark alley, and you feel a little uneasy—a slight discomfort, a version of what the fire commander called his "sixth sense." Your inner voice, your adaptive subconscious, says, "Don't go down this alley." But you're in a hurry, so you do, albeit nervously. If your intuition is right, the consequences could be severe.

Or let's say you are interviewing to fill a vacant position at work. You feel a slight twinge of unease with a prospective candidate—but you're in a hurry, and the individual's qualifications seem strong on paper. The position has been open for a while and it must be filled, so you override your intuition and hire the person. That is how so many hiring mistakes are made. Or you're talking to your child and, distracted by other thoughts or a text you just received, you ignore a little niggle about something she was saying—or was not saying.

Sometimes what your intuitive response signals is that you need more information. But our modern, hyperconnected world throws up roadblock after roadblock between us and our intuition. It can get buried under a groaning email in-box, the constant chirping of our smartphones, or our running from appointment to appointment, stressed and burned out. If our intuitive voice had the same strength-of-signal bars our phones do, we'd often see that we're out of range of our wisdom.

"The longer we wait to defend our intuitions, the less we

will have to defend," Gary Klein writes. "We are more than the sum of our software programs and analytical methods, more than the databases we can access, more than the procedures we have been asked to memorize. The choice is whether we are going to shrink into these artifacts or expand beyond them."

For me, the easiest way to lose touch with my intuition is to be sleep deprived. As we saw in the Well-Being section, sleep deprivation lowers not just our attention span, focus, and memory, it also affects our emotional intelligence, self-esteem, and empathy toward others. And when we're sleep deprived we're more likely to cross ethical lines, because lack of sleep depletes our self-control. Our behavior and our character are not set in stone—they can be affected by how recharged and centered we are.

Meditation, yoga, and mindfulness can help us to still the noise of the world so we can listen to our inner voice. During my pregnancies with Christina and Isabella, I practiced yoga every day. It was a discipline I inherited from my mother, who could stand on her head for what seemed like hours when we were growing up in Athens. So it was a kind of family tradition, though one I rebelled against before finally embracing it. In the concentration and relaxation, the inner discipline and outer postures, I feel aligned, a balance that stays with me long after the yoga mats are rolled away.

One of the people who helped popularize meditation and yoga in the West was Paramahansa Yogananda. Here's how he put the need to take care of our intuitive inner selves in his 1946 *Autobiography of a Yogi:* "Intuition is soul guidance, appearing naturally in man during those instants when his mind is calm. Nearly everyone has had the experience of an inexplicably correct 'hunch,' or has transferred his thoughts effectively to another person. The human mind, free from the static of restlessness, can perform through its antenna of intuition all the functions of complicated radio mechanisms sending and receiving thoughts, and tuning out undesirable ones."

This was the book that Steve Jobs had asked to be given out at his memorial. Jobs had spent some time in India and was particularly taken with the role of intuition in our lives. "The people in the Indian countryside don't use their intellect like we do, they use their intuition instead, and their intuition is far more developed than in the rest of the world," Jobs said. "Intuition is a very powerful thing, more powerful than intellect, in my opinion. That's had a big impact on my work."

Intuition is about connections—but connections that aren't obvious and that can't be reasoned into existence. Our intuition connects us both to our inner selves and to something larger beyond ourselves and our lives. But it's incredibly easy to become disconnected from it. And with the pressures and pace of modern life, without deliberate effort, it's more likely than not that we will stay disconnected. Our intuition is like a tuning fork that keeps us in harmony—if we learn to listen. It helps us live more of our lives from that still center in us that Marcus Aurelius called our "inner citadel."

What is beyond doubt is that we spend most of our life outside that citadel. The key is course correcting. The ability to do that, and recognize that we need to, are skills we can learn and get better at simply through practice. Indeed, we can learn to course correct faster and faster, and bring ourselves back to that place of stillness, imperturbability, and loving—until it becomes second nature to return quickly to what is our true nature.

You learn to speak by speaking, to study by studying, to run by running, to work by working; and just so you learn to love . . . by loving.

—Francis de Sales

In that quiet center there is perspective and balance and a recognition of what really matters. I sadly saw this unfold when, in his seventies, my father began to lose his eyesight until—and this, he said, was his greatest regret—he could no longer tell his two granddaughters apart. He had survived a German concentration camp, years of financial hardship, divorce, and myriad disappointments. He had a brilliant intellect and the soul of a poet, but also an erratic temper and a love affair with gambling and drinking. When his diabetes led to macular degeneration and he was unable to read or write, he was devastated. These had been the great passions he thought would occupy his later years. Instead, he was forced to turn inward. And, as my sister put it, "Inside him was a neglected garden that had not been watered or weeded for a long, long time, with a gate to his heart firmly closed. If we could read the sign on the gate, it would probably say 'No entry—explosive materials inside.'" There were brief moments when he would let his guard down and let the gate open a little, but then it would promptly close shut. It took something as tragic as losing his eyesight before he could start tending his inner garden.

iParadox: Your Smartphone Isn't Making You Wiser

One of the things that makes it harder and harder to connect with our wisdom is our increasing dependence on technology. Our hyperconnectedness is the snake lurking in our digital Garden of Eden.

"People have a pathological relationship with their devices," says Kelly McGonigal, a psychologist who studies the science of self-control at Stanford's School of Medicine. "People feel not just addicted, but trapped." We are finding it harder and harder to unplug and renew ourselves.

Professor Mark Williams sums up the damage we're doing to ourselves:

> What we know from the neuroscience—from looking at the brain scans of people that are always rushing around, who never taste their food, who are always going from one task to another without actually realizing what they're doing—is that the emotional part of the brain that drives people is on high alert all the time. . . . So, when people think "I'm rushing around to get things done," it's almost like, biologically, they're rushing around just as if they were escaping from a predator. That's the part of the brain that's active. But nobody can run fast enough to escape their own worries.

Mindfulness, on the other hand, "cultivates our ability to do things knowing that we're doing them." In other words, we become aware that we're aware. It's an incredibly important tool—and one that we can't farm out to technology. There are some who believe the increasing power of Big Data (using powerful computers to sift through and find patterns in massive amounts of information) is going to rival the human consciousness at some point. But there's also growing skepticism about how effective Big Data is at solving problems.

As Nassim Taleb, the author of *The Black Swan: The Impact of the Highly Improbable*, writes, "Big data may mean more information, but it also means more false information." And even when the information is not false, the problem is "that the needle comes in an increasingly larger haystack."

"There are many things big data does poorly," writes David Brooks. "When making decisions about social relationships, it's foolish to swap the amazing machine in your skull for the crude machine on your desk." The quest for knowledge may be pursued at higher speeds with smarter tools today, but wisdom is found no more readily than it was three thousand years ago in the court of King Solomon. In fact, ours is a generation bloated with information and starved for wisdom.

At the Aspen Ideas Festival in 2013, one of the best speeches I heard was by Harvard Business School professor Nancy Koehn. What we need, said Koehn, is wisdom, because "information . . . does not equal knowledge, and knowledge does not equal understanding, and understanding does not equal wisdom. . . . Aren't we searching like frisky pilgrims through the desert for that right here, right now?"

At *HuffPost* we started a section titled Screen Sense, devoted to our addiction to our devices, and publishing the latest scientific studies, reports, and explorations about how technology is impacting our lives, our health, and our relationships. The price for this addiction is high. More than three thousand deaths and four hundred thousand injuries nationwide are caused by distracted driving and especially texting, which the National Highway Traffic Safety Administration calls "by far the most alarming distraction."

In her opening post titled "Mom's Digital Diet," Lori Leibovich, *HuffPost*'s executive lifestyle editor, wrote about the family vacation she recently took that included a vacation from her phone. She told her kids, "If you see me doing anything on my iPhone besides taking pictures, take it away from me." Like all diets, it wasn't always easy to stay on. But there were rewards. "Yes," she writes, "there were moments when I felt existentially lost without the iPhone's Pavlovian ping alerting me to a new message or tweet. But it also felt exhilarating to use my hands for digging tunnels in the sand and turning the pages of a novel instead of just for tapping away on a screen. For the first time in I don't know how long, I was really seeing my kids. And they were relishing being seen."

Disconnection is a two-way street. Caroline Knorr from Common Sense Media wrote about a study conducted by her nonprofit that found that 72 percent of children under the age of eight and 38 percent of children under the age of two have already started using mobile devices.

According to Stephanie Donaldson-Pressman, clinical

director of the New England Center for Pediatric Psychology, "Clinically, we are seeing an increase in symptoms typically associated with anxiety and depression," which include "short-term memory problems, decreased attention span, sleep deprivation, excessive moodiness and general dissatisfaction."

While "the average eight- to ten-year-old spends nearly eight hours a day with a variety of different media, and older children and teenagers spend more than eleven hours per day," the American Academy of Pediatrics recommends children and teens have no more than one to two hours a day of entertainment screen time. And screen media exposure of any kind is discouraged for children under two years old. The key to these recommendations is having parents model healthy, nonaddictive behavior.

Louis C.K. has put a brilliant comedic mirror in front of us and our screen addictions. In one of his routines, he captures the absurdity of children's events where none of the parents is actually able to watch the soccer game or school play or kindergarten graduation because they're straining to record it on video with their devices, blocking "their vision of their actual child." We are so hell-bent on recording our children's milestones that we miss them altogether. "The resolution on the kid is unbelievable if you just look," he jokes. "It's totally HD."

File it under Be Careful What You Wish For. Big Data, unfettered information, the ability to be in constant contact, and our growing reliance on technology are all conspiring to create a noisy traffic jam between us and our place of insight and peace. Call it an iParadox: Our smartphones are actually blocking our path to wisdom.

Hurry Sickness and Time Famine

In the summer of 2013, a blog post on *The Huffington Post* became an unexpected overnight sensation, with more than 7 million page views and nearly 1.2 million Facebook likes. It was entitled "The Day I Stopped Saying 'Hurry Up,'" and was written by Rachel Macy Stafford, a special education teacher and mother of a six-year-old girl. Rachel's life, as she writes, was "controlled by electronic notifications, ringtones, and jam-packed agendas." But one day she painfully realized the impact she was having on her daughter—"a laid-back, carefree, stop-and-smell-the-roses type of child": "I was a bully who pushed and pressured and hurried a small child who simply wanted to enjoy life." The reason the post struck such a chord, beyond our guilt about the way we parent, was because so many recognized the damage we do when we constantly tell not just our children but ourselves to "hurry up." Children are much more connected to the moment, and much less connected—yoked, actually—to the artificial constructs of time that we've imposed on ourselves (and for which we've appointed our devices as rigid enforcers). Rachel's story was a reminder of just how much we can learn from our children when it comes to the importance of living in the moment.

My heart leaps up when I behold
A rainbow in the sky:
So was it when my life began;
So is it now I am a man;

So be it when I shall grow old,
Or let me die!
The Child is father of the Man;
And I could wish my days to be
Bound each to each by natural piety.

—WILLIAM WORDSWORTH

It turns out that, not surprisingly, mastering the art of slowing down doesn't happen quickly. Learning the wisdom of slowing down, of truly living, is itself a journey. But it is also a prescription for better health. A study led by Lijing L. Yan at Northwestern University found that young adults exhibiting time urgency and impatience had a higher risk of developing hypertension. And rushing can lead to packing on the pounds when we bring our obsession with speed to the table. As nutrition expert Kathleen M. Zelman says, "It takes approximately 20 minutes from the time you start eating for your brain to send out signals of fullness. Leisurely eating allows ample time to trigger the signal from your brain that you are full. And feeling full translates into eating less." New studies have confirmed that eating more slowly leads to lower calorie consumption. Even sex is better when slow since stress from rushing inhibits production of dopamine, a chemical that affects libido.

Research published in the *Harvard Business Review* shows that speed adversely affects creativity and work: "When creativity is under the gun, it usually ends up getting killed. . . . Complex cognitive processing takes time, and, without some reasonable time for that processing, creativity is almost impossible."

Our culture is obsessed with time. It is our personal deficit crisis. We always think we're saving time, and yet we feel like we never have enough of it.

In order to manage time—or what we delude ourselves into thinking of as managing time—we rigidly schedule ourselves, rushing from meeting to meeting, event to event, constantly trying to save a bit of time here, a bit there. We download apps for productivity and eagerly click on articles with time-saving life hacks. We try to shave a few seconds off our daily routine, in hopes that we can create enough space to schedule yet another meeting or appointment that will help us climb the ladder of success. Like airlines, we routinely overbook ourselves, fearful of any unused capacity, confident that we can fit everything in. We fear that if we don't cram as much as possible into our day, we might miss out on something fabulous, important, special, or career advancing. But there are no rollover minutes in life. We don't get to keep all that time we "save." It's actually a very costly way to live.

We suffer from an epidemic of what James Gleick's book *Faster: The Acceleration of Just About Everything* calls "hurry sickness": "Our computers, our movies, our sex lives, our prayers—they all run faster now than ever before. And the more we fill our lives with time-saving devices and time-saving strategies, the more rushed we feel."

Harvard professor Leslie Perlow has given this feeling a name: "time famine." Feeling like you're experiencing time famine has very real consequences, from increased stress to diminished satisfaction with your life. On the flip side, the feeling of having enough time, or even surplus time, is called "time affluence." And though it may be hard to believe, it's actually possible to achieve.

Her heart sat silent through the noise and concourse of the street. There was no hurry in her hands, no hurry in her feet.

—CHRISTINA ROSSETTI

Some people are naturally time affluent. My mother, for instance. In fact, when it came to time, she was filthy rich. She moved through her days like a child does, living in the present, stopping, literally, to smell the roses. A trip through the farmers' market might be an all-day affair with little thought of All the Things That Must Be Done. I still often think of the advice she'd give my sister and me when we were faced with a hard decision: "Darling, let it marinate." In other words, give yourself the time to think about and live with the consequences of the decision.

She was a towering example of the joys of slowing down. Until her death in 2000, she and I had an unspoken deal: Hers would be the rhythm of a timeless world, a child's rhythm; mine was the rhythm of the modern world. While I had the sense every time I looked at my watch that it was later than I thought, she lived in a world where there were no impersonal encounters, and never a need to rush. She believed that rushing through life was a sure way to miss the gifts that come only when you give 100 percent of your-self to a task, a conversation, a dinner, a relationship, a moment. Which is why she despised multitasking.

As it turns out, it's my mother's luxurious sense of time, rather than my own struggle against perpetual time famine, that's apparently closer to the scientific reality of time. As physicist Paul Davies wrote in *Scientific American*, though most of us feel time is something that flows—always coming at us and then rushing behind us—that's not actually what happens: "physicists prefer to think of time as laid out in its entirety—a timescape, analogous to a landscape—with all past and future events located there together. It is a notion sometimes referred to as block time." I love this because "block time" helps me see the big picture—there is literally both no time and all the time in the world.

Sadly, I am living proof that time affluence is not an inherited trait. But if you're not born time affluent, there are things you can do to turn your time famine into a feast. Studies have shown that, as Keith O'Brien wrote in *The Boston Globe*, "Small acts, simple emotions such as awe, and even counterintuitive measures like spending time doing tasks for someone else—essentially giving time away," can make us feel more time affluent. "It's not just that people felt less impatient," said Jennifer Aaker, a Stanford business professor and coauthor of a study on people's perception of time, "but . . . they reported higher levels of subjective well-being. . . . They actually felt better in their lives."

Just as money can't buy happiness, neither can it buy time affluence. According to a 2011 Gallup poll, the more money you have, the more likely you are to suffer from time famine. The study concluded that "those at the top of the income spectrum are among the most likely to be time-poor."

Not surprisingly, when it comes to winning the war on time famine, we are our own worst enemies. To win the war, first we have to declare that we want to change. According to a 2008 Pew report, when asked what was important to them, 68 percent of Americans replied "having free time." It ranked even higher than having children, which came in at 62 percent, and a successful career, at 59 percent. Yet the way many of us choose to live doesn't reflect those priorities. As long as success is defined by who works the longest hours, who goes the longest without a vacation, who sleeps the least, who responds to an email at midnight or five in the morning—in essence, who is suffering from the biggest time famine—we're never going to be able to enjoy the benefits of time affluence.

And while time affluence isn't inherited, it's clear that we're doing a pretty good job of passing our self-destructive relationship with time on to our children. Not getting enough sleep definitely puts you on the road to time famine. Vatsal Thakkar, a psychiatry professor at the NYU School of Medicine, has suggested that many cases of attention deficit/hyperactivity disorder in children are, in fact, sleep disorders. According to the Centers for Disease Control and Prevention, an astounding 11 percent of school-age children have received a diagnosis of ADHD. Sleep-deprived children, writes Thakkar, "become hyperactive and unfocused." In one study he cites, a sleep disorder was found in every single one of thirty-four children diagnosed with ADHD. Sleep, he notes, is especially crucial for children, who need the deep, slow-wave type of sleep called "delta sleep." Compared to a hundred years ago, today's children get a full hour less of sleep per night. And the answer is not as simple as choosing an earlier bedtime. It's about changing how we overschedule our children's days so that they can begin their nights sooner.

We protect our children in unprecedented ways—from car seats, to packing their lunches in containers made with BPA-free plastic, to shopping for organic food. But we apply less care and vigilance to our children's time diets, even though the benefits of time affluence outweigh all those trips to soccer and violin practice. In William Faulkner's book *The Sound and the Fury*, Quentin Compson's father gives him a watch. "I give it to you not that you may remember time, but that you might forget it now and then for a moment and not spend all your breath trying to conquer it."

So what can we do to fight back against "hurry sickness"? You can walk—don't run—to join the slow movement. As Carl Honoré, the author of *In Praise of Slowness*, put it: "Speed can be fun, productive and powerful, and we would be poorer without it. What the world needs, and what the slow movement offers, is a middle path, a recipe for marrying la dolce vita with the dynamism of the information age. The secret is balance: instead of doing everything faster, do everything at the right speed. Sometimes fast. Sometimes slow. Sometimes in between."

For Honoré, the turning point that led him to become one of the godfathers of the burgeoning slow movement happened nearly ten years ago. He was at the airport in Rome, waiting for his flight home and talking to his editor on his cell phone. Like far too many of us, he says, at the time he was wired and harried, a "Scrooge with a stop-watch, obsessed with saving every last scrap of time, a minute here, a few seconds there."

While in line and on the phone, to make his time even more "productive," he started skimming a newspaper when a headline caught his eye: "The One-Minute Bedtime Story." The article was about a volume in which classic children's books are condensed down to sixty seconds. Eureka, he thought to himself. As the father of a two-year-old son, he saw the book as a great bedtime time-saver. He started making a mental note to order the book as soon as he got home. Suddenly, he caught himself wondering: "Have I gone completely insane?"

The Slow Food movement was launched in Italy in 1989 with a manifesto to push back against the spread of fast food, focusing on local food, sustainability, and eating as a social act of connection. (Italians have other great traditions to draw from in preventing burnout: the *riposo*, the period of rest in the afternoon; and the evening stroll, the *passeggiata*, a time to disconnect from the pressures of the day.)

And now the slow movement has widened to include slow travel, slow living, slow sex, slow parenting, slow science, slow gardening, slow cities, and, now, slow thinking. "Slow Thinking is intuitive, woolly and creative," wrote Carl Honoré. "It is what we do when the pressure is off, and there is time to let ideas simmer on the back burner. It yields rich, nuanced insights and sometimes surprising breakthroughs. . . . The future will belong to those who can innovate—and innovation comes from knowing when to slow down."

We are not going to eliminate watches, appointments, and deadlines, although it's worth remembering that the word "deadline" has its American origin in Civil War prison camps; instead of a physical perimeter, there would often be an imaginary line—the deadline—that the prisoners were not to cross. Our current use of the word isn't too far from its origin. Today we often use deadlines—real and imaginary—to imprison ourselves.

Everything changed the day she figured out there was exactly enough time for the important things in her life.

—Brian Andreas

Gaining a sense of time affluence can help lead us to both greater well-being and deeper wisdom—not a bad thing to put on top of our ever-expanding to-do lists. But to do that we'll have to address the relationship between our sense of time and technology. Our digital devices both reflect and amplify our hurry sickness. We use technology to save time (or so we think), but we also impose our distorted sense of time on our technology and use of social media.

There are countless examples of how social media have been a force for good. They can accelerate raising awareness about issues and leading people to action. From Tahrir Square to Tripoli to Tehran to Tucson, social media have made it easier to organize, share information, and protest injustice. During natural disasters, they have served as a lifeline to vital information, and as Eric Schmidt and Jared Cohen put it in their book *The New Digital Age*, they "strengthen the bonds of culture, language and perspective" between diaspora communities and their home countries. Whether it's CollegeHumor teaming up with Malaria No More and raising over $750,000 to fight malaria, or tens of thousands of people contributing videos to the "It Gets Better" campaign to prevent LGBT suicides, or people rallying to raise money through GoFundMe for Glen James, a homeless Boston man who returned a lost backpack with $40,000 in it, social media have made it easier to harness our collective power for good.

But going viral has gone viral, and is taken to be a big sign of success independently of the value of the thing going viral. It doesn't matter, is often the assumption, as long as it's viral. And social! Indeed, in the media world the fetishization of social media has reached idol-worshipping proportions. Media conference agendas are filled with panels devoted to social media and how to use social tools to amplify coverage. But you rarely hear anyone discussing the value of the story that they want so badly to go viral.

Our media culture is locked in the Perpetual Now, constantly chasing ephemeral scoops that last only seconds and that most often don't matter or have any impact in the first place, even for the brief moments that they're "exclusive." Michael Calderone, *HuffPost*'s senior media reporter, writes, "Nothing is too inconsequential to be made consequential." The ersatz urgent has overtaken the truly important.

"We are in great haste," wrote Thoreau in 1854, "to construct a magnetic telegraph from Maine to Texas; but Maine and Texas, it may be, have nothing important to communicate." Today, we are in great haste to celebrate something going viral, but seem completely unconcerned whether the thing that went viral added one iota of anything good or worthwhile—including just simple amusement—to our lives. We treat virality as a good in and of itself, moving forward for the sake of moving.

"Hey," someone might ask, "where are you going?"

"I don't know—but I'm moving really fast!" Not a very effective way to end up in a better place.

Of course, our team at *HuffPost* is as aggressive as any media outlet in using social media. But maybe because we've been doing "social" well for a while, I hope we're better able and more willing to see it for what it is—a tool, not a magical feat.

How many times is the discussion of a topic justified by the fact that it's "trending on Twitter"? Is it really meaningful that "sentiment on Twitter is breaking 80 to 1 against such and such"? Is something important because it has three thousand "likes" on Facebook?

In fact, trending on Twitter may not mean much of anything at all, except an indication of what's dominating the conversation at that particular moment. (There were 24.1 million tweets during the 2013 Super Bowl, for example, and 10,901 tweets per second during Adele's Record of the Year win at the Grammys.) But as Twitter's Rachael Horwitz wrote to me, "Twitter's algorithm favors novelty over popularity."

The bottom line is that you can use Twitter to talk obsessively about Miley Cyrus twerking at the Video Music Awards (there were an astounding 306,000 tweets per minute). Or you can use Twitter as sites such as Kickstarter and

DonorsChoose do: to make a difference by leveraging the power of social media to crowdfund creative projects, or to help teachers fund urgent classroom needs.

As we adopt new and better ways to help people communicate, it is important to ask what is being communicated. And what's the opportunity cost of what is *not* being communicated while we're locked in the perpetual present chasing whatever is trending?

Social media are a means, not an end. Going viral isn't "mission accomplished."

Fetishizing "social" has become a major distraction. And we love to be distracted. I believe our job in the media is to use the social tools at our disposal to tell the stories that matter—as well as the stories that entertain—and to keep reminding ourselves that the tools are not the story. When we become too obsessed with our closed, circular Twitter or Facebook ecosystem, we can easily forget that poverty is on the rise, or that downward mobility is trending upward, or that millions of people in the United States and even more so in Europe and around the world have fallen into chronic unemployment. And that 400 million children around the world are living in extreme poverty. On the other side of the spectrum, too often we ignore the great instances of compassion, ingenuity, and innovation shown by people who are changing lives and communities by trying to address these problems.

Our times demand a better response. These new social tools can help us bear witness more powerfully—or they can help us be distracted more obsessively.

We all have a relationship with technology. The question is this: How healthy is that relationship going to be?

It's an important question, because it affects how healthy and how wise we ourselves will be.

Our attention is the fuel that drives our lives. Or as Viral Mehta, cofounder of ServiceSpace, put it, "the clay with which we mold our days." No matter what people say about what they value, what matters is where they put their attention. When technology eats up our attention, it's eating up our life. And when we accumulate projects on our to-do list, they eat up our attention, even if unconsciously, and even if we never start them.

I did a major "life audit" when I turned forty, and I realized how many projects I had committed to in my head—such as learning German and becoming a good skier and learning to cook. Most remained unfinished, and many were not even started. Yet these countless incomplete projects drained my energy and diffused my attention. As soon as the file was opened, each one took a little bit of me away. It was very liberating to realize that I could "complete" a project by simply dropping it—by eliminating it from my to-do list. Why carry around this unnecessary baggage? That's how I completed learning German and becoming a good skier and learning to cook and a host of other projects that now no longer have a claim on my attention.

Evicting the Obnoxious Roommate in Your Head

Even our worst enemies don't talk about us the way we talk to ourselves. I call this voice the obnoxious roommate living in our head. It feeds on putting us down and strengthening our insecurities and doubts. I wish someone would invent a tape recorder that we could attach to our brains to record everything we tell ourselves. We would realize how important it is to stop this negative self-talk. It means pushing back against our obnoxious roommate with a dose of wisdom. My personal obnoxious roommate is incredibly sardonic. Once when I was on Stephen Colbert's show, I told Stephen that my obnoxious roommate sounded exactly like him! "I had to find a place to crash," he replied.

I have spent many years trying to evict my obnoxious roommate and have now managed to relegate her to only occasional guest appearances in my head. What makes our liberation from these voices harder is that so much of the news and information directed at women these days seems determined to reinforce our obnoxious roommates and make us feel that our lives are somehow lacking. We are constantly made to feel that we should be prettier, thinner, sexier, more successful, make more money, be better moms, better wives, better lovers, et cetera. Though often wrapped in a "You go, girl!" message, the subtext is clear: We should feel bad because we have fallen short in so many ways from some imagined ideal—we have tummies, not abs; we are undesirable because we don't always feel like sex kittens (or because we do); we are incompetent because we don't have a color-coded filing system for our recipes or papers; we are not trying hard enough because we are not a senior vice president or on a corporate board or in a corner office. Even the very existence of the phrase "having it all," no matter how it's debated, is, in effect, implying that we're somehow not measuring up.

Educating our obnoxious roommate requires redefining success and what it means to live a life that matters, which will be different for each of us, according to our own values and goals (and not those imposed upon us by society).

Humor helps in dealing with that constant inner critic. "Angels fly because they take themselves lightly," my mother used to tell my sister and me, quoting G. K. Chesterton. What also worked was sending myself a consistent and coherent alternative message. Since my roommate fed on my fears and negative fantasies, the message that resonated with me the most was the message with which John-Roger ends all his seminars: "The blessings already are." Or as Julian of Norwich, the fifteenth-century English mystic, put it, "And all shall be well and all manner of things shall be well." Or as Sophocles' Oedipus cried out, "Despite so many ordeals, my advanced age and the nobility of my soul make me conclude that all is well." I keep repeating it to myself until I am bathed in this calm and reassuring message—which has the added advantage of being true. So find your own message. Don't let your constant critic filibuster your dreams.

If you walk in with fear and anger, you'll find fear and anger. Go into situations with what you want to find there. . . . When you worry, you're holding pictures in your mind that you want less of. . . . What you focus upon, you become. What you focus on comes to you. So hold in your mind what you want more of.

—John-Roger

Breaking Bad Habits: What We Can Learn from Minotaurs, Seat Belts, and the Stoics

I've always been fascinated by the story of Ariadne, Theseus, and the Minotaur, not just because Ariadne is my given name but because of the role of the thread in mythology and in our everyday lives. Theseus could be saved and be free to return to Athens only if he entered the labyrinth and slew the Minotaur. All who had gone before him had perished, but Theseus, guided by the thread Ariadne had given him, was able to make his way into the labyrinth and come out of it alive and victorious. Ariadne's thread is our way in and our way out. It connects this world with the other, the outer with the inner, mortality with eternity.

As we are liberating ourselves, building new habits, and slaying our old habits—our own Minotaurs—it is critical to find the thread that works for us. When we do, no matter what life throws our way we can use the thread to help us navigate the labyrinth of daily life and come back to our center.

For me, the thread is something as simple as my breath. I have worked to integrate certain practices into my day—meditation, walking, exercise—but the connection that conscious breathing gives me is something I can return to hundreds of times during the day in an instant. A conscious focus on breathing helps me introduce pauses into my daily life, brings me back into the moment, and helps me transcend upsets and setbacks. It has also helped me become much more aware when I hold or constrict my breath, not just when dealing with a problem, but sometimes even when I'm doing something as mundane as putting a key in the door, texting, reading an email, or going over my schedule. When I use my breath to relax the contracted core of my body, I can follow this thread back to my center.

After all, computers crash, people die, relationships fall apart. The best we can do is breathe and reboot.
— CARRIE BRADSHAW IN *Sex and the City*

As psychologist Karen Horneffer-Ginter asks: "Why are so many of us so awful at taking breaks? What is it about our culture and conditioning as adults that prevents us from stepping away from our seemingly important tasks in order to briefly recharge? . . . If I were to make up banners and flyers in support of the break movement, they'd have to speak to our tendencies to exhaust ourselves . . . to continue on past the point that's really in our best interests, or even in the best interests of the project we're working on."

Habits are habits for a reason. Humans lead complex lives, and one of the traits we've developed that has allowed us to be such productive creatures is the ability to make many learned traits and responses an automatic part of our lives, buried so deeply in the inner workings of our subconscious that they no longer require conscious thought. As mathematician Alfred North Whitehead wrote in 1911, "It is a profoundly erroneous truism that we should cultivate the habit of thinking of what we are doing. The precise opposite is the case. Civilization advances by extending the number of important operations which we can perform without thinking about them." Indeed, research by John Bargh of Yale and Tanya Chartrand of Duke suggests that the lion's share of a person's behavior is dictated by mental processes that aren't conscious.

Some of these habits are useful and some are not. Some start out being useful and become destructive later on or in different contexts. But the internal machinery we've developed to create them doesn't discriminate. And whether good or bad, once established, habits rapidly grow roots and entrench themselves in our lives. And that's the problem— habits are a lot easier to learn than to unlearn, easier to bury than to exhume.

An old Cherokee is teaching his grandson about life. "A fight is going on inside me," he said to the boy. "It is a terrible fight and it is between two wolves. One is evil—he is anger, envy, sorrow, regret, greed, arrogance, self-pity, guilt, resentment, inferiority, lies, false pride, superiority, and ego."

He continued, "The other is good—he is joy, peace, love, hope, serenity, humility, kindness, benevolence, empathy, generosity, truth, compassion, and faith. The same fight is going on inside you—and inside every other person, too."

The grandson thought about it for a minute and then asked his grandfather, "Which wolf will win?" The old Cherokee simply replied, "The one you feed."

—CHEROKEE LEGEND

The puzzle of habits—of learning and unlearning them—has been a focus of humanity since the dawn of civilization. Of the Ten Commandments, several are about resisting bad habits, such as coveting, and some are about cultivating good habits, such as honoring your parents. To Aristotle, "Habit's but a long practice," which "becomes men's nature in the end." To Ovid, "Nothing is stronger than habit." And as Benjamin Franklin put it, "'Tis easier to prevent bad habits than to break them."

Charles Duhigg explains in *The Power of Habit* that scientists at MIT have, in essence, mapped the habit genome. What they've found is that the nucleus of a habit is made up of a neurological loop, which has three parts. It begins with a cue that sends the message to the brain to switch on the automatic mode. Next comes the routine—what we think of as the habit itself, which can be psychological, emotional, or physical. And last is the reward, the cue that tells the brain to reinforce this process. This is the "habit loop," and it's easy to see why as time goes on it becomes more and more automatic, more and more difficult to break. Of course, our primary goal shouldn't be merely breaking bad habits as much as replacing them with new, healthier habits that help us thrive.

The poet Mark Nepo defines sacrifice as "giving up with reverence and compassion what no longer works in order to stay close to what is sacred." So recognizing when habits are no longer working for us and sacrificing them is a cornerstone of wisdom.

We might think we're in charge of our thoughts and behavior—captains of our ship, turning the wheel this way and that—but so often it's actually our autopilot that's in control. It reminds me of the time a friend took a family trip on a cruise ship. Her ten-year-old son kept pestering the crew, begging for a chance to drive the massive ocean liner. The captain finally invited the family up to the bridge, whereupon the boy grabbed hold of the wheel and began vigorously turning it. The boy's mother panicked—until the captain leaned over and whispered to her not to worry, that the ship was on autopilot; her son's maneuvers would have no effect.

In the same way, if we're not able to reprogram our autopilot, all our protestations of wanting to change will be as pointless as the little boy furiously turning the wheel on the cruise ship. Reprogramming the autopilot takes different amounts of time for each of us. What makes it easier is focusing on "keystone habits"; when you change one of them, it makes changing other habits easier. "Keystone habits start a process that, over time, transforms everything," Duhigg writes. "Keystone habits say that success doesn't depend on getting every single thing right, but instead relies on identifying a few key priorities and fashioning them into powerful levers." For me, the most powerful keystone habit has been sleep. Once I changed the amount of sleep I was getting, and started regularly getting seven to eight hours of sleep a night, other habits, such as meditation and exercise, became easier. Willpower alone is not enough. As a number of psychological studies have shown, willpower is a resource that gets depleted the more it's used.

Dr. Judson Brewer of Yale has summed up the common signs of resource depletion in the acronym "HALT," which stands for hungry, angry, lonely, tired. It also happens to be a good summation of the standard state of being for so many of us in our current workplace culture, which almost seems designed to create resource depletion. We work through mealtimes, don't see our children, conduct most social contact electronically, and work late—that pretty much touches all four bases of HALT.

When the habits that lead to resource depletion are the very habits we're incentivized to cultivate, it makes for a tough environment for change. "We get a sense of belonging that is important to us," says Cindy Jardine, professor of sociology at the University of Alberta. "We can see ourselves as part of a social structure; it's very hard to change a behavior if it is still accepted socially. For instance, stress is bad for us, yet we wear it as a badge of honor. It is seen as a socially desirable thing to be overworking. We don't seem to have the same respect for people who work a 40-hour week." This kind of thinking feeds on itself, creating a downward bad habit spiral.

This is all the more reason it's important to create a positive keystone habit, to gain some leverage to take back our lives. And given that we're social creatures, and that social support is one of our primary resources, it's much easier to create and reinforce new, positive habits in a social network, with a group of friends or colleagues who can band together for mutual encouragement. This is why Alcoholics Anonymous is so successful and has helped an estimated ten million people to date. But even if the culture of your workplace still operates with the traditional definition of success, you can gather around you a group of like-minded people who want to thrive and not just "succeed."

At the same time, we can work to change social culture and habits on a large scale. In 1984, 86 percent of the public did not wear a seat belt. By 2012 that number was flipped, with 86 percent of Americans buckling up. This is an example of an "upstream" intervention. Policies at the top can be changed—through laws, tax incentives, and the provision of services—that will gradually change habits on a wide scale. "Downstream" interventions are aimed directly at individuals and they are most effective when people are going through transitions, such as when moving or starting a new job.

But we don't have to wait until we move or change jobs to change our lives. Nor do we have to wait for large-scale, upstream change. We can initiate change right now. There are endless starting points. For me, one of them was reading the Stoics.

Stoicism is a school of philosophy founded in Athens in the third century BC. Though Zeno of Citium is often credited with its founding, Stoicism is now more widely known through the work of the first-century Roman philosopher Seneca and the second-century Greek Epictetus. Stoicism teaches that unhappiness, negative emotions, and what we would today call "stress" are not inflicted on us by external circumstances and events, but are, rather, the result of the judgments we make about what matters and what we value. To the Stoics, the most secure kind of happiness could therefore be found in the only thing that we are in control of—our inner world. Everything outside us can be taken away, so how can we entrust our future happiness and well-being to it?

Stoicism is hugely relevant to our time. "Stoicism took off because it offered security and peace in a time of warfare and crisis," write Rob Goodman and Jimmy Soni, authors of a biography of the Stoic Cato the Younger. "The Stoic creed didn't promise material security or a peace in the afterlife; but it did promise an unshakable happiness in this life."

Around two centuries after Cato the Younger, one of Stoicism's most famous practitioners—and philosophers—arrived, the emperor Marcus Aurelius, who reigned for nearly twenty years as the last of the so-called Five Good Emperors until his death in AD 180. Marcus Aurelius was a true paradox—an emperor with almost unlimited power to control his world and circumstances, who nevertheless had a deep understanding that happiness and peace do not lie in the outside world.

For Marcus Aurelius, the quality of our day is up to each one of us. We have little power to choose what happens, but we have complete power over how we respond. It all starts with setting the expectations that make it clear that no matter how much hardship we encounter—how much pain and loss, dishonesty, ingratitude, unfairness, and jealousy—we can still choose peace and imperturbability. And from that place of imperturbability—or *ataraxia*, as the Greeks called it—we can much more effectively bring about change. In the W. C. Fields movie *Never Give a Sucker an Even Break*, Fields's niece is about to throw a rock at someone. He tells her to count to ten. As she counts, she gets more and more relaxed. When she reaches ten, he tells her to throw, because now "you got a good aim!"

In his *Meditations*, Marcus Aurelius did not sugarcoat life: "When you wake up in the morning, tell yourself: The people I deal with today will be meddling, ungrateful, arrogant, dishonest, jealous and surly. They are like this because they can't tell good from evil. But I have seen the beauty of good, and the ugliness of evil and have recognized that the wrongdoer has a nature related to my own—not of the same blood or birth, but the same mind, and possessing a share of the divine. And so none of them can hurt me."

Not a bad solution to road rage. Or rudeness at the supermarket. Or to the many travails of modern office life.

So much of the time, what is standing between us and satisfaction is . . . us. This isn't to say we control whether we get that promotion, or how our kids are going to act, or if a relationship is going to work out. Nor is it saying that things like that are not important. It's saying that we can control how much we're controlled by things outside ourselves. So the first goal, as the first-century Stoic philosopher Agrippinus put it, is not to be "a hindrance to myself." Or, in the classic comic strip Pogo's famous turn of phrase, "We have met the enemy and he is us!"

Stoicism is not just a tool for staving off unhappiness when we don't get a much-desired promotion—it also teaches us to put that promotion and all our success in its proper perspective. Too often, Stoicism is confused with indifference, but it's really about freedom. As Seneca said, "Once we have driven away all that excites or affrights us, there ensues unbroken tranquility and enduring freedom."

Sometimes people let the same problem make them miserable for years when they could just say "so what." That's one of my favorite things to say.

—ANDY WARHOL

Some might look at these practices as a luxury—that it's all very well for emperors and the financially independent, for people who have their basic needs met and have what are known as "first world problems." What about those without a job who are struggling to put food on the table? In fact, it's in extreme circumstances that Stoicism has the most to offer us. It is in times of great adversity when we are pushed and challenged that these principles become essential.

Viktor Frankl was a Holocaust survivor whose parents, brother, and pregnant wife all perished in the camps. What he took away from that unimaginable horror became the basis for his timeless book *Man's Search for Meaning*. "We who lived in the concentration camps," he wrote, "can remember the men who walked through the huts comforting others, giving away their last piece of bread. They may have been few in number, but they offer sufficient proof that everything can be taken from a man but one thing: the last of the human freedoms—to choose one's attitude in any given set of circumstances, to choose one's own way." To Frankl, "Every day, every hour, offered the opportunity to make a decision, a decision which determined whether you would or would not submit to those powers which threatened to rob you of your very self, your inner freedom."

And what Frankl did with that freedom was to find meaning in his suffering, and, by extension, all suffering. "If there is a meaning in life at all, then there must be a meaning in suffering," he wrote. "Suffering is an ineradicable part of life, even as fate and death. Without suffering and death human life cannot be complete."

One of the great texts on the relationship of suffering, acceptance, wisdom, and transformation is the book of Job, which asks how we should respond when circumstances seem to be at their most unfair and capricious. In other words, what do we do when bad things happen to good people? Job, a wealthy farmer, was the subject of a debate between Satan and God. Satan believed that Job was faithful only because he was prosperous; if Job's good fortune was removed, Job would renounce God. And so the two agreed to an experiment of sorts.

In short order Job's livestock was destroyed, his sons and daughter were killed when the house they were in collapsed, and Job broke out in sores all over his body. But Job's reaction was to proclaim, "Naked I came from my mother's womb, and naked I shall return there. The Lord gave and the Lord has taken away. Blessed be the name of the Lord praised." In the end, not only did God restore Job's fortunes; he increased them. The message of the parable is that there is a hidden purpose—and alchemy—in suffering that's transmuted into wisdom and strength.

As Francine and David Wheeler, who lost their six-year-old son, Ben, in the shooting at Sandy Hook Elementary School in Newtown, Connecticut, in December 2012, told Oprah, "The mistake is looking at life and thinking, 'I have nothing, life has nothing left to give me because of my tragedy.' And, you know, in our darkest moments, we have been there. Yes, but the key is it doesn't really matter what you expect from life. And to be able to see that and accept that is a very important step to finding your way out of the dark. . . . You've got to make your heart bigger than the hole. You just have to make your decisions out of love. And when we make the decisions out of fear, that's when we have problems."

Nelson Mandela captured the imagination of the entire world, not because he was a political prisoner for twenty-seven years who then became president, but because of the transcendent wisdom he demonstrated after his release: "As I walked out the door toward the gate that would lead to my freedom, I knew if I didn't leave my bitterness and hatred behind, I'd still be in prison."

Such equanimity and grace in the face of real suffering are in sharp contrast to the way we often react to the trivial challenges we let disturb us. The truth is that even in everyday adversity, the principles—though, of course, not the immediate stakes—remain the same.

How we respond to adversity can make a huge difference to our health and to our lives. Psychologist Salvatore Maddi and his colleagues at the University of Chicago studied more than twenty-five thousand employees of Illinois Bell Telephone, after the company was downsized 50 percent in one year in what was considered the largest upheaval in corporate history. "Two-thirds of our sample broke down in various ways. Some had heart attacks or suffered depressive and anxiety disorders. Others abused alcohol and drugs, were separated and divorced, or acted out violently. In contrast, a third of our employee sample was resilient. These employees survived and thrived despite the stressful changes. If these individuals stayed, they rose to the top of the heap. If they left, they either started companies of their own or took strategically important employment in other companies."

What the researchers found is that those who were able to make the transition a success used, as they put it, the "three C attitudes." First, there was commitment: deciding to join in and try to be a part of the solution. Next was control: fighting to maintain a sense of resolve as opposed to resignation. And last was challenge: finding ways to use the crisis to strengthen themselves, to build resilience and grow.

According to Laurence Gonzales, author of *Deep Survival: Who Lives, Who Dies, and Why*, when faced with life-threatening situations, 10 percent of us will stay calm, focused, and alive. The other 90 percent of us will panic. What's the difference? Those who are most likely to survive, he says, are those who are able to find opportunity in the situation. For instance, they are more likely to see beauty around them. "Survivors are attuned to the wonder of the world," he writes. "The appreciation of beauty, the feeling of awe, opens the senses."

He cites the experience of Antoine de Saint-Exupéry, the aviator and author of *The Little Prince*. After his plane crashed in the desert in Libya, Saint-Exupéry kept calm by finding something to focus positive energy on. "Here we are, condemned to death, and still the certainty of dying cannot compare with the pleasure I am feeling," he wrote. "The joy I take from this half an orange which I am holding in my hand is one of the greatest joys I have ever known."

By finding something—anything—to enable us to keep the pathways of hope open and a positive attitude alive, we can deal with loss, suffering, and tragedy bit by bit. "Survivors take great joy from even their smallest successes," writes Gonzales. "Count your blessings. Be grateful—you're alive."

So, yes, it's a blessing to be healthy. It's a lucky thing if we live near a park or have access to the great outdoors. But no matter what our situation is, life will inevitably challenge us. What is important is to know that we have the inner tools to meet those challenges.

There is a big difference between stoic acceptance and resignation. Cultivating the ability to not be disturbed by our lives' obstacles, disappointments, and setbacks doesn't mean not trying to change what we can change. The serenity prayer, adapted from the one written by the theologian Reinhold Niebuhr in 1942, sums up stoic wisdom: "God, grant me the serenity to accept the things I cannot change, the courage to change the things I can, and the wisdom to know the difference."

And the wisdom to know the difference comes from our ability to move from our narrow, self-absorbed world to a world that encompasses a larger perspective and a higher altitude. And it all starts with daily, tiny, positive changes that move us in the direction we want to go. Let me suggest three that have made a big difference in my life:

1. Listening to your inner wisdom, let go of something today that you no longer need—something that is draining your energy without benefiting you or anyone you love. It could be resentments, negative self-talk, or a project you know you are not really going to complete.

2. Start a gratitude list that you share with two or more friends who send theirs to you.

3. Have a specific time at night when you regularly turn off your devices—and gently escort them out of your bedroom. Disconnecting from the digital world will

help you reconnect to your wisdom, intuition, and creativity. And when you wake up in the morning, don't start your day by looking at your smartphone. Take one minute—trust me, you do have one minute—to breathe deeply, or be grateful, or set your intention for the day.

Wonder

Men go forth to wonder at the heights of mountains, the extent of the oceans, and the courses of the stars, and omit to wonder at themselves.

—St. Augustine

Blast-off on a Journey to Inner Space

O N T H E morning after the launch of *HuffPost Germany* in October 2013, I was in a car on my way to the airport from the center of Munich. It was raining, which gave everything a beautiful, almost magical, shimmer. All the buildings and trees seemed wrapped in wonder. Yet when I arrived at the airport, everyone I talked to was complaining about the rain. We were all experiencing the same weather but with very different results.

Wonder is not just a product of what we see—of how beautiful or mysterious or singular or incomprehensible something may be. It's just as much a product of our state of mind, our being, the perspective from which we are looking at the world. At a different time, in a different city (maybe even most times in most cities), I, too, might have been annoyed by the rain. But at this particular time, in this particular city, what came to my mind instead was a poem by Albert Huffstickler (I know his name sounds German, but he's from Texas):

> *We forget we're*
> *mostly water*
> *till the rain falls*
> *and every atom*
> *in our body*
> *starts to go home.*

Countless things in our daily lives can awaken the almost constant state of wonder we knew as children. But sometimes to see them we must look through a different set of eyes. The triggers are there. But are we present enough to experience them?

When my girls were just a few years old, I remember one of those clear California evenings when the stars seemed close enough to touch. Christina and Isabella were cradled in the crook of each of my arms as we lay on the grass in the backyard, watching the universe go by. While Isabella was stretching out her little hands, trying to peel a star off the rind of heaven, Christina was, as usual, asking questions: "Mommy, what makes it go?"

Her question was as old as time itself. When men began to wonder about the hidden causes of things, they were on their way to the discovery of science. Our proud scientific age is rooted in wonder. "Men were first led to the study of philosophy," wrote Aristotle, "as indeed they are today, by wonder." Physicist James Clerk Maxwell's first memory was "lying on the grass, looking at the sun and wondering."

That sense of wonder is often stronger when it's provoked by things ordinary and unassuming—our children's faces, rain, a flower, a seashell. As Walt Whitman said, "After all, the great lesson is that no special natural sights—not Alps, Niagara, Yosemite or anything else—is more grand or more beautiful than the ordinary sunrise and sunset, earth and sky, the common trees and grass."

Ten thousand flowers in spring, the moon in autumn,
a cool breeze in summer, snow in winter.
If your mind isn't clouded by unnecessary things,
this is the best season of your life.

—WU MEN

At the root of our secular age is the fatal error that has led us to regard organized religion and the spiritual truth that man embodies as one and the same thing. This has caused millions to deny the reality of the latter because they have rejected the former. The impulse to know ourselves—which, after all, is a key component of spiritual seeking—is as deeply imprinted within us as our instincts for survival, sex, and power.

As Goethe wrote, "This life, gentlemen, is too short for our souls." The preoccupations of our daily life can never satisfy our deepest needs. "Atheist that I am," philosophy professor Jesse Prinz wrote, "it took some time for me to realize that I am a spiritual person." And a growing number of people who proclaim themselves atheists because they're uncomfortable with organized religion and its depictions of God (especially the image of the bearded figure in the sky), acknowledge experiencing awe and wonder in their lives—experiences that stop them in their tracks, transport them to hidden worlds, and give them a glimpse of the fathomless mystery of life.

Einstein defined wonder as a precondition for life. He wrote that whoever lacks the capacity to wonder, "whoever remains unmoved, whoever cannot contemplate or know the deep shudder of the soul in enchantment, might just as well be dead for he has already closed his eyes upon life." Throughout history, great scientists—whom Arthur Koestler described as "peeping Toms at the keyhole of eternity"—have shared this sense of childlike wonder.

I completely understand the sense of wonder that has led men and women through the ages to explore outer space, but I've personally always been much more fascinated with exploring inner space. There is, of course, a connection between the two. Astronauts have often reported transformational experiences when they looked back at Earth, a phenomenon that has been called "the overview effect." As Edgar Mitchell, the sixth man on the moon, described it, "There was a startling recognition that the nature of the universe was not as I had been taught . . . I not only saw the connectedness, I felt it. . . . I was overwhelmed with the sensation of physically and mentally extending out into the cosmos. I realized that this was a biological response of my brain attempting to reorganize and give meaning to information about the wonderful and awesome processes that I was privileged to view."

What can we gain by sailing to the moon if we are not able to cross the abyss that separates us from ourselves? This is the most important of all voyages of discovery, and without it all the rest are not only useless but disastrous.

—THOMAS MERTON

Elon Musk, the founder of Tesla and SpaceX, who is intent on colonizing Mars, has also given expression to the other age-old human yearning: "I came to the conclusion that we should aspire to increase the scope and scale of human consciousness in order to better understand what questions to ask. Really, the only thing that makes sense is to strive for greater collective enlightenment." But there is no collective enlightenment without personal enlightenment. And spiritual teachers, poets, and songwriters alike have in so many ways, through so many centuries, told us that unconditional loving is both at the heart of the human mystery and the only bridge from our sacred inner world into the frenetic outer world. Or, as Kurt Vonnegut put it in his book *The Sirens of Titan*, "A purpose of human life, no matter who is controlling it, is to love whoever is around to be loved."

And now we have the empirical data to back up what the songs and sacred texts have told us. As Professor George Vaillant, who oversaw the Harvard Grant Study, which followed the lives of 268 male Harvard undergraduates beginning in 1938, put it, "The seventy-five years and twenty million dollars expended on the Grant Study points, at least to me, to a straightforward five-word conclusion: 'Happiness is love. Full stop.'" It is the same conclusion reached without spending seventy-five years and $20 million by the English poet Ted Hughes: "The only thing people regret is that they didn't live boldly enough, that they didn't invest enough heart, didn't love enough. Nothing else really counts at all."

Nature and art are two of the most fertile grounds for experiencing wonder. Essayist and philosopher Alain de

Botton describes art as "an apothecary for the soul." "Art," he writes, "enjoys such financial and cultural prestige that it's easy to forget the confusion that persists about what it's really for." In describing Claude Monet's *The Water-Lily Pond*, one of the most popular works at the National Gallery in London, he writes that some worry "that the fondness for this kind of art is a delusion: Those who love pretty gardens are in danger of forgetting the actual conditions of life—war, disease, political error, immorality." But the real problem in our lives, he argues, is elsewhere: "The real risk is that we will fall into depression and despair; the danger is that we will lose hope in the human project. It is this kind of despondency that art is uniquely well suited to correct. Flowers in spring, blue skies, children running on the beach . . . these are the visual symbols of hope."

Museums and galleries remain among the few oases that can deliver what has become increasingly rare in our world: the opportunity to disconnect from our hyperconnected lives and experience the feeling of wonder. Museums are where we go to commune with the permanent, the ineffable, and the unquantifiable. And it's an especially rare, and thus precious, experience in our technology-besieged lives. Maxwell Anderson, the CEO of the Indianapolis Museum of Art, describes a museum's mission as providing visitors with "resonance and wonder . . . an intangible sense of elation—a feeling that a weight was lifted." Or as my fellow countryman Aristotle put it: "catharsis."

"Every era has to reinvent the project of 'spirituality' for itself," wrote Susan Sontag in "The Aesthetics of Silence." And museums offer a pathway for that reinvention. Sometimes, of course, reinvention means going back to something that's always been there. What makes it harder today is our obsession with photographing everything before we've even experienced it—taking pictures of pictures, or of other people looking at pictures.

Sherry Turkle, MIT professor and author of *Alone Together*, has written about the cost of constantly documenting—i.e., photographing—our lives. These interruptions, she writes, "make it hard to settle into serious conversations with ourselves and with other people because emotionally, we keep ourselves available to be taken away from everything." And by so-obsessively documenting our experiences, we never truly have them. Turkle is optimistic, however, that the generation that has been hit the hardest by this will also be the one to rebel against it. She recounts the thoughts of a fourteen-year-old boy who told her, "Don't people know that sometimes you can just look out the window of a car and see the world go by and it is wonderful. You can think. People don't know that."

My younger daughter, Isabella, came to the same realization when, as an art history major, she was given an assignment to spend two hours in a museum in front of a painting and write down her experience. She described the assignment as both "exhilarating and unsettling: unsettling because I realized I have never really seen a painting and exhilarating because I was finally seeing one." She had chosen to look at J. M. W. Turner's *The Fighting Temeraire* in the National Gallery in London, and she describes the process of looking at the painting for two hours as "parallel to going on a long run. As odd as it sounds, looking at a painting for two hours requires you to push yourself and go past the point of what is comfortable. But what was so interesting was that when I was finished I had what felt like a runner's high. I felt like I had just experienced something magical, like I had created a tie between the art piece and me." She'd had an experience that cannot be captured on Instagram or Twitter.

After she had been looking at *The Fighting Temeraire* for about an hour, a security guard came up to her and asked what she was doing. "I found this hilarious because what I was doing was looking at a painting. But, we have gotten to the point where someone standing in front of a painting just looking at it for a long period of time is suspect."

Fully giving our attention to anything—or anyone—is precisely what is becoming more and more rare in our hyperconnected world, where there are so many stimuli competing for our time and attention and where multitasking is king.

The museum experience provides us with mystery, wonder, surprise, self-forgetfulness—vital emotions most undermined by our always-connected 24/7 digital culture, which makes it a lot easier to shy away from introspection and reflection. Increasingly, the world around us, or at least the one that's presented to us by the tools we choose to surround ourselves with, is designed—and very well, at that—to take that element of surprise out of our path. The ever-more-sophisticated algorithms on the social media sites where we live our lives know what we like, so they just keep shoveling it to us. It's celebrated as "personalization," but it often caters to a very shriveled part of who we really are. They know what we like but they don't know what we don't know we like—or what we need. They don't know our possibilities, let alone how vast they are.

In *The Shallows: What the Internet Is Doing to Our Brains*, Nicholas Carr writes that "there needs to be time for efficient data collection and time for inefficient contemplation, time to operate the machine and time to sit idly in the garden." There's not a lot of garden left in the world. And this is why museums need to guard against the danger of using social media in a way that reduces the essential art experience to more apps providing more data. Ultimately, this is as laughable as reducing the experience of going to church down to parishioners tweeting: "At church, pastor just mentioned loaves and fishes. Anyone have some sushi recs for later?" Or whipping out their iPads to quickly look up the fact that the Sermon on the Mount took place near the Sea of Galilee, which, following a link, I see is the lowest freshwater lake in the world. . . . I should totally tweet that! Or, even better, I can just imagine the tweet if social media had been around two thousand years ago. (Hey, I might have just tweeted it myself.) "Just checked in at Gethsemane. Cool garden. Anyone want to meet up?"

Of course, social media have a role to play in museums as in life. They can provide access to a much wider audience, let potential visitors know what's going on, and extend the museum visit by allowing users to continue the aesthetic experience after leaving the museum and share it with their friends and community. It's when we move social media from the background to the foreground that we undermine the artistic experience.

Museums all across the world are making good use of new media technologies. The Los Angeles County Museum of Art has *Unframed*, a blog that showcases the voices of museum curators and visitors alike. It also launched a first-of-its-kind digital reading room, offering important out-of-print publications. The Museum of Modern Art in New York (MoMA) started an online course for teachers titled "Museum Teaching Strategies for Your Classroom," enrolling more than seventeen thousand participants. The Indianapolis Museum of Art created ArtBabble.org, an online community that showcases art-based video content. The Walker Art Center in Minneapolis has a website featuring the Walker Channel, which presents live streams of museum events. The Tate Modern in London offers iPhone apps ranging from the "Tate Guide to Modern Art Terms" to "Pocket Art Gallery," which allows users to curate and share their own virtual galleries. And the Rijksmuseum in Amsterdam launched Rijksstudio to allow enthusiasts to engage with over 125,000 works from its collection through sharing images, ordering prints on materials ranging from aluminum to Plexiglas, or downloading high resolution images that can be used on anything—from tattoos to upholstery. The museum even launched a contest encouraging people to "remix, reuse and reinvent the masterpieces," offering awards for the best designs and the opportunity for them to be sold in the museum's store.

But when museums forget their DNA and get their heads turned by every new tech hottie that shimmies by, they undercut the point of their existence. Too much of the wrong kind of connection can actually disconnect us from an aesthetic experience.

To me, the key question is this: Does the technology deepen the experience, or does it diminish it? Clearly, it can do both. It's great to take advantage of new media tools to reach new audiences and provide platforms for greater engagement with the arts. But we should not forget that while technology will constantly change, the need to transcend ourselves through great art never will.

From a centered state of being, every encounter with an object, however ordinary, can be an opportunity for transcendence. But if we don't give our full attention to a deeper experience at a museum or exhibit, what are the chances that we'll give it to a passing cloud, a tree, or a clay jug?

Inside this clay jug there are canyons and pine mountains,
and the maker of canyons and pine mountains!
All seven oceans are inside, and hundreds of millions
  of stars.

—KABIR

Of course, the visual arts are only one of art's voices. Music, sculpture, photography, cinema, architecture, literature, drama, poetry, dance—each can ignite the deeper truth, and awaken the sense of wonder that slumbers within us. Even the ancient art form of rhetoric can pierce through the crusts of our everyday preoccupations and spark the memory of who we are. When Socrates in Plato's *Apology* addressed his accusers for the last time—"Now it is time that we were going, I to die and you to live; but which of us has the happier prospect is unknown to anyone but God";

or when John F. Kennedy stood within walking distance of the Berlin Wall and declared, on behalf of all who treasure freedom, *"Ich bin ein Berliner"*; or when Martin Luther King, Jr., stood on the steps of the Lincoln Memorial and cried out, "I have a dream," something was stirred in our souls that transcends words and time.

Music has always been a big part of my life. In my twenties, living in London, I became a classical music reviewer for *Cosmopolitan* so I could get free records to review (yes, vinyl records—I know I'm dating myself). I would play them for hours. Indeed, I wrote my second book listening to Haydn's 106 symphonies. And then I fell in love with a man whose idea of heaven was traipsing around Europe from music festival to music festival.

So having spent countless hours in darkened auditoriums, often with my eyes closed, meditating, I have found myself transported by music no matter what the quality of the performance. I remember at Covent Garden in London a performance of *The Marriage of Figaro* under a guest conductor. I was sitting with a group of friends that included a brilliant English conductor when, very early into the performance, we realized that this would be a painful affair—especially for him. When the string section was attentive to the guest conductor's unfamiliar rhythm, the brass was not. Soloists bolted off in their own directions, often taking a good share of the chorus—never, unfortunately, the whole lot—with them. It finally ended. And our conductor friend was the first on his feet, applauding loudly and long with what certainly appeared to be genuine appreciation. As he applauded, a regular patron seated behind us leaned forward and hollered, "What a terrible performance!" Over his shoulder, applauding even more enthusiastically, our conductor friend shouted back, "What a great work!"

A symphony or an opera is such a metaphor for life. As philosopher Alan Watts put it, "No one imagines that a symphony is supposed to improve in quality as it goes along or that the whole object of playing it is to reach the finale. The point of music is discovered in every moment of playing and listening to it. It is the same, I feel, with the greater part of our lives, and if we are unduly absorbed in improving them we may forget altogether to live them."

And sometimes there are great philosophy lessons in the simplest popular song. I fell in love with the lyrics to the Beatles' classic "Let It Be" when I was at Cambridge—an ode to acceptance written by Paul McCartney and John Lennon that could have been written by Marcus Aurelius:

> *When I find myself in times of trouble*
> *Mother Mary comes to me*
> *Speaking words of wisdom, let it be*

There is sadness in many popular songs, and there is plenty of darkness in great art, whether Shakespeare's *Tempest* or Mozart's *Magic Flute*, but in the end it is overcome by love. There is chaos and ugliness, but a new order of harmony and beauty evolves out of them; there is evil, but it is cast out by good.

And there is plenty of darkness in the drawings of children trapped in the violence and the poverty of the inner city. I remember one such drawing by a child in South Central LA. It was no less dark than any of the others, but through the darkness it was clear that this child had seen something beyond, and by seeing it, had given the rest of us access to that vision. In the same way, a collection of poems and whimsical butterfly drawings by children at the Theresienstadt concentration camp, far from diminishing the horror, makes it starker and more horrible when set against the glimpse of another reality.

Along with music and the visual arts, another art form that often offers a direct road map to our inner lives is storytelling. Humans are hardwired for narrative; we may be the only creatures who see our own lives as part of a larger narrative. Though we're told by physicists that time doesn't exist as we think it does, we're still very much creatures of time. And time inherently creates a story. Things begin and they end. How they end is the story. Or maybe it's what happens between when they begin and end that's the story.

Jung called the universal language of stories "archetypes." He described them as "ancient river beds along which our psychic current naturally flows." Our conscious minds relate to these archetypes through stories. Far from simply serving as entertainment or diversion, stories are a universal language about the purpose of life itself. And that purpose is self-actualization—integrating the Third Metric into our lives. Christopher Booker identifies seven kinds of stories: Overcoming the Monster, Rags to Riches, The Quest, Voyage and Return, Comedy, Tragedy, and Rebirth. But though there are seven plots, in one way or another they're all about the same thing: the personal transformation of the protagonist and his or her journey through challenges, ordeals, and wrong turns to a place of wisdom. As in our own lives, the story's outward form must track the inner journey of the hero. When we disconnect from our inner selves and identify exclusively with our ego, that's when we lose our connection with life's meaning and purpose and are left facing a void that we try to fill with more money, more sex, more power, more fame. And as we see in all modern literature, when the ego separates itself from the self, the end is always frustration and destruction—whether in Herman Melville's *Moby-Dick* or Stendhal's *The Red and the Black*.

We can use the power of story, and our primal need for it, to redefine our own narrative. We're all on a journey, a voyage, a quest to slay the monster, free the princess, and return home. But too often the goals we seek—those that the conventional notions of success tell us we should be seeking—take us down dead ends, searching for the meaning of our lives in all the wrong places. Mindfulness helps us become aware of our own story.

Hello, Silence, My Old Friend

The silence in our lives is under assault on all fronts: blaring headline news, squawking car alarms, buzzing and chirping smartphones, wailing sirens (especially if you live in New York, as I do), numbing elevator music, and screens fitted into every available space. We are wired, plugged in, constantly catered to, and increasingly terrified of silence, unaware of what it has to offer. We drown out the big but simple questions of life with the simplistic sound bites of our 500-channel-and-nothing-on universe.

I used to walk into my apartment or a hotel room and immediately turn on the news. And then, one day, not too long ago, I stopped. And I realized two things. First, that I didn't miss anything—not even anything helpful in running a 24/7 media operation—except hearing the same regurgitated talking points being repeated again and again by different people. But the second and more important thing is that I allowed some silence into my day, in which I could hear that still, small voice that we rarely give our time and attention to. I lost nothing, but I gained a lot. And then I got better at listening to others—my children, my colleagues, my friends.

"Ask your soul!" pleads German poet and novelist Hermann Hesse in *My Belief*:

> Ask her who means freedom, whose name is love. Do not inquire of your intellect, do not search backwards through world history. Your soul will not blame you for having cared too little about politics, for having exerted yourself too little, hated your enemies too little, or too little fortified your frontiers. But she will perhaps blame you for so often having feared and fled from her demands, for never having had time to give her, your youngest and fairest child, no time to play with her, no time to listen to her song, for often having sold her for money, betrayed her for advancement. . . . You will be neurotic and a foe to life—so says your soul—if you neglect me, and you will be destroyed if you do not turn to me with a wholly new love and concern.

What is success? It is being able to go to bed each night with your soul at peace.

—PAULO COELHO

Many postmodern pilgrims, seeking to find quiet and learning to listen to the silence and make room for the soul to awaken, are taking the path into retreats, monasteries, temples, and the "cathedral of the outdoors."

Holidays were traditionally intended as a time to recharge ourselves spiritually as well as physically—to make ourselves slow down, tap into our inborn but suppressed ability to wonder, and to make us recognize the breadth and the bounty in our lives. I remember one such holiday when my daughters were little, in a small village on the island of Rhodes. That same week, coincidentally, *Time* magazine had run a cover story about the healing power of faith. The people in the village where we stayed would have giggled at the thought of needing scientific experiments with control groups to prove the power of silence, of contemplation, of prayer—and of God. Women would come from all over Greece to climb the nearby mountain to the little Tsambika Monastery, where they prayed to the Virgin Mary—for a child, for healing, for a job. The villagers were full of stories of her miracles. The naturalness with which everyone there spoke of miracles was, in itself, a cause for wonder—flushing away the dross of our everyday lives.

I could completely identify. I think I was three when, with no parental prompting, I knelt by my bed and prayed to the Virgin Mary. Whenever I felt alone and afraid, I prayed to her. When schoolyard squabbles broke out, when my sister got sick, when my father moved away and didn't come home one night, I prayed to her. And when I started meditating at thirteen, I kept praying to her. Whether I was in India studying comparative religion, learning Buddhist meditation, or exploring the Kabbalah, I kept coming back to her. She was a mother figure, a guide—unconditional love personified. Throughout my childhood, my two favorite summer days were July 15, my birthday, and August 15—the date when the whole of Greece paid homage to the Virgin Mary. I fasted on her feast day, even though no one else in my family did. And even if I didn't go to church any other day of the year, I went on her Assumption Day and sat quietly among the widows in black kerchiefs and younger women smelling of summer wool and candle smoke—heads bent in prayer, communing.

One day when we were on Rhodes, we went to the nearby Tharri Monastery, a vine-covered tenth-century monastery that its abbot, Father Amfilochios, had brought back to life. Steeped in Orthodox theology, the abbot (who is now head of the Greek Orthodox Archdiocese of New Zealand) exuded a mischievous joy that clearly did not come from his divinity degrees. Monks and children alike called him Geronda, which means "old man." The identification of old age in Greece with wisdom and closeness to God is a startling contrast with the way we often treat aging today: like a disease, to be quarantined and forgotten.

Geronda was not even that old—he was probably in his late fifties then. "Old man" was a title bestowed on him because of the love and respect he inspired. His eyes sparkled, but his enthusiasm was tempered by humility: "Thank God," he said of what he'd accomplished. "God willing," he would say of what he had yet to do. His spirituality was filled with a reverence for nature. "There are other countries as beautiful as our homeland," he told me on a morning walk in the hills. "But there is no country with the perfumes of Greece." Every few steps, he stopped to pick up a sprig of thyme or rosemary, a twig from a pine tree, or any number of wildflowers, which he, unlike me, was on a first-name basis with.

Being with the monks on Rhodes was food for the soul. Listening to Father Christodoulos, another monk at Tharri, speak about his faith strengthened my own. Born in Denver, of Greek parents, he had moved to Los Angeles to try to leverage his talent at impersonation into a Hollywood career. Instead, he waited tables at the Old Spaghetti Factory and whiled away his time at celebrity parties, where cocaine was passed around like Greek olives. Finally, through a series of coincidences—known around the monastery as the miracles God performs anonymously—he entered the monastery in Tharri. His days started at four in the morning with matins and the Divine Liturgy. He worked with those in need in the community, and, in his time alone, he painted icons—exquisite Byzantine images into which he poured all his devotion. He gave a small icon to my children and in return, Isabella, then five years old, drew a picture of him, long and thin with a beard down to his waist—artistic license—and a smile from ear to ear. She offered it to him at the beach while sitting on his lap—she in her pink bikini, he in his gray monk's habit. He asked if she had slept well the previous night. "No, I had a nightmirror," little Miss

Malaprop replied. "A big mosquito in tennis shoes running all over me."

That was the kind of week that puts the "holy" back in holidays. But for far too many of us, vacations often serve only to amplify our stress and busyness and desire to do and accomplish—with our smartphones keeping us fully connected to the world we've ostensibly left behind. We all know the feeling of coming back from a vacation more drained than when we set off. In fact, according to a study by Fierce Inc., which provides leadership development and training, 58 percent of workers feel absolutely no reduction in stress from their vacations, and 28 percent return even more stressed than they were before they left.

No matter where you go, there you are.

—BUCKAROO BANZAI

For me, whether I'm on a visit to a monastery in Greece or an elaborately planned staycation (that involves disengaging from all my devices, going on long hikes or walks, yoga classes and unhurried meditations, sleeping in with no alarms, and reading actual books you can underline that have nothing to do with work), the essential element is to regain that sense of wonder. It means disconnecting from the outside world and setting out—for however short a time—on an inner journey.

Without such spiritual renewal, we may be left with only negative experiences to draw from. And as Dr. Rick Hanson, a neuropsychologist at the University of California, Berkeley, and author of the book *Hardwiring Happiness*, writes, "The brain is very good at building brain structure from negative experiences." But our brains are relatively poor at doing the same thing with positive experiences. To fight this, he explains, we need to "install" the positive experiences, "taking the extra 10, 20 seconds to heighten the installation into neural structure." In other words, we need to take the time to wonder at the world around us, feel gratitude for the good in our lives, and overcome our natural bias toward focusing on the negative. And in order for it to "take," to become part of us, we need to slow down and let wonder do its job, at its own pace.

Coincidences: Life's Secret Door to Wonder

One pathway to awakening wonder in our lives is the serendipity of coincidence. In fact, if we're open to it, it's not just a pathway, but a fast track. Coincidences, however prosaic, elicit our curiosity about the nature of the universe and all that we don't yet know or understand.

There is something about coincidences that delights us. There are thousands upon thousands of examples to choose from—yet not so many that they lose their strange power over us. And that's the point—the combination of improbability, timing, and felicity has a kind of magic power. To the philosopher Arthur Schopenhauer, coincidences were the "wonderful pre-established harmony" of the universe. To Carl Jung, they were "acts of creation in time." To author and journalist Arthur Koestler, they were "puns of destiny."

So here are a couple of puns of destiny: A woman named Mrs. Willard Lowell locks herself out of her house in Berkeley, California. While she is trying to figure out what to do, the mailman arrives. Included in the mail for her is a letter from her brother, who had visited recently and accidentally left with the spare key. Inside the letter is the key.

And then there is the man doing surveys at a mall in which he has to ask people for their phone numbers. One man being questioned makes up a number and gives it to him. "No, sir, I'm sorry. That's not your phone number," the surveyor replies. "Well, why isn't that my phone number?" the man asks. "Because," the surveyor says, "the phone number that you just made up is actually my phone number."

We don't have to know what coincidences mean, or arrive at some grand conclusion when we encounter them. But they serve as sporadic reminders to maintain our sense of wonder, to stop every now and again and allow ourselves to be fully present in the moment and open to life's mystery. They're a sort of forced reboot.

In my experience, whatever your spiritual beliefs, whether you believe in something larger than yourself in the universe or not, we all love coincidences. (There may be some curmudgeons who don't, but I haven't met them yet.) "Coincidences are kind of like shortcuts to very big questions about fate, about God, even to people who don't believe in either one," said Sarah Koenig, producer of public radio's *This American Life*. "The notion that somewhere out there, someone or something is paying attention to your life, that there might be a plan conjured through coincidences."

In an episode on coincidences, the producers asked listeners to send in their stories. The listeners responded—and the producers read through 1,300 submissions. One was from a man named Blake Oliver. He mentioned to his friend Camille that he wanted a new screensaver for his phone, so she emailed him a photo of her as a child. But in the photo, Oliver also saw his own grandmother. He had grown up in Michigan; Camille in Utah. But when the photo was taken, Camille was in Vancouver on vacation and Oliver's grandmother happened to be there visiting relatives—and walking through the back of a photo Oliver would see years later. A cosmic photo bomb. "It's crazy," said Oliver, "not only just in the picture, but perfectly behind her."

Also on the show was the story of a man named Stephen Lee, who told of inviting his girlfriend Helen's parents to meet his parents just after the two became engaged. As it happens, they found out that Stephen's late father had actually dated and proposed to Helen's mother in Korea back in the 1960s. This coincidence had real meaning for Stephen: "I didn't have the time with my dad that I wished I had, and then suddenly to kind of have him be an active part of my life again. To think that I can talk to my mother-in-law and hear what he was like in his twenties, something that my mom doesn't even know."

Another example came from Paul Grachan, who recounted a story about the day he was considering becoming more serious with his girlfriend Esther. He was thinking about it while buying a sandwich in a deli. As he pulled out his money to pay, he noticed that the name "Esther" was written on one bill. So he kept it. He then framed it and gave it to her. She was taken aback but didn't say much at the time. Years later, when they're married and moving to a new apartment, she unpacked it and revealed to him why she reacted like she did. When she was nineteen, she was unhappily dating somebody. "I just thought, how do people know who's the right person that they're meant to be with?" she said, recounting that time. "I said, you know what? I'm not going to worry about that. I'm just going to put my name on this dollar bill. And the guy that gets this dollar bill is going to be the guy that asks me to marry him . . . and I knew that we were going to be married the day that you gave me this dollar bill." The reason she didn't tell him at the time was because she didn't want to "freak this guy out" by raising the idea of marriage so soon.

When he finally found out, he was suitably stunned: "I just thought, what does this mean for us? Are we going to invent a time machine? Or are our kids going to bring world peace? Like, what's the point? Because there's some sort of bigger thing that we're not seeing here."

And that, of course, is the point. There *is* a bigger thing that we're not seeing here! I've always had a deep love of the mysteries of coincidence and how they can give us tiny glimpses of the structure of the universe—or even a glimpse into the fact that there's a structure at all. One of my favorite Bible verses comes from Matthew: "Not a single sparrow can fall to the ground without God knowing it"—a marvelous challenge to the existentialist belief that we live isolated and alienated in an indifferent universe.

As my sister, Agapi, recounts in her book *Unbinding the Heart*, coincidences were strewn all over our lives growing up. "I was raised in Greece with olive oil, feta cheese, and the principle of synchronicity as fare," she writes. "I had a mother who lived it, breathed it, and affirmed it daily. And my own life was synchronicity in action, from the very start."

She then tells a story about that start. Five months after I arrived, our mother became pregnant again. But my parents' marriage was not a happy one (they later ended up divorcing). So they decided not to keep the baby. "But on the morning of the doctor's appointment," writes Agapi, "my father had something else on his mind (another kind of transcendence). Their intimate moment in bed that morning made my mother miss her appointment, and she never made another one. She ended up having the baby—me. Synchronicity working in my favor!"

And in mine—since it gave me a sister who has always been my closest friend. And since then synchronicity has never stopped popping into my life. Years later, when I was in my last year at Cambridge, a British publisher who had published Germaine Greer's *The Female Eunuch* happened to see me on TV debating. He sent me a letter wondering if I'd be interested in writing a book. My plans at the time were to go on to grad school at the Kennedy School of Government, so I sent him a letter politely declining. He wrote back and said, what about just having lunch? So I thought, why not? Well, by the end of lunch he was offering me a contract and a small (probably smaller than the lunch tab) advance, which I accepted—and which put me on an entirely different career path. And all because the publisher wasn't into watching more entertaining television!

There are also plenty of uncanny historical coincidences, including Thomas Jefferson and John Adams dying on the same day in 1826, which also happened to be not only July 4, but also the fiftieth anniversary of the signing of the Declaration of Independence. John Adams's son, John Quincy Adams, who was then the president, wrote in his diary that the coincidence was a "visible and palpable" sign of "divine favor." A fellow cosigner of the Declaration, Samuel Smith, said in his eulogy of the pair that the coincidence was due to "All-seeing Providence, as a mark of approbation of their well spent lives." In her examination of possible explanations for the coincidence, Margaret Battin, professor of philosophy at the University of Utah, writes, "What we say about Adams and Jefferson, in the absence of compelling historical evidence, may in the end reflect what we want to say about ourselves."

Research has shown that our willingness to let ourselves experience the wonder of coincidence really does say something about us. According to Martin Plimmer and Brian King, coauthors of *Beyond Coincidence*, "People who notice coincidences most tend to be more confident and at ease with life. Every coincidence they experience—even the minor ones—confirms their optimism," they write. And according to Ruma Falk, professor at the Hebrew University of Jerusalem, events in our lives that are not part of a coincidence are less likely to be remembered than those that are.

Plimmer and King note the important role that coincidence plays in narrative. "Allegory and metaphor work by linking together two normally unconnected ideas in order to startle the reader into seeing something they thought they knew in a different light," they write. "Strictly speaking metaphors aren't coincidences, as they are man-made, but they work the same trick: fusing unrelated entities to power a revelation." As an old Chinese saying goes, "No coincidence, no story."

Carl Jung used the term "synchronicity" to describe events that are "other than causal"—the product of "a falling together in time, a kind of simultaneity." Jung grew interested in synchronicity by hearing stories of his patients that he "could not explain as chance groupings," and "which were connected so meaningfully that their 'chance' concurrence would represent a degree of improbability that would have to be expressed by an astronomical figure."

To Jung, synchronicity wasn't just about a chance event, but about the interplay between the chance event and a person's psychological state at the time. "Synchronicity," he wrote, "therefore means the simultaneous occurrence of a certain psychic state with one or more external events which appear as meaningful parallels to the momentary subjective state—and, in certain cases, vice versa." He concluded that "we must regard them as creative acts, as the continuous creation of a pattern that exists from all eternity, repeats itself sporadically, and is not derivable from any known antecedents."

The concept of simultaneity is especially interesting. By making us rethink the linear nature of time, it actually nudges us closer to how physicists describe time—with past, present, and future laid out together. So coincidences can be thought of as those moments when the invisible threads connecting and binding that timescape become momentarily visible.

One of those threads popped loose as I was working on this very section on coincidences. On my way to the airport for my return flight to New York after Christmas, I gave this part of the book one final read before it went to press. Later, while going through security, TSA officer Jay Judson told me he had a Greek wife and we made small talk about how good her spanakopita was. And then he suddenly said to me, "Do you have a moment for me to tell you a story?" And he began to tell me a coincidence tale!

"My wife's cousin Mark works at a Greek deli opposite St. Sophia's church," he said. "He was born on the Greek island of Zakynthos, and was six months old when the terrible earthquake of 1953 hit. During the earthquake, he was separated from his family, put in foster care, and then sent to live with a couple in the United States who ended up adopting him. More than fifty years later, he was setting up tables in the deli with a part-time waiter who had just started. It turned out that the waiter was his cousin who immediately put Mark in touch with his brother in Zakynthos. 'You know, you have a big, fat Greek family here that's dying to meet you!' his brother told him. Every time I tell this story, I get goose bumps."

And he pulled up his sleeve to show me the goose bumps on his arm. Here was this big, burly man, visibly moved by a coincidence that hadn't even happened to him, but to his wife's cousin—right in the midst of my finishing this section on coincidences (cue the *Twilight Zone* theme song!).

That's perhaps why in *Beyond Coincidence*, the examples used by a majority of respondents when asked about religious or spiritual moments in their lives were about coincidences. But if coincidences are a sign that there is meaning and design in the universe, there are consequences for how we live our lives. Because if there is meaning in the universe, there is meaning in our daily lives and the choices we make. And so we can choose to live in ways that help us live fuller, more complete lives, aligned with what matters: A life that isn't defined by our salaries and résumés. A life that encompasses all that we are and can become.

Of course, statisticians can, without much difficulty, explain away coincidence as nothing more than, as Yale scientist Pradeep Mutalik put it, "an interaction of mathematics and human psychology. May your coming week," he wrote, "be blessed with many interesting coincidences. And may you not assign cosmic significance to them." To which I say: Assign all the significance you want! And use the significance as an entry point for living a Third Metric life.

What's the downside, as long as you don't assign a dogma to them (if x happens it must mean y and you therefore have to do z)? The upside, however, is obvious: Maintaining a childlike sense of awe and curiosity is part of the fun and intense mystery of being alive. Coincidences connect us across time, to one another, to ourselves, and to an invisible order in the universe. We can't choose where or when they grace us with their presence, but we can choose to be open to their power.

Memento Mori

In mythology, death is always described in terms of transformation and renewal.

No matter how good and fulfilling a life we have, no matter how successful we are at filling our lives with well-being, wisdom, wonder, and giving, at some point our life is going to end. And no matter what we believe happens after we die, whether our souls live on, whether we go to heaven or hell, whether we're reincarnated or folded back into the energy of the universe or simply cease to exist altogether, our physical existence and our lives as we know them will end. Whether death is final or simply a transition to something else, it's definitely a stopping point. It might not be the end of the story, but it's definitely the end of a chapter. And as *The Onion* headline summed it up: "World Death Rate Holding Steady at 100 Percent."

In today's highly polarized times, in which so much media ink (or pixels) is spent highlighting how divided and disconnected we are, death is the one absolutely universal thing we all have in common. It's the ultimate equalizer. And yet we talk so little about it. At a soulless airport waiting area, we can bond with someone we've never met before over the meager shared experience of a ten-minute flight delay, and we can develop an entire relationship based on our common devotion to *Mad Men*, yet it seldom occurs to us to bond over the massive dying elephant in the room: our shared mortality.

Certainly in the West, we mostly sweep it under the rug. And the closer death comes, the deeper we bury it, desperately putting machines and tubes and alarms and railings between us and the person stepping over to the other side of the mortality line. The medical machinery has the effect of making the person—the patient—seem less human, and therefore his or her fate less relevant to us, the lucky and alive. It allows us to not think about it, to put it off endlessly like something on our to-do lists we never quite get to, like changing our wireless calling plans or thinning out the contents of our closets. Rationally, we know we'll get to it—or run smack into it—eventually. But we figure we don't need to deal with it until we really have to. Thinking about death is like shopping for a new water heater before the current one breaks down. Why do it now? How would it change things? What good would it do us?

A lot, actually. In fact, there may be no single thing that can teach us more about life than death. If we want to redefine what it means to live a successful life, we need to integrate into our daily lives the certainty of our death. Without "dead" there is no "alive." Death is the sine qua non of life. As soon as we're born, we're also dying. The fact that our time is limited is what makes it so precious. We can spend our lives feverishly accumulating money and power as some sort of irrational, subconscious hedge against the inevitable. But that money and power will be no more permanent than we are. Yes, you can pass on an inheritance to your children, but you can also pass down the shared experience of a fully lived life, rich in wisdom and wonder. To truly redefine success we need to redefine our relationship with death.

I vividly recall all the preparations I went through during my pregnancies: the Lamaze classes, the breathing exercises, the endless reading on the subject. How strange, I thought to myself one day, to spend hour upon hour learning how to bring life into the world, but hardly a minute learning how to leave it. Where are our culture's preparations for leaving life with gratitude and grace?

Indeed, we seem obsessed with using social media to memorialize our experiences as if photographing everything we do will make our lives less ephemeral. In fact, while the remnants of our virtual selves might linger on past our physical selves, they are just as fleeting.

I remember a dinner in New York, at a time when visiting the Egyptian temples on the Nile seemed to be the "in" vacation. I was sitting next to a man who had just returned from one such vacation. "Ramses," he told me incredulously, "spent all his life preparing for death." Looking around the room, I thought this was certainly a wiser choice than ours: spending our lives desperately pretending death would never come. "Maybe they were onto something," I said. "A life lived without taking death into account seems to me to be missing the point in a big way." "Death bores me," he replied disdainfully, drawing appreciative murmurs. "In Central Europe they have coffeehouses for that stuff—*Kaffee mit Schlag* and soul baring about death and the hereafter. There is something very undignified about such confessions. I don't want to know more about myself." There was laughter and relief all around, and on cue, our perfect hostess changed the subject.

But it's getting harder and harder to change the subject, harder and harder to believe in the splendor of the naked emperor's clothes as the price we're paying for the way we define a successful life rises higher and becomes more painful.

In the 1980s, I wrote a biography of Pablo Picasso. Avoiding death was a driving force for Picasso as he grew older and death inched closer. I spent a lot of time when I was researching my biography trying to understand this impulse to command death out of his orbit. What made it harder for him, as it makes it harder for all of us, was when key people in his life would die. For Picasso, two essential people in his long life died in 1963: painter Georges Braque in August and writer Jean Cocteau in October. He buried his head and went on working. If work could not defeat death, then what could? His children, far from giving him a sense of life going on through them, were only a grim reminder of his own life coming to an end. During the Christmas holidays that year, he told his son Claude that this would be the last time he could visit him: "I am old and you are young. I wish you were dead." In his work, he had thrown the glaring light of his genius into the darkness and evil in man. But in his life, he was overpowered by that same darkness.

There is a reason the subject of death has been central to every religion and philosophy throughout history. "The one aim of those who practice philosophy in the proper manner," Socrates says in Plato's *Phaedo*, "is to practice for dying and death." Since our body "fills us with wants, desires, fears, all sorts of illusions and much nonsense," we can only achieve true wisdom when our soul is liberated from our bodies by death. And this is why philosophy, he says, is about "training for dying."

From ancient Rome, we have been given the phrase "memento mori"—remember death, MM for short—carved on statues and trees. Tradition has it that the phrase goes back to an ancient Roman victory parade in which the triumphant commander had a slave cry out, "Remember that you are mortal." Another Roman, Michelangelo, once said: "No thought exists in me which death has not carved with his chisel."

In Judaism, mourning is divided into four stages: three

days of profound mourning; seven days of *shiva*, in which guests come to be with the mourner; thirty days of *shloshim*, in which the bereaved gradually reconnects with the community; and then a year of *shneim asar chodesh*, in which certain rituals continue as a remembrance. Christianity, of course, is based upon Jesus going through the most defining human rite of all—death—and overcoming it, through his resurrection.

In Buddhism, there is no separate self distinct from the rest of existence, so death is simply a rebirth to another manifestation of life and energy in the universe. In the West, by avoiding conversations about death and making it an almost taboo subject, we have separated ourselves from what death can teach us. As Dr. Ira Byock wrote in *Dying Well: The Prospect for Growth at the End of Life*, "Our society reserves its highest accolades for youth, vigor, and self-control and accords them dignity, while their absence is thought to be undignified. The physical signs of disease or advanced age are considered personally degrading, and the body's deterioration, rather than being regarded as an unavoidable human process, becomes a source of embarrassment."

Since we have very efficiently removed death—and the dying—from our homes and our daily lives, those with the closest view of these lessons are end-of-life caregivers. And when you read their accounts, it's remarkable how consistently they say that being so enmeshed in death has taught them a great deal about life.

Joan Halifax is a Zen Buddhist priest, anthropologist, and hospice worker. In her book *Being with Dying: Cultivating Compassion and Fearlessness in the Presence of Death*, she writes that the very American notion of the "good death," one that often means a "life-denying, antiseptic, drugged up, tube entangled, institutionalized" final stage, denies us valuable lessons about life. She found that being up close with death and giving care "enjoins us to be still, let go, listen, and be open to the unknown."

That's not to say being around death all the time is easy. "Working so closely with death often scared me," she writes. "I was afraid I might get what the dying person had. When I recognized, however, that I already have what dying people have—mortality—I stopped being afraid of catching it. Recognizing this very interconnectedness is the beginning of compassion."

One particular lesson she learned was how taking care of others meant also taking care of herself. She writes of witnessing many caregivers leave the profession because of overwork and burnout. "Keeping your personal life together is not an optional indulgence but an absolute necessity when it comes to being of use to others in the world," she writes. "We aren't separate from everything else; when we suffer, others suffer. Our well-being is the well-being of others. So make time to connect with your heart, for as the Zen saying goes, 'If you take care of your mind, you take care of the world.'"

For Halifax this means embracing meditation and spiritual care. She describes it as "integral to our realizing the developmental task of transcendence that is possible at death." Where she had once seen death as an "enemy," she learned to see death as a teacher and guide.

Elisabeth Kübler-Ross writes in her book *Death: The Final Stage of Growth* about how being so close to death enriched her life. "Working with dying patients is not morbid and depressing," she writes, "but can be one of the most gratifying experiences possible, and I feel now that I have lived life more fully in the last few years than some people do in a whole lifetime." She calls death a "highly creative force. . . . Facing death means facing the ultimate question of the meaning of life. If we really want to live we must have the courage to recognize that life is ultimately very short, and that everything we do counts."

Kübler-Ross is, of course, most famous for her five stages of grief: denial, anger, bargaining, depression, and acceptance, the last of which, she writes, is "not a happy stage, but neither is it unhappy . . . it's not a resignation, it's really a victory."

Even if we stubbornly refuse to allow death to influence our lives, our lives will definitely influence our death. Stan Goldberg, author of *Lessons for the Living: Stories of Forgiveness, Gratitude, and Courage at the End of Life*, writes that "the ideas and emotions people carry with them through life often determine the quality of their death." In other words a "good death" is more likely if you have had a good life. "I've come to believe the baggage I'll tote with me to my death will determine its quality," he writes. "I've learned the importance of doing simple things—telling my family and friends I love them; expressing gratitude for even the smallest kindnesses shown to me; being accepting of the unskillful words and actions of others; and asking for forgiveness when I screw up."

We often read very moving accounts from the dying themselves—those at the threshold of dying, I should say, unlike the rest of us, who are simply in earlier stages of dying—about the profound lessons that seem so obvious at the end of life. In March 2010, Andy Whitfield, the star of the television show *Spartacus: Blood and Sand*, was diagnosed with non-Hodgkin's lymphoma. His quest for treatment took him to India, New Zealand, and Australia. While awaiting results of a test, he and his wife got matching tattoos that read "Be Here Now": "In my heart I am convinced that this is all meant to be," he said. "I'm supposed to be right here right now and I'm open to the journey and to the discoveries and to the adventure of all of this. 'Be Here Now' is all about being present and not fearing what you don't know."

He died in September 2011. But the lesson lives on. Being fully present in our lives is as important to a good life as it is to a good death.

British historian Tony Judt died of amyotrophic lateral sclerosis, or Lou Gehrig's disease, in 2010. In an extraordinary interview with Terry Gross on NPR's *Fresh Air*, Judt explained that with a severe condition like ALS, in which you're surrounded by equipment and health professionals, the danger isn't that you'll lash out and be mean. But, rather, it's that you'll disconnect from those you love. "It's that they lose a sense of your presence," he says, "that you stop being omnipresent in their lives." And so, he said, his responsibility to his family and friends was not to be unfailingly positive and "Pollyanna," which wouldn't be honest. "It's to be as present in their lives now as I can be so that in years to come they don't feel either guilty or bad at my having been left out of their lives, that they feel still a very strong . . . memory of a complete family rather than a broken one."

Asked about his spiritual beliefs, he replied: "I don't believe in an afterlife. I don't believe in a single or multiple godhead. I respect people who do, but I don't believe it myself. . . . So no god, no organized religion, but a developing sense that there's something bigger than the world we live in, including after we die, and that we have responsibilities in that world."

That sense that there's something bigger than the world we live in dramatically changes our priorities about what is truly important in life.

Although Western culture, which fetishizes youth and celebrity, has never been comfortable talking about death, there is a growing movement to incorporate a discussion of death into our daily lives. *The Huffington Post*'s religion reporter Jaweed Kaleem has been covering death as his beat. He wrote about the "Death Over Dinner" movement, in which, much like it sounds, people get together to discuss death and dying over dinner. And where better to discuss death than over the primary activity we do to stay alive? The idea has spread to more than 250 cities worldwide. "People talk about death in the doctor's office, awkward family gatherings, lawyers' offices, all of these awful places that are not designed for a conversation that requires a great deal of humanity and often humor, reverence," says Seattle artist Michael Hebb. "But historically, it's over food where ideas have come alive."

The Death Over Dinner movement comes on the heels of the Death Café movement, which began in Switzerland in 2004. Like Death Over Dinner, the Death Café is about informal gatherings to discuss ideas about death. "There's a growing recognition that the way we've outsourced death to the medical profession and to funeral directors hasn't done us any favors," says Jon Underwood, who hosts a Death Café in London. As Pulitzer Prize–winning journalist Ellen Goodman, whose "encore career" was founding The Conversation Project to get people talking about death, put it, "People are not dying the way they choose. Seventy percent of people say they want to die at home, but 70 percent are dying in hospitals and institutions." Goodman went "from covering social change to making social change," spurred into action by the pain of not knowing her mother's wishes during her illness and death. "The best part of The Conversation Project," she told me, "is that we are asking people to talk about their end of life wishes at the kitchen table and not in the ICU. We are asking them to talk about what matters to them, not what's the matter with them. The conversations turn out to be some of the most intimate and caring ones that families have ever had."

In talking to others about their experiences with death, Goodman has concluded that "the difference between a good death and a difficult death seemed to be whether the dying person had shared his or her wishes." But most of the time this doesn't happen because "elderly parents and adult children often enter into a conspiracy of silence. Parents don't want to worry their children. Children are reluctant to bring up a subject so intimate and fraught; some worry their parents will think they're expecting or waiting for them to die. We often comfort ourselves with the notion that doctors are 'in charge' and will make the right decisions. And we all think it's too soon to speak of death. Until it's too late."

And in most major cities, there are also groups called "deathbed singers" in which "threshold choirs" sing to patients in hospices, hospitals, and homes for free. The choirs consist mostly of women, who go to the patient's bedside and simply sing, inviting any of those assembled to sing along. And there's a field of science, music thanatology, which studies the effects of music on respiration, heart rate, and stress levels. Research has shown that we often keep our hearing until the very end. "Words are good for many things, but they don't seem sufficient when it comes to death," says Ellen Synakowski, who started a Washington, D.C., threshold choir. "But music can reach those places where words alone can't go."

What, then, is the role technology plays at the end of life? Much of the discussion about the intersection of technology and death has been about how it has enabled us to stave off death (and, increasingly, about the cost-benefit calculations of extreme and costly measures that add little quality—or even quantity—to our lives). But technology is also being used to deepen our relationship with death.

In July 2013 a Kickstarter campaign was launched for a game called My Gift of Grace, created by the design firm Action Mill. In the game, nobody wins or loses (in death, everybody ties and gets a participation ribbon). Players use cards that facilitate discussion, answering questions such as: What makes you feel most alive? What do you fear about the end of your life? There are "action" cards that spur activities such as visiting a funeral home and talking with funeral workers. "A lot of people think a game about death and dying sounds sad and scary," says firm partner Nick Jehlen, "but our experience is the more you do it, the more it allows you to be joyful about day-to-day life."

Social media sites mostly encourage us to spend a huge

amount of energy and time creating and maintaining our virtual selves, distinguishing ourselves from others based on what we watch, what we listen to, what we recommend, what we like. But they, too, have been used of late to widen the conversation about our most universal shared experience. NPR's Scott Simon started a national dialogue about death when he began essentially live-tweeting his mother's death to his 1.2 million followers. His moving and almost real-time chronicle of her final decline was a lesson in what's important. A few selections:

> July 27, 2:38 a.m.: "Nights are the hardest. But that's why I'm here. I wish I could lift my mother's pain & fears from her bones into mine."
>
> July 27, 6:41 a.m.: "No real sleep tonight. But songs poems memories laughs. My mother: 'Thank you God for giving us this night & each other.'"
>
> July 28, 2:02 p.m.: "And: listen to people in their 80s. They have looked across the street at death for a decade. They know what's vital."

And the final one:

> July 29, 8:17 p.m.: "The heavens over Chicago have opened and Patricia Lyons Simon Newman has stepped onstage."

"In journalism, when we want to get a story over the jumps, we refer to it as a universal experience, but it almost never is," Simon said later. "There is one universal experience, that's death. That is something we are all going to experience at some distance in the lives of loved ones, strangers and friends, people around us and certainly our own. I think it should be something we are comfortable talking about. Insofar as we can talk about it comfortably, we can reset the clocks in our own lives."

And you don't have to wait until—to borrow from John Donne—the bell tolls for thee to reset your clock. Allowing the reality of death into our everyday reality can keep us from veering off course.

Psychology professor Todd Kashdan has found that avoiding the reality of death leads us to adhere to customs and beliefs that give us a feeling of stability, including identification with groups based on race or gender. "Clinging to our 'culture worldview' gives us a sense of symbolic immortality," he writes. "I know this sounds weird, but by defending the groups that we identify with, we have a second strategy to manage the fear of death." These groups feel more permanent than we feel, but this strategy is disastrous for society, leading to ostracism, racism, and other ways in which we demonize outsiders to glorify our own group and identify with it.

Professor Kashdan goes on to cite research that shows that when reminded about death, people tend to give responses that are more racist toward groups other than their own. So Kashdan and his colleagues wondered about what could possibly mitigate or check these responses. Specifically, they wanted to find out if the practice of mindfulness could alter the phenomenon. Or, as Kashdan put it, "If mindful people are more willing to explore whatever happens in the present, even if it's uncomfortable, will they show less defensiveness when their sense of self is threatened by a confrontation with their own mortality?"

The answer was a resounding yes. After being reminded about their own death and then asked to describe the decomposition of their bodies (as reminders of death go, a pretty good one), more mindful participants showed less hostility toward groups with different beliefs than their own. The mindful group also wrote for a longer amount of time and used more words related to death, suggesting "that a greater openness to processing the threat of death allows compassion and fairness to reign." Kashdan concludes: "Mindfulness alters the power that death holds over us. Pretty cool."

What the experiment also showed is that it's not enough for us to bump up against death now and again. To be able to incorporate the clock-resetting, course-correcting, empathy-building, perspective-giving power of death into our lives, we need to be in shape for it, much the way those who are in shape can experience profound pleasure from running a marathon. For those not in shape, the experience will likely be a painful struggle. Our relationship with death is just that—a relationship. The dynamic flows both ways. Death can bring something to our lives and, in turn, how we live our lives can bring something to our death.

On October 27, 2013, musician Lou Reed died at his home in Southampton, New York. By his side was his partner of twenty-one years, Laurie Anderson. She described their final moments together. Having been out of the hospital for only a few days, Reed insisted on being taken outside into the morning sun.

"As meditators," she wrote, "we had prepared for this—how to move the energy up from the belly and into the heart and out through the head. I have never seen an expression as full of wonder as Lou's as he died. His hands were doing the water-flowing 21-form of tai chi. His eyes were wide open. I was holding in my arms the person I loved the most in the world, and talking to him as he died. His heart stopped. He wasn't afraid. I had gotten to walk with him to the end of the world. Life—so beautiful, painful and dazzling—does not get better than that. And death? I believe that the purpose of death is the release of love."

It's a powerful, moving example of how a mindful life can fuse with a mindful death: "We had prepared for this." And, of course, the release of love isn't just the purpose of death, but also the purpose of life. Yet, for too many of us, the purpose of life is the avoidance of death—by a thousand distractions, by endless busyness, by relentless narcissism, by obsessive overwork. For some, there will come a time when the specter of death brings clarity to what life is all about. But that clarity is available to us now. As Joan Halifax writes, "We are all terminal." And we are all caregivers—of others and of ourselves.

We spend so much time searching for tips on how to extend our lives and eke out a little bit more time. But whether we believe there's something after this life or not, death has much to teach us about redefining how we live this one earthly life, however long.

My mother died on August 24, 2000. The day of her passing was one of the most transcendent moments of my life.

That morning, she told my sister and me: "I want to go

to the international food market in Santa Monica." That was like Disneyland for her; she'd leave with baskets full of food, fruit, and goodies for everyone. So we took her there. My mother in her fragile little body, still filled with a zest for life, bought salamis and cheese, olives, halvah, Viennese and Greek chocolates, and nuts, and by the end, we had bags and bags of food to haul home. It was surreal, taking her out into the world after all the time she had spent in the hospital and then at home with congestive heart failure. We wanted to say to the checkout clerk: "You don't seem to understand what is happening here. This is our mother! And she's going! Can you please take care of her? Can you please take care of us?" But instead, we kept pretending that it was just like any other day. Deep down, we knew that we were shopping for the last supper, but we were not admitting it, even to ourselves.

Back at home, my mother spread out the most amazing lunch in the kitchen, inviting her daughters, her granddaughters, our housekeeper, Debora Perez, and everyone who worked in my home office at the time: "Sit now and let us enjoy our food!" It was a feast. My sister looked at me with renewed hope: "Look at her appetite for food and love and sharing! This is not a woman who is going to die!"

Early that evening, she was sitting at a little table in her bedroom, shelling shrimp and eating them. "Sit and eat some shrimp!" she said. She had her hair in little pigtails and she was playing beautiful Greek music. She was like a happy child. It was as if her spirit was calling her back, and she was ready. There was no struggle. There was simply grace. Christina and Isabella—then eleven and nine—kept going in and out of the room on Razor scooters we had just gotten for them. My mother standing, looking at them, pouring all her love into them.

And then she fell.

I tried to help her get back in her bed, but she said no. This was a woman who, however weakened, still had the authority of the twenty-two-year-old who during the German occupation of Greece fled to the mountains as part of the Greek Red Cross, taking care of wounded soldiers and hiding Jewish girls. This was a woman who, when German soldiers arrived at their cabin and threatened to kill everyone if they didn't surrender the Jews they were hiding, told them categorically to put down their guns, that there were no Jews in their midst. And they did.

So I obeyed. She asked me instead to bring her lavender oil to put on her feet. And then she looked me in the eye and in a strong, authoritative voice that I had not heard for months, she said, "Do not call the paramedics. I'm fine." Agapi and I felt completely torn. So instead of calling an ambulance, we called the nurse who had taken care of my mother at home. And we all sat on the floor with her, her granddaughters still going in and out of her room on their scooters making happy noises, completely oblivious to what was happening, because that's how my mother wanted it to be. The nurse kept taking her pulse, but her pulse was fine. My mother asked me to open a bottle of red wine and pour a glass for everyone.

So we all sat there having a picnic on the floor telling stories for an hour or more waiting for her to be ready to get up. There she was on the floor with a beautiful turquoise sarong wrapped around her, making sure we were all having a good time. It sounds surreal now, and it was surreal then. I had the sense that something larger was moving all of us, keeping us from taking any action, so that my mother would have the chance to pass the way she wanted to pass. Then suddenly her head fell forward and she was gone.

Later, I found out my mother had confided to Debora that she knew that her time had come. She asked her not to tell us, and Debora, who had known and loved my mother for thirteen years, understood why, and honored her wishes. My mother knew that we would insist on getting her to the hospital, and she didn't want to die in the hospital. She wanted to be at home with her daughters and her precious granddaughters around her, in the warmth of those she loved and who loved her. She didn't want to miss the moment.

We scattered my mother's ashes in the sea with rose petals, as she had asked. And we gave her the most beautiful memorial, with music, friends, poetry, gardenias, and, of course, food, lots of food: a memorial that truly honored her life and her spirit. Everyone felt her presence there, hosting, presiding, shining her light on us. In our garden, we planted a lemon tree in her honor that has been producing juicy lemons ever since. And we installed a bench engraved with one of her favorite sayings that embodied the philosophy of her life: "Don't Miss the Moment."

I keep coming back to this lesson again and again. And however many times I backtrack, I return to the basics. I remember reading how Mikhail Baryshnikov, an absolute master at his art, was always at the barre with the rest of the corps, every morning, even on performance days and on days after a performance—doing the basics. There are three basics, three simple practices, that help me live more in the moment—the only place from which we can experience wonder:

1. Focus on the rising and falling of your breath for ten seconds whenever you feel tense, rushed, or distracted. This allows you to become fully present in your life.

2. Pick an image that ignites the joy in you. It can be of your child, a pet, the ocean, a painting you love— something that inspires a sense of wonder. And any time you feel contracted, go to it to help you expand.

3. Forgive yourself for any judgments you are holding against yourself and then forgive your judgments of others. (If Nelson Mandela can do it, you can, too.) Then look at your life and the day ahead with newness and wonder.

Giving

I slept and dreamt that life was joy. I awoke and saw that life was service. I acted and behold, service was joy.

—Rabindranath Tagore

Widening the Boundaries of Our Caring: What Are We Going to Do This Weekend?

WELL-BEING, WISDOM, wonder: All are critical to redefining success and thriving, but they are incomplete without the fourth element of the Third Metric: giving. Giving, loving, caring, empathy and compassion, going beyond ourselves and stepping out of our comfort zones to help serve others—this is the only viable answer to the multitude of problems the world is facing. If well-being, wisdom, and wonder are our response to a personal wake-up call, service naturally follows as the response to the wake-up call for humanity.

We are in the midst of multiple crises—economic, environmental, and social. And we cannot wait for a leader to ride in on a white horse to save us. We all need to find the leader in the mirror, and take the steps needed to make a difference, both in our own communities and at the other end of the world.

What makes service so powerful is that its benefits go two ways. When my younger daughter, Isabella, was five years old, we were living in Washington, D.C. One day we were volunteering at Children of Mine, a center for children in need in Anacostia, a struggling part of town. The day before we had celebrated Isabella's fifth birthday with a mermaid cake, presents, balloons, and a birthday party. By coincidence, at the center that day there was a little girl also having her fifth birthday. This little girl's entire birthday celebration consisted of a chocolate chip cookie with a candle—the cookie served as both her birthday cake and her only gift. I remember watching my daughter from across the room, her eyes welling with tears. Something clicked for her, something that I could not have taught her. When we returned home, Isabella rushed to her room, collected all the presents she had gotten for her birthday, and told me that she wanted to take them to the little girl. Now it's not as if Isabella was suddenly transformed into Mother Teresa—she has had many moments of selfishness since then. But it was a profound moment nonetheless, whose impact will always be with her.

That's why I'm so passionate about families making volunteering together a regular part of their lives. I dream of a day when families look at their weekend plans and say, What are we going to do this weekend—are we going to shop, see a movie, volunteer? A day when volunteering is just a natural thing—not something exceptional or something that makes us feel particularly noble. Just something that we do. Something that connects us with one another. It is the only way we, as individuals, will ultimately make a real difference in the lives of millions of children who are homeless, hungry, or living in inner cities where random violence is a daily occurrence.

That little girl in Anacostia is one of more than sixteen million kids in America living in poverty, in conditions that compromise their health, their school performance, and their chances for the future. And the problem is getting worse. The percentage of children living in low-income families in the United States went from 37 percent in 2000 to 45 percent in 2011. Until compassion and giving become part of our daily lives, these are statistics that we will continue to uncomfortably brush aside with world-weary explanations that offer no answers: "The system is broken," or "Government has become too polarized to pass meaningful reform." Yes, there is a lot governments need to do, but we cannot just delegate our compassion to government and sit on the sidelines bemoaning the fact that it's not doing enough.

From the depths of our compassion, we can free ourselves of all that limits our imagination about what is possible. It's the only way to counteract the excessive greed and narcissism that surround us. Since the cultivation of compassion is crucial for societies to thrive, it is very good news that new scientific studies confirm the claims of contemplative traditions that compassion can indeed be enhanced with meditation training. As a 2012 study at the University of Wisconsin concluded, "Compassion and altruism can be viewed as trainable skills, rather than as stable traits." And a 2013 study by researchers from Harvard University, Northeastern University, and Massachusetts General Hospital also found that "meditation enhances compassionate responding," providing "scientific credence to ancient Buddhist teachings that meditation increases spontaneous compassionate behavior." If these findings are taken as seriously as they should be, the impact on how we educate our children, live our lives, and solve collective problems will be nothing short of revolutionary.

Evidence of the power of compassion is all around us. In the wake of the 2008 financial crisis, we saw many people who had lost their jobs turn around and offer their skills and talents to help others in need. In Philadelphia, for example, Cheryl Jacobs, a lawyer who had been laid off from a large firm, opened her own practice to help people avoid foreclosure. So service is not only about going to homeless shelters and food banks—vitally important as that is. It's also about offering whatever special skills and talents and passions we have. And being of service can help people who've lost their jobs rebuild their own confidence and sense of purpose.

When a friend of mine in Los Angeles lost her job early in the economic downturn, I suggested that as she was looking for another job, she might think about volunteering, and I offered to connect her with A Place Called Home, which offers education, art, and well-being programs to underserved youth in South Central Los Angeles. She thought I did not empathize enough with what she was going through. I asked her to trust me, simply give a few hours a week while she was looking for a job, and just see what happens. She did, and she immediately started feeling much better about herself as she came out of the fog she'd been in after not having a job for the first time in her adult life. She also found herself exposed to a whole other world.

She shared her experience going through a self-awareness seminar with others at A Place Called Home. She found herself sitting in a circle, forgiving her daughter for forgetting her birthday, while someone next to her was forgiving her mother for shooting her father. And she realized what separate but parallel lives we're living, which only further feeds our self-absorption. She saw firsthand that what people who are struggling economically need as well as money, food, clothing, and material necessities, is to feel that someone cares.

"To feel the intimacy of brothers," wrote Pablo Neruda, "is a marvelous thing in life. To feel the love of people whom we love is a fire that feeds our life. But to feel affection that comes from those whom we do not know, from those unknown to us, who are watching over our sleep and solitude, over our dangers and our weaknesses—that is something still greater and more beautiful because it widens out the boundaries of our being and unites all living things." And that's really what we are engaged in when we are engaged in service and volunteering—widening the boundaries of our being.

It Shouldn't Take a Natural Disaster for Us to Tap into Our Natural Humanity

Jacqueline Novogratz, the founder of the Acumen Fund, a nonprofit devoted to tackling poverty around the world, and a heroine of mine, tells a beautiful story that demonstrates how connected we all are. "Our actions—and inaction—touch people every day, people we may never know and never meet," she says. Her story centers on a blue sweater. It was given to her by her uncle Ed when she was twelve. "I loved that soft wool sweater with its striped sleeves and African motif—two zebras in front of a snow-capped mountain—across the front," she says. She even wrote her name on the tag. But in her freshman year of high school, her classmates turned out not to be as enamored of the sweater and kept mocking her for it. So she donated it to Goodwill. Eleven years later, she was jogging in Kigali, Rwanda, where she was working to set up a microfinance program for poor women. Suddenly, she spotted a little boy wearing a similar sweater. Could it be? She sprinted over to him and checked out the tag. Yep, there was her name. A coincidence that served to remind Jacqueline—and the rest of us—of the threads of our connection to one another.

Hurricane response is another reminder of how connected we all are. When superstorm Sandy struck during the heat of the 2012 presidential campaign, it didn't just knock the campaign off the front pages; it transformed it as well. Suddenly, the artificial walls that our political process erects to separate us into little demographic microgroups to make us believe that we have no mutual interests were blown away. At a moment of extreme polarization, Mother Nature brought us together.

The collective recovery effort, the we're-all-in-this-together spirit, was great to see. We know that spirit is always there. After every disaster—natural or man-made—whether Hurricane Sandy or the Haiti earthquake or the Newtown shooting, we hear again and again how the disaster brought out the best in us.

But it shouldn't take a natural disaster to make us tap into our natural humanity. After all, we know that there are people desperately in need all the time, in every community, in every country, even when it's not on the front pages.

Two thousand children under the age of five die every day from diseases that could have been prevented with clean water and proper sanitation, 3 million children die every year from poor nutrition, and 1.4 million from diseases that could be prevented by vaccination.

So how can we sustain all year round the best-self spirit that comes forward during natural disasters? How can we make it a part of our lives so it becomes as natural as breathing? In very real ways, the need to take care of our planet and those who are hurting, and the need to build our inner resilience and spiritual infrastructure, are connected.

It is something I found myself thinking about by candle-light each night for nearly a week after Hurricane Sandy when the electricity was out, and I was forced to disconnect from the day-to-day minutiae that I would have ordinarily considered important. It's amazing how quickly one's priorities get completely reordered when the power goes out. Not having much ability to connect with my outer world, I decided to embrace the moment and connect with my inner one. Many of the things that I thought at first were indispensable, I barely missed after a week. A famous passage from Matthew particularly spoke to me:

> Therefore everyone who hears these words of mine and puts them into practice is like a wise man who built his house on the rock. The rain came down, the streams rose, and the winds blew and beat against that house; yet it did not fall, because it had its foundation on the rock. But everyone who hears these words of mine and does not put them into practice is like a foolish man who built his house on sand. The rain came down, the

streams rose, and the winds blew and beat against that house, and it fell with a great crash.

Building our home upon a rock is about much more than protecting us from devastating storms; it's about building and maintaining our spiritual infrastructure and resilience every day. And to keep our inner world strong it's essential that we reach out to our outer world through compassion and giving.

Watching Oprah Winfrey interview Diana Nyad on *Super Soul Sunday*, I was struck by a story the distance swimmer told about community. A man on the street where she lives lost his wife, and was left to both earn a living and take care of his young family. Another neighbor, who already worked two jobs, took it upon herself to organize everyone in the neighborhood to rally around and help. So Diana got a note that said, "Diana, you've got to deliver dinner to that guy every other Wednesday night. If you can't do it, get somebody else to do it. You've got—we've got—to help."

What I love about that story is that it exemplifies making our giving instinct a part of our everyday lives. So often we think of giving as donating time or money to relief efforts for catastrophes in faraway places, helping people who have nothing. And that's obviously critical to do when disaster strikes. But we forget that every day we are surrounded by opportunities to act on that same instinct for giving. These chances are always "under foot." As the nineteenth-century naturalist John Burroughs put it, "The great opportunity is where you are. Do not despise your own place and hour. Every place is under the stars, every place is the center of the world."

On the question of his own enlightenment the Master always remained reticent, even though the disciples tried every means to get him to talk. All the information they had on this subject was what the Master once said to his youngest son, who wanted to know what his father felt when he became enlightened. The answer was, "A fool."

When the boy asked why, the Master had replied, "Well, son, it was like going to great pains to break into a house by climbing a ladder and smashing a window—and realizing later that the door of the house was open."

—ANTHONY DE MELLO

And every place is full of openings to make a real difference in the life of another human being. There are millions of small missed opportunities at home, in our offices, on the subway, on the street where we live, in the grocery store—what David Foster Wallace called "being able truly to care about other people . . . over and over in myriad petty, unsexy ways, every day." When we flex our giving muscles every day, the process begins to transform our own lives. Because however successful we are, when we go out in the world to "get things," when we strive to achieve a goal, we are operating from a perceived deficit, focused on what we don't have and are trying to obtain—until the goal is achieved. And then we go after the next goal. But when we give however little or much we have we are tapping into our sense of abundance and overflow.

When I was growing up in Athens, we lived in a one-bedroom apartment and had little money. But my mother was a magical improviser. She was always able to conjure up what we needed, including a good education and healthy food. She only owned two dresses and never spent anything on herself. I remember her selling her last pair of little gold earrings. She borrowed from anyone she could so that her two daughters could go to college, and no matter how little we had she never failed to give to others with even less, and to make us feel that we were bigger than our circumstances.

It may be somewhat counterintuitive, but it is gravity that enables us to stand tall—that which seems to pull us down to earth and limit us actually enables us to expand upward. In the same way, it is when we give that we feel most abundant. Giving sends a message to the universe that we have all we need. We become virtuous by the practice of virtue, responsible by the practice of responsibility, generous by the practice of generosity, compassionate by the practice of compassion. And we become abundant by giving to others.

Giving and service mark the path to a world in which we are no longer strangers and alone, but members of a vast yet tightly knit family. "From everyone to whom much is given, much shall be required" is the biblical admonition at the heart of the good life. The Bible goes even further and tells us that we'll be judged by what we do for the least among us.

The Bhagavad Gita draws attention to three different kinds of life: a life of inertia and dullness with no goals and achievement; a life full of action, busyness, and desire; and a life of goodness, which is not just about ourselves but about others. "'Through selfless service, you will always be fruitful and find the fulfillment of your desires': this is the promise of the Creator," according to the Gita. The second life—which is how we have been defining success—is obviously a big improvement on the first, but by itself it becomes driven by a hunger for "more" that's never satisfied, and we become disconnected from who we truly are, and the riches inside us.

What living the third kind of life and making a difference in the life of even one other human being means is perfectly expressed in this story by Rabbi David Wolpe:

> My paternal grandfather died when my father was eleven years old. His mother was a widow at 34, and he—an only child—bore much of his grief alone. In accordance with traditional Jewish practice, he began to walk very early to synagogue each morning to say prayers in his father's memory, a practice lasting for a year after a parent's death. At the end of his first week, he noticed that the ritual director of the synagogue, Mr. Einstein, walked past his home just as he left to walk to synagogue. Mr. Einstein, already advanced in years, explained, "Your home is on the way to the synagogue. I thought it might be fun to have some company. That way, I don't have to walk alone." For a year my father and Mr. Einstein walked through the New England seasons, the humidity of summer and the snow of winter. They talked about life and loss, and for a while my father was not so alone.
>
> After my parents married and my oldest brother was born my father called Mr. Einstein, now well into his 90s, and asked if he could meet my father's new wife and child. Mr. Einstein agreed, but said that in view of his

age, my father would have to come to him. My father writes: "The journey was long and complicated. His home, by car, was fully twenty minutes away. I drove in tears as I realized what he had done. He had walked for an hour to my home so that I would not have to be alone each morning. . . . By the simplest of gestures, the act of caring, he took a frightened child and he led him with confidence and with faith back into life."

Go-Getters Are Good; Go-Givers Are Better

Imagine how our culture, how our lives, will change when we begin valuing go-givers as much as we value go-getters. Social entrepreneurs are classic go-givers. They build their work on a foundation of adding value to people's lives.

Bill Drayton coined the term "social entrepreneur" to describe individuals who combine the practical gifts of a business entrepreneur with the compassionate goals of a social reformer. He came up with the term as a college student after taking a trip to India to witness a man named Vinoba Bhave lead the effort to peacefully redistribute seven million acres of land across India to his most destitute compatriots. Today Drayton leads Ashoka, the largest network of social entrepreneurs worldwide. Sally Osberg, CEO of the Skoll Foundation, is at the forefront both of investing in some of the most game-changing social entrepreneurs across the globe, and of rethinking "how we carry out business, construct and hold our governments accountable, tap and replenish natural resources—how we survive and thrive, together."

At *The Huffington Post* we are collaborating with the

Skoll Foundation to create a new model for giving in the digital era, based on our belief that media organizations have a responsibility to spotlight the work of social entrepreneurs and nonprofits so that we can accelerate scaling and replicating what is working. In 2013, we launched three projects together—Job Raising, RaiseForWomen, and the Social Entrepreneurs Challenge—that raised more than $6 million and empowered our readers to donate to specific causes, as well as to blog about the stories of the people being helped and those giving.

Even in everyday business dealings, giving is becoming an increasingly valuable coin. As author and entrepreneur Seth Godin put it:

> The irony of "getting in return for giving" is that it doesn't work nearly as well as merely giving. . . . Bloggers who measure the return on investment of every word, twitterers who view the platform as a self-promotional tool instead of a help-others tool, and those that won't contribute to Wikipedia and other projects because there's no upside . . . these folks are all missing the point. . . . It's not that difficult to figure out who's part of the online community for the right reasons. We can see it in your writing and in your actions. And those are the people we listen to and trust. Which, of course, paradoxically, means that these are the people we'll choose to do business with.

Philosophers have long known that our well-being is deeply connected to our compassion and giving. "No one can live happily who has regard for himself alone and transforms everything into a question of his own utility," wrote Seneca in AD 63. As a more modern-day philosopher, David Letterman, said in AD 2013, "I have found that the only thing that does bring you happiness is doing something good for somebody who is incapable of doing it for themselves."

In practically every religious tradition and practice, giving of oneself is a key step on the path to spiritual fulfillment. Or, as Einstein put it, "only a life lived for others is the life worth while."

Since Einstein, theoretical physicists have been trying to come up with a "theory of everything" that would explain our entire physical world by reconciling general relativity with quantum physics. If there were an analogous theory of everything in the study of our emotional universe, empathy and giving would be at the center of it. Modern science has overwhelmingly confirmed the wisdom of those early philosophers and religious traditions. Empathy, compassion, and giving—which is simply empathy and compassion in action—are the molecular building blocks of our being. With them we expand and thrive; without them we wither.

Science has, in fact, broken this down on the biological level. A crucial component is the hormone oxytocin. It is known as the "love hormone," and is released naturally in our bodies during experiences such as childbirth, falling in love, and sex. Researchers have found that giving people oxytocin can lower their anxiety and mitigate shyness. In a study by neuroscientist Paul Zak, a squirt of oxytocin into the nose increased the amount of money participants offered one another. "Oxytocin, in particular," Zak said, "promotes empathy, and when the chemical is inhibited in someone, they become more prone to sinful, or selfish, behavior."

Oxytocin, the "love hormone," is in a constant battle in our bodies with cortisol, the "stress hormone." Of course, we can never completely eliminate stress from our lives. But nurturing our natural empathy is a great way to reduce it and protect ourselves from its effects.

Of course, there are different kinds of empathy and compassion, and some are more beneficial to us than others. As professor of psychiatry Richard Davidson told me, "Oxytocin increases the compassion towards one's family and the groups one identifies with, as opposed to the higher level of universal compassion." And psychologist Paul Ekman has identified three kinds of empathy: first, there's "cognitive empathy," which is knowing how someone else is feeling or thinking. But simply understanding another's position doesn't mean we've internalized what they're feeling. So there's also "emotional empathy," in which we actually feel what another person is feeling. This is triggered by so-called mirror neurons. Given the amount of suffering we're so frequently exposed to, it would be too draining to live in a constant state of emotional empathy. "This can make emotional empathy seem futile," writes Daniel Goleman, author of *Emotional Intelligence*. But there's a third type, "compassionate empathy," in which we know how a person is feeling, we can feel their feelings along with them, and we're moved to act. Compassionate empathy is a skill we can nurture, and one that leads to action.

And this is the kind of empathy we're fueled by when we're giving back. But even the term "giving back" can be misleading. It implies that service and volunteering are important only in terms of what they do for the recipient or the community. Just as important is what they do for the giver or volunteer, and the science on this is unambiguous. Essentially, giving is a miracle drug (with no side effects) for health and well-being.

One study demonstrated that volunteering at least once a week yields improvements to well-being tantamount to your salary increasing from $20,000 to $75,000. A Harvard Business School study showed that "donating to charity has a similar relationship to subjective well-being as a doubling of household income." This is the case in poor countries and rich countries alike. And the same study found that students who were told to spend a small amount of money on someone else were happier than students who were told to spend it on themselves.

Indeed, we're so wired to give that our genes reward us for giving—and punish us when we don't. A study by scientists from the University of North Carolina and UCLA found that participants whose happiness was mostly hedonic (i.e., focused on self-gratification) had high levels of biological markers that promote inflammation, which is in turn linked to diabetes, cancer, and other conditions. Those whose happiness included service to others had health profiles showing reduced levels of these markers. Of course, we all experience a mixture of both kinds of happiness, but our bodies' internal systems are subtly pushing for us to augment the kind based on giving. Our bodies know what we need to do to make us healthy and happy, even if our minds don't always hear the message.

If you bring forth what is within you,
what you bring forth will save you.
If you do not bring forth what is within you,
what you do not bring forth will destroy you.

—THE GOSPEL OF THOMAS

Many other studies show the positive health boost provided by giving. A 2013 study led by Dr. Suzanne Richards of the University of Exeter Medical School found that volunteering was connected to lower rates of depression, higher reports of well-being, and a significant reduction in mortality risk. And a 2005 Stanford study found that those who volunteer live longer than those who don't.

Science Proves: Love Grows Brains

The effects of giving as we age are especially dramatic: A study from Duke University and the University of Texas at Austin found that senior citizens who volunteered had significantly lower rates of depression than nonvolunteers. And a Johns Hopkins study found that volunteering seniors were more likely to engage in brain-building activities that lower the risk of Alzheimer's disease. Those who have suffered the loss of their defining roles as parents or wage earners were able to regain a sense of purpose in their lives.

Studies of the effects of giving in the workplace are equally dramatic and show the impact of volunteering on creating a healthier, more creative, and collaborative workforce. At AOL and *The Huffington Post*, we offer our employees three paid volunteer days each year to serve in their communities and we match up to $250 a year of charitable contributions per employee. A 2013 study by UnitedHealth Group found that employee volunteer programs increased engagement and productivity. Among the study's other findings:

- More than 75 percent of the employees who had volunteered said they felt healthier.
- More than 90 percent said volunteering had put them in a better mood.
- More than 75 percent reported experiencing less stress.
- More than 95 percent said that volunteering enriched their sense of purpose in life (which, in turn, has been found to strengthen immune function).
- Employees who volunteered reported improved time-management skills and enhanced ability to connect with peers.

Another 2013 study, this one by researchers at the University of Wisconsin, found that employees who give back are more likely to assist their colleagues, more committed to their work, and less likely to quit. "Our findings make a simple but profound point about altruism: helping others makes us happier," says Donald Moynihan, one of the study's authors. "Altruism is not a form of martyrdom, but operates for many as part of a healthy psychological reward system."

It is a reward system that should be incorporated into

how we think about health care. "If you want to live a longer, happier, and healthier life, take all the usual precautions that your doctor recommends," says Sara Konrath of the University of Michigan, "and then . . . get out there and share your time with those who need it. That's the caring cure."

Givers also end up getting ahead at work. (Nice guys don't finish last!) In his best-selling book *Give and Take*, Wharton professor Adam Grant cites studies that show that those who give their time and effort to others end up achieving more success than those who don't. Salespeople with the highest annual revenue are those who are the most motivated to help their customers and coworkers; the engineers with the highest productivity and fewest errors are those who do more favors for colleagues than they receive. The highest achieving negotiators are those who focus not only on their own goals, but also on helping their counterparts succeed. Grant also cites research indicating that companies led by CEOs who are "takers" end up having more fluctuating, volatile returns.

CEOs who are "givers" identify their companies' goals as going beyond short-term profits. Starbucks, under the leadership of Howard Schultz, for instance, not only instituted Create Jobs For USA—a job creation initiative that has raised over $15 million and created and sustained more than five thousand jobs—but the company also sponsored more than a million hours of community service by employees and customers over the past two years. Schultz explained that behind these policies lies his belief that "profitability is a shallow goal if it doesn't have a greater purpose behind it." For Schultz, that purpose is to drive performance through the lens of humanity by delivering value to shareholders while simultaneously sharing the company's success, reaching out to the communities it serves, and consistently delighting its customers. In 2013, during the shutdown of the U.S. government, customers who bought a beverage for someone else were rewarded with a free brewed coffee in return. In a letter to Starbucks employees, Schultz wrote, "Every day in our stores, we bear witness to small acts of human kindness that reflect the generosity of spirit at the core of our guiding principles. Most often, these are the little gestures that best embody our commitment to our communities and our care for our customers, and one another."

Given the unmistakable benefits of putting empathy into action, how do we strengthen that impulse? And how do we pass it on to our kids? Parents are constantly thinking about how to help their children succeed in life, earn a good salary, advance in their profession, or simply be happy. But it's just as important to pass down a rich capacity for compassion, especially if we really want them to be happy. This is all the more true in a world where we are beset on all sides by technological distractions and the lure of ersatz connections that can disrupt our pathways of empathy.

A 2010 San Diego State University study found a fivefold increase in depression among children in the United States since the 1930s. To teach children about emotional literacy and empathy, Mary Gordon, a former kindergarten teacher and an Ashoka fellow, founded Roots of Empathy. She believes empathy is best nurtured by example. "Love grows brains," Gordon says. "We need to show children a picture of love as we raise them. Learning is relational and empathy is constructed, not instructed. . . . The baby reflects the emotional state of the parents." In her program, classrooms "adopt" a baby and carefully observe and try to determine what the baby is trying to tell them through the sounds it makes. Instructors educate students on how to recognize the baby's emotions through these physical cues, and, in turn, the students learn to explore their own emotions. Spending time mindful of how a baby communicates deepens students' understanding not only of the patience and love needed to parent a child properly but also of the kind of attention and connection necessary to develop empathy. It's not enough to tell our children about empathy; we have to show them—which means, of course, that we have to demonstrate it ourselves. Parents teach empathy the same way they help their children learn to talk.

Of course, not everybody is blessed with parents who model empathy. But, fortunately, the effects of growing up in a family that is not rich in empathy can be reversed. It's never too late to transcend our childhoods. Any entry point of giving and service can lead to benefits for our well-being—and for our community.

Bill Drayton emphasizes that empathy is an increasingly important resource for dealing with the exponential rate of change we are experiencing. "The speed at which the future comes upon us—faster and faster—the kaleidoscope of constant change contexts," he says, "requires the foundational skill of cognitive empathy."

And the best way to build that internal foundation is to reach out to others. Compassion and giving don't have to involve getting on a plane to build houses or teach school in a remote part of the world. It may involve helping people across town. Or helping your neighbors. And it doesn't just mean giving money. As Laura Arrillaga-Andreessen put it in her book *Giving 2.0: Transform Your Giving and Our World*, it may involve donating "skills in areas such as strategic planning, management, human resources, marketing, design, or IT to nonprofits in need of those skills," as the Taproot Foundation does.

Press 1 to Donate: Technology Meets Philanthropy

Today's technology has leveled the giving playing field. Dennis Whittle, founder of GlobalGiving, says technology has the potential to make "all donors equal in the eyes of philanthropy" and turn us all into "ordinary Oprahs": "If you have $10 or $100 or $1,000," he says, "you can come [online], find a school in Africa to support, and you can get updates from the field to get responses to your support." Social media helped make Giving Tuesday, which now follows Black Friday and Cyber Monday, a huge success. In 2013, Giving Tuesday brought together well over ten thousand nonprofit, institutional, and corporate partners from around the world. Social media influencers from the White House to Bill Gates spread the word to their followers, and Giving Tuesday was featured all day on the Google home page. *HuffPost* joined media organizations, including *The Wall Street Journal* and CNN, in featuring articles and blogs. There was a 90 percent increase in online giving compared to the inaugural Giving Tuesday in 2012, with an average donation of $142.05. The City of Baltimore raised more than $5 million; the United Methodist Church raised over $6 million. But giving wasn't just limited to big cities and churches. On the local level, for instance, the Second Harvest Food Bank of Central Florida reached its $10,000 goal by 9 a.m. and decided to double its goal. The Bethesda Mission in Harrisburg, Pennsylvania, which expected to raise $400, raised $2,320 in online donations. And though Giving Tuesday comes five days after the American celebration of Thanksgiving, its partners included international organizations ranging from the Galapagos Conservancy to the Girls Empowerment Project of Kenya to the Goodwill Social Work Centre in Madurai, India, to Ten Fe in Guatemala.

Of course, giving can be as simple as giving joy to others—sharing our talents and skills to help them tap into their own ability to experience wonder. Improv Everywhere, in collaboration with Carnegie Hall, set up an empty podium on the streets of New York in front of an orchestra with the sign "Conduct Us"—allowing bystanders to conduct some of the most talented young musicians in the world. The musicians responded to the amateur conductors and altered their tempo and performance accordingly.

Monica Yunus and Camille Zamora, who met while studying singing at Juilliard, founded Sing for Hope to share their love of music with their community. They have been planting dozens of "pop-up pianos" in the middle of parks and street corners in New York City so passersby can play music or simply listen to it and build connections with strangers they would have otherwise silently passed by on the street.

Robert Egger took the skills he honed from running music clubs to found the D.C. Central Kitchen, which redirects leftover food from local businesses and farms, prepares the food in kitchens that employ the homeless, and then delivers it to feed the needy. He is now working to launch the L.A. Kitchen. "My attitude," Egger says, "is that food isn't just gasoline for the body; food is community."

We tend to identify creativity with artists and inventors, but, in fact, creativity is in each and every one of us, as David Kelley, the founder of the world-famous design firm Ideo and the d.school at Stanford University, writes in *Creative Confidence*, a book he coauthored with his brother Tom. We simply need to claim it back and share it. We are too quick to censor or judge our natural creative impulses as not being good enough. But we need to give ourselves permission to follow what makes us feel most alive. And when we are most alive we are most compassionate and vice versa. If you love to sing, sing—you don't have to sing in a choir or become a soloist. If you love to write poems or short stories, write them—you don't have to become a published author. If you love to paint, paint. Don't squash your creative instincts because you're not "good enough" to turn what you love to do into a career.

As David and Tom Kelley write, "When a child loses confidence in his or her creativity, the impact can be profound. People start to separate the world into those who are creative and those who are not. They come to see these categories as fixed, forgetting that they too once loved to draw and tell imaginative stories. Too often they opt out of being creative."

Every man, when he gets quiet, when he becomes desperately honest with himself, is capable of uttering profound truths. We all derive from the same source. There is no mystery about the origin of things. We are all part of creation, all kings, all poets, all musicians; we have only to open up, to discover what is already there.

—HENRY MILLER

A friend of mine has a ritual: He writes a poem every day with his morning coffee. "It centers me," he says, "and then I ride that wave during the day—it helps me stay connected." My sister graduated from the Royal Academy of Dramatic Art in London with many awards and accolades. But after years of auditions and not getting the parts she hoped to get, she began to feel lost and discouraged. In her book *Unbinding the Heart*, she describes a moment of epiphany on a New York bus:

After auditioning for a six-hour play adaptation of many Greek tragedies combined, and not getting a part—not even in the chorus—disappointed and distraught I got on the bus to go to my singing lesson on the Upper West Side when I started to notice the faces of the other passengers. Each one of them looked burdened, their worries the only thing showing in their expressions. As I looked at everyone around me, I was filled with compassion, and the understanding that their disappointments were probably much bigger than mine. If only I could bring some joy onto this bus, I thought.

And then I realized that I could. I could act right here! I could entertain these people for a brief moment. I could do a song and dance right here and now!

And with that thought, I broke down the barriers. I reached out to the woman next to me, struck a conversation, and asked her if she liked the theater. We started talking about our favorite plays and characters, and I told her that I had just performed the part of Saint Joan for an audition. She knew the play, and we had an unexpectedly wonderful conversation. In my enthusiasm, I said to her, "Would you like me to do Joan's monologue for you?"

"I would love that," she replied.

The first words of the monologue are: "You promised me my life, but you lied. You think that life is nothing but not being stone dead." As I said the words, the woman's face started to change. I could see that she was being touched; I was being touched as well, sharing my talent for a moment, on a New York bus.

By the time I finished, the woman on the bus had tears in her eyes. As she got off at her stop, she thanked me. I felt elated. I felt a release, as if a door had opened that I didn't even know was there. Here I was thinking that I had this wonderful gift that was not being recognized by the world. And then it dawned on me how many conditions I had put on my gift. That moment of sharing without an agenda of getting a part wasn't about the outcome but about the joy of touching others and giving unconditionally what was mine to give. And that brought with it a tremendous sense of fulfillment.

Your gift may simply be making a beautiful meal for someone down the street who is sick or has suffered a loss. The phrase "To know even one life has breathed easier because you have lived" crystalizes giving.

The day before she died, Scott Simon's mother had a message for the hundreds of thousands of people who were following his live blog about her journey toward death.

> July 28, 2:01 p.m.: "I think she wants me to pass along a couple of pieces of advice, ASAP. One: reach out to someone who seems lonely today."

Technology has made it possible for us to live in a self-contained, disconnected bubble twenty-four hours a day, even while walking down the street listening to music on our smartphones. Our devices might seem like they're connecting us, and they do to a degree, but they're also disconnecting us from the world around us. And without being connected to the people we encounter, it's hard to activate our hardwired instinct for empathy.

Millennials—the first generation that's truly native to the digital world (unlike those of us who are digital immigrants, who come to this moment from the land of the analog)—will most likely be the ones to figure out how to manage the influence of technology and use it to amplify, rather than diminish, their capacity for empathy. John Bridgeland, co-chair of the Franklin Project, a national service movement, believes millennials could "rescue the civic health of our nation after decades of decline." Recent studies corroborate his sentiments. Millennials lead the way in volunteering, with 43 percent of them engaging in service.

The numbers are even higher among college students: 53 percent have volunteered in the past year, and over 40 percent of them volunteer more than once a month.

What if that desire to connect and give back could be scaled up and institutionalized? That's the goal of the Franklin Project: to establish national service as a "common expectation and common opportunity for all Americans to strengthen our social fabric and solve our most pressing national challenges." Think of it as the ultimate shovel-ready infrastructure project—one that can literally help to rebuild our country from the inside out.

It taps into the incredible outpouring of community and compassion we experienced after 9/11—a yearning to rebuild not just what had physically been destroyed, but to rebuild a spirit of community and service that had been eroding for decades. It's an idea that is at the heart of the founding of this country, connected to the very pursuit of happiness described in the Declaration of Independence.

When Thomas Jefferson expressed our right to the pursuit of happiness, he was not simply referring to the right to pursue personal, momentary pleasure fueled by a culture of material goods. The happiness he was referring to was the right to build our life within a strong and vibrant community.

Throughout our history, the spirit of giving, of service, and of civic engagement helped build a country of disparate parts and races and languages, and has continued to bring us closer to a more perfect union. The fading of that spirit is behind the feeling so many Americans have that the country is breaking apart, hopelessly polarized and no longer indivisible.

Every U.S. president—with the exception of William Henry Harrison, who died a month after taking office, having given the longest inaugural address in history—has recognized the importance of this connective tissue and made an effort to reinforce it in one way or another. FDR created the Civilian Conservation Corps, which led to three million unemployed young people working on public lands across the country; JFK launched the Peace Corps; George H. W. Bush started the Daily Point of Light Award, which inspired the Points of Light Foundation; and Bill Clinton created AmeriCorps.

Ray Chambers, Points of Light's founding chairman (who invited me to join its board in the early nineties), has been for me a model for redefining success and prioritizing service and giving. After achieving success in business, instead of being content to simply amass wealth and power, he turned his remarkable skills and passion toward finding solutions to problems all over the world—from funding college education for hundreds of students in Newark, New Jersey, to founding Malaria No More and serving as the United Nations Secretary-General's Special Envoy for Financing the Health Millennium Development Goals. He has even put his mind, skills, and connections to work, solving an overlooked problem that is affecting millions of young people, moved by watching children in the urban programs he supports drop out and become physically and emotionally scarred because of acne—something I've experienced in my own family, as Isabella suffered from acne as a teenager. He's an example of private sector leadership at its best.

Clearly, there's a hunger in the world to serve. And the millennials are leading the way in large numbers. A robust national service program would help both to bring down the unacceptably high youth unemployment rate and give them a clear sense of purpose. "Our generation wants to push and dream for something big," Matthew Segal, co-founder of Our Time, a national advocacy group for young people, said. "And few policies make more sense than allowing idealistic young Americans to serve their country via nursing, teaching, disaster relief, park restoration, and infrastructure repair." And in Appendix C, you'll find some of my favorite sites connecting you to volunteering opportunities in your community and around the world.

So what is it going to take to transform service from something people do around Thanksgiving or Christmas—from something people talk about at commencement addresses—to an everyday reality?

As Dr. Ervin Staub, who studied men and women who risked their lives during World War II to protect Jews hiding from the Nazis, put it, "Goodness like evil often begins in small steps. Heroes evolve; they aren't born. Very often the rescuers made only a small commitment at the start, to hide someone for a day or two. But once they had taken that step they began to see themselves differently, as someone who helps. What starts as mere willingness becomes intense involvement."

Yaya Lessons in Giving: "It's Not a Trade, Darling, It's an Offering"

I was blessed to have a mother who was incapable of having an impersonal relationship with anyone. This doesn't mean my mother was perfect, but she did live in a constant giving mode. If the FedEx man arrived to drop off a package, my mom—or Yaya, as everyone called her—would have him come in, sit down at the kitchen table, offer him something to eat. If you went to the farmers' market with my mother, or to a department store, you'd better be prepared for a long discussion with the shop assistant or the farmer about their lives before she even got around to asking about something she wanted to buy. That intimacy with strangers, that empathy toward everyone she encountered, was something I had been surrounded with since I was a little girl in Athens.

Her life was filled with giving moments. Wherever she was—in an elevator, a taxi, an airplane, a parking lot, a supermarket, a bank—she would reach out to others. Once, a stranger admired the necklace she was wearing; my mother took it off and gave it to her. When the astonished woman asked, "What can I give you in return?" my mother said, "It's not a trade, darling, it's an offering." Toward the end of her life, she would always arrive at the doctor's office with a basket of fruit or a box of chocolates for the nurses. She knew that in an office where patients brought their anxiety and pain, the gesture would help change the atmosphere. Her tenacity in breaking through the barriers that people put up around their hearts was both enchanting and comical. If one of the nurses was, as she put it, "on automatic" and didn't take the time to be friendly or personal, my mother would whisper to me, "This one doesn't want to budge," and would start looking for a way to give her extra attention. She might produce a little treat from her purse—a package of nuts, a special kind of chocolate—and give it to the woman, knowing she would get a smile. Giving was a way of being for her.

When she died, my mother left no will and no prized possessions, which is not surprising, considering her habit of giving things away. I remember the time we tried to give her a second watch; within forty-eight hours she had given it to someone else. What she left us with is the treasure house of her spirit. It's as though certain gifts can be bequeathed only at one's death—that while she was alive she so embodied the qualities of nurturing, giving, and unconditional loving that it felt as if those dimensions of life were taken care of for all those blessed to be in her orbit. Why learn how to cook when you live with the Iron Chef? After her death it became much clearer to my sister and me that if our life's journey is to evolve as human beings, there's no faster way to do it than through giving and service.

We mostly focus on the good giving does for others—the good it does for our community. But just as profound is what it does for us. Because it is really true that while we grow physically by what we get, we grow spiritually by what we give.

Ever since I became a mother, I've been moved by the need to make volunteering and service part of children's lives from very early on. And I've seen the impact it had on my own children's lives. When one of my daughters was dealing with an eating disorder and started volunteering at

A Place Called Home, I saw how it began to change the way she saw herself—her own perception of her problems and difficulties. There's nothing like putting your own problems in perspective. When you become involved in the lives of children for whom drive-by shootings are a regular occurrence, where one out of three fathers is in jail, and where there isn't enough to eat, it's much harder to worry about how you look, whether you're wearing the right clothes, whether you're pretty enough, and how thin you are. My daughter learned these lessons not by being lectured at (though I tried), but by absorbing them firsthand.

The Fire Gets in the Poker, Too

People are already doing an enormous amount of good every day. So how do we put the spotlight on it? How do we help scale and replicate it until we achieve a critical mass? My dream in the 1990s was to create a new TV channel, a kind of C-SPAN3—back when there was only C-SPAN covering Congress and C-SPAN2 covering the Senate. So I put together a proposal to create C-SPAN3 to cover what nonprofits, NGOs, and volunteers were doing 24/7 so that service could become part of our everyday reality—as much a part of the business of the country as the doings of the House and the Senate and thus deserving of the same coverage. Well, my version of C-SPAN3 didn't happen, but the Internet did. And at *The Huffington Post* we now have multiple sections—Impact, Good News, and What Is Working, among them—covering the moving stories of people reaching beyond themselves to help others, sometimes right next to them, sometimes at the other end of the world. Just as important, we have the go-givers themselves tell their stories in text, in pictures, and in video. The magic happens when people respond to the stories by getting involved—by being inspired to move from observers to givers.

The Reverend Henry Delaney spent a lifetime transforming crack houses in Savannah, Georgia. He said something to me that captures what happens with service. "I want to get people involved," he said. "It's like putting a poker in a fire; after a while the fire gets in the poker, too." And that's how we're going to get to a critical mass.

To a physicist, a critical mass is the amount of radioactive material that must be present for a nuclear reaction to become self-sustaining. For the service movement, a critical mass is when the service habit hits enough people so that it can begin to spread spontaneously around the country and the world. Think of it as an outbreak of a positive infection, with everyone as a potential carrier.

"There are doors in space you look for," a friend told me once, "and doors in time you wait for." We are facing such a door in time right now—an opening for great possibilities. The modern equivalent of the pre-Copernican vision of the world as flat has been our secular view of man as an exclusively material being. This error has dominated how we live our lives and what we consider success. But today this is all changing. We have increasingly come to realize—partly due to the growing price we have been paying and partly due to new scientific findings—that there are other dimensions to living a truly successful life. And these dimensions, the four pillars of the Third Metric, impact everything we do and everything we are, from our health to our happiness. As a result, something as vast and epic as the destiny of humanity depends on something as intimate and personal as the shape of our individual lives—the way each one of us chooses to live, think, act, and give.

Transforming our narcissistic habits and awakening our giving nature—which is what both the world and we ourselves need—is the work of a lifetime. But once again, it starts with small daily steps. And once again our daily life is the ultimate training. If you told yourself that the goal is to write the great American novel, you might never begin. But you would be far more likely to begin if you told yourself to write one hundred words a day. It's the same with transforming ourselves:

1. Make small gestures of kindness and giving a habit, and pay attention to how this affects your mind, your emotions, and your body.

2. During your day make a personal connection with people you might normally tend to pass by and take for granted: the checkout clerk, the cleaning crew at your office or your hotel, the barista in the coffee shop. See how this helps you feel more alive and reconnected to the moment.

3. Use a skill or talent you have—cooking, accounting, decorating—to help someone who could benefit from it. It'll jumpstart your transition from a go-getter to a go-giver, and reconnect you to the world and to the natural abundance in your own life.

Epilogue

WE HAVE, if we're lucky, about thirty thousand days to play the game of life. How we play it will be determined by what we value. Or, as David Foster Wallace put it, "Everybody worships. The only choice we get is what to worship. And the compelling reason for maybe choosing some sort of god or spiritual-type thing to worship—be it JC or Allah, be it Yahweh or the Wiccan Mother Goddess, or the Four Noble Truths, or some inviolable set of ethical principles—is that pretty much anything else you worship will eat you alive."

We now know through the latest scientific findings that if we worship money, we'll never feel truly abundant. If we worship power, recognition, and fame, we'll never feel we have enough. And if we live our lives madly rushing around, trying to find and save time, we'll always find ourselves living in a time famine, frazzled and stressed.

"Onward, upward, and inward" is how I ended my commencement speech at Smith. And in many ways, this book is bearing witness, both through my own experience and through the latest science, to the truth that we cannot thrive and lead the lives we want (as opposed to the lives we've settled for) without learning to go inward.

My goal is for this book to chart another way forward—a way available to all of us right now, wherever we find ourselves. A way based on the timeless truth that life is shaped from the inside out—a truth that has been celebrated by spiritual teachers, poets, and philosophers throughout the ages, and has now been validated by modern science.

I wanted to share my own personal journey, how I learned the hard way to step back from being so caught up in my busy life that life's mystery would pass me by. But it was also important to me to make it clear that this was not just one woman's journey. There's a collective longing to stop living in the shallows, to stop hurting our health and our relationships by striving so relentlessly after success as the world defines it—and instead tap into the riches, joy, and amazing possibilities that our lives embody. It doesn't matter what your entry point is or what form your wake-up call takes. It could be burnout, sickness, addiction, the loss of a loved one, the ending of a relationship, a line of poetry that stirs something ineffable in you (I've sprinkled plenty of those throughout the book), or a scientific study about the power and benefits of slowing down, or sleep, or meditating, or mindfulness that speaks to you (I've scattered more than plenty of those throughout the book too). Whatever your entry point is—embrace it. You will find you have the wind at your back because that's what our times are calling for. And I hope I've shown that there are many tools in our inner tool box to help us get back on track when we veer off. And we undoubtedly will. Again and again.

But remember that while the world provides plenty of insistent, flashing, high-volume signals directing us to make more money and climb higher up the ladder, there are almost no worldly signals reminding us to stay connected to the essence of who we are, to take care of ourselves along the way, to reach out to others, to pause to wonder, and to connect to that place from which everything is possible. To quote my Greek compatriot Archimedes again: "Give me a place to stand, and I will move the world."

So find your place to stand—your place of wisdom and peace and strength. And from that place, remake the world in your own image, according to your own definition of success, so that all of us—women and men—can thrive and live our lives with more grace, more joy, more compassion, more gratitude, and yes, more love. Onward, upward, and inward!

Appendices

Appendix A

The "No Distraction" Dozen: 12 Tools, Apps, and Resources to Help You Stay Focused

Steve Jobs said, "focusing is about saying no." Here are some of my favorite tools that can help you maintain focus, filter out distractions . . . and say no, assembled by our *HuffPost* Third Metric features editor, Carolyn Gregoire:

Anti-Social

Social-media anxiety disorder may not yet be recognized by the medical community, but as many of us know, it can feel very real. And it truly does have addictive qualities: In 2012, Harvard researchers found that sharing information about ourselves activates the same part of the brain associated with the pleasure we experience from eating food, receiving money, and having sex.

If you have a hard time peeling yourself away from

Facebook, Twitter, and Pinterest during the workday (or during your leisure time, for that matter), try Anti-Social, a social network–blocking software that allows you to avoid distracting sites. You can choose the times you don't want to be distracted and the sites you want to restrict.

Available for $15 from Anti-Social.cc.

Nanny

Like Anti-Social, the Chrome extension Nanny blocks distracting sites from your browser so that you can keep your mind on the task at hand. In addition to blocking specific URLs for set periods of time (such as restricting You-Tube from 9 a.m. to 5 p.m.), you can also set a limit for your browsing time on certain sites so that, for example, you only give yourself 30 or 60 minutes total to spend on Facebook per day.

Available for free download from the Chrome Web Store.

Controlled Multi-Tab Browsing

Having thirty tabs open in a single window of Google's web browser Chrome can be incredibly distracting—not to mention stress-inducing—and it could keep you jumping from one page to another without really focusing on any one task. Limit your tabs and keep your focus using Controlled Multi-Tab Browsing, a Chrome plug-in. Set a maximum number of tabs (say, four or six), and the plug-in will prevent you from opening any more than that set number until you're done. If you're a cyber-loafer or an incorrigible multitasker, this tool can help you improve your productivity and focus on what you need to complete.

Available for free download from the Chrome Web Store.

Siesta Text and BRB

The downside of unplugging and recharging is that you run the risk of being seen as ignoring friends and family. In our culture of constant connectivity, a three-hours-later response can be taken as a slight.

"The social norm is that you should respond within a couple of hours, if not immediately," David E. Meyer, University of Michigan psychology professor, told *The New York Times* in 2009. "If you don't, it is assumed you are out to lunch mentally, out of it socially, or don't like the person who sent the email."

Now, there's an app for that. If you want to unplug from your email and texts without worrying that your friends and family will think you're ignoring them, set an away message on your mobile device using Siesta Text for Android, or BRB for iPhone. Siesta features customizable away messages for both texts and calls ("I'm driving—text you back later," or "On vacation, will respond when I return next Monday.") Store up to twenty messages and select specific recipients from your contacts to receive the away message.

Siesta Text is available for Android for $0.99 from Google Play, and BRB for iPhone is available for free download from the App Store.

Self Control

The application Self Control can keep your computer offline for preset blocks of time and can also temporarily stop incoming email. And even rebooting your computer won't bring the online distractions back. Or, if there are certain sites that are particularly tempting, you can single them out for blacklisting.

Available for free for Mac from selfcontrolapp.com.

RescueTime

RescueTime presents you with a readout tracking your online activity at the end of each day. With greater awareness of how your time is being spent, you can set goals (to spend only an hour checking email, for instance) and create alarms to go off when you've spent too much time on a particular site or activity—the online equivalent of staging an intervention.

Available for free, or $9 a month for the pro version, for Mac at rescuetime.com. Also available for free on Android from Google Play.

Freedom

You don't have to head off to a remote corner of the world to escape WiFi. If you're a writer, Freedom might just be your new best friend. Freedom completely blocks the Internet from your computer for a set period of time so that checking social sites or getting sucked into Reddit or *HuffPost* simply isn't an option. If the Internet is a big time drain for you, Freedom is a great way to eliminate the temptation.

Available for $10 for Mac, Windows, and Android from macfreedom.com.

Time Out

Taking breaks is a scientifically backed way to help you focus and be more present, but so often we spend hours upon hours in front of a computer screen, pausing only to peruse Facebook or Twitter. If you have trouble remembering to take real breaks, try the Mac app Time Out, a tool that encourages you to stop what you're doing and get up at regular intervals. Time Out reminds you to take a 10-minute break every 50 minutes, and a 10-second "micro-break"—a brief pause to take a deep breath, look away from your screen, and recenter yourself—every 10 minutes. Make your break even more effective by queuing up your most relaxing songs on iTunes to alert you to your upcoming break.

Available for free for Mac from the App Store.

Concentrate

Concentrate packs several different productivity tools into one. The Mac software allows you to designate various activities (studying, writing, et cetera) and then set your computer so that it will only allow certain actions during those times. For example, while in "writing" mode, you can set the software to block social networking sites while allowing you to access relevant documents and websites, set a timer for how long you'll be writing, and add a sound alert to remind you to come back to the task at hand if your mind has wandered.

Available for $29 for Mac from getconcentrating.com.

Digital Detox App

This app could revolutionize your vacations—or even your weekends. Using Digital Detox, you can force your phone to shut down for a set period of time ranging from 30 minutes to one month (and no, the decision is not reversible).

But the app comes with a disclaimer: Only those who are truly serious about unplugging need apply.

Available for free for Android from Google Play.

Isolator

If you have trouble tuning out desktop clutter and distractions, try Isolator, a menu-bar app for Macs that hides desktop clutter and helps you tune out everything but the Word doc in front of you. This app is another great tool for anyone who needs to eliminate digital distractions while focusing on a project. It covers your desktop with a dark overlay so that your full attention is on the present task, with an easy shortcut key to allow you to turn the focus feature on and off.

Available for free for Mac at macupdate.com.

Higby

When you want to put away your email, camera, texts, and playlists in order to be fully present in the moment— whether you're concentrating on a task or being with friends—you might need a physical contraption, not just an app, to do it. Enter Higby, a rubber iPhone holder that covers up your phone's camera and headphone jack. It can also be used for two phones, with the rubber arms holding the devices together so that you can avoid both distractions!

"With our heads, our hearts, and our hands busy with so much digital input, we're losing the downtime we need to observe the world around us, nurture our relationships, and make new things," Higby's creators wrote.

Higby will be available for iPhone from Wolff Olins later in 2014.

Appendix B

Transcendent Tool Box: 12 Tools, Apps, and Resources for Meditation and Mindfulness

Here are a dozen meditation and mindfulness tools to help you start or deepen your practice, compiled by Carolyn Gregoire:

Headspace

Former Buddhist monk Andy Puddicombe founded Headspace as a way to make mindfulness meditation easily available. Headspace's "Take 10" starter program—10 days' worth of 10-minute meditations—is a simple, straightforward introduction to starting a meditation practice. Through short animated videos, the app breaks down the basic principles of meditation and mindfulness, and the recordings take beginners through brief mindfulness practices and guided meditations each day. There is now even a Headspace channel available for passengers on board Virgin Atlantic flights.

Available for free download for iPhone and Android at getsomeheadspace.com.

Mark Williams's Mindfulness Meditation Recordings

Mark Williams, professor of clinical psychology, director of the Oxford Mindfulness Centre, and author of *Mindfulness*, offers a range of free audio meditations for new and experienced meditators and includes instructions for a number of variations on the practice, including a three-minute minibreak, a meditation for depression, silent meditations with bells, and a fun "chocolate meditation." "We must get out of our heads and learn to experience the world directly, experientially, without the relentless commentary of our thoughts," Williams wrote in *The Mindful Way Through Depression*. "We might just open ourselves up to the limitless possibilities for happiness that life has to offer us."

Available for free at franticworld.com.

Buddhify

Touted as the "urban meditation app," Buddhify offers a fun, game-ified approach to creating a meditation practice. Buddhify uses bright graphics and simple language (no Sanskrit or mention of chakras), and is designed to be used on the go. The app has different settings, like home, traveling, walking, and gym, offering audio and video meditations suited to wherever you are. Buddhify "actually changes one's life in big-little ways," wrote one user. "It's the Google Maps of the interior world."

Available for free download for iPhone and Android.

Movement of Spiritual Inner Awareness
Online Meditation Classes

The Movement of Spiritual Inner Awareness, founded by John-Roger, offers a 12-lesson online course on meditation and spiritual exercises for beginners consisting of readings, audio, and video. MSIA's teachings consist of "active meditations," or spiritual exercises, with an emphasis on connecting with our inner source of wisdom and peace. The step-by-step guides include instruction on using a mantra, keeping a journal, and meditative breathing.

Available for free on msia.org.

Chopra Center Meditation Podcast

Deepak Chopra's Chopra Center for Well-Being offers many resources for aspiring and experienced meditators, including a collection of 24 free meditation podcasts. The podcasts include inspiring talks and audio meditations for releasing stress, healing, gratitude, self-empowerment, and more. Download the podcasts on iTunes and listen to them at home, during your commute, or while out on a walk to bring more mindfulness to your day.

Available for free on iTunes.

Oprah & Deepak Chopra's Meditation Master Trilogy

Chopra joined forces with Oprah Winfrey on a series of 21-day online meditation challenges, which have attracted nearly two million participants. Now, they have made all three of their challenges—on the subjects of desire and destiny, perfect health, and miraculous relationships—available through Oprah and Deepak's Meditation Master Trilogy, a gift set containing 66 audio meditations and an interactive journal.

Available for $99 on chopracentermeditation.com/store.

Calm.com

Watch waves crashing, brooks babbling, snow falling, and the sun setting while you enjoy a short, timed meditation—without ever leaving your desk. Calm.com is also available in app form.

Available for free on calm.com and free download for iPhone from the App Store.

Do Nothing for 2 Minutes

Donothingfor2minutes.com, brought to you by the creators of calm.com, is simply a full-screen video of waves crashing at sunset with a timer counting down for two minutes, along with the instructions, "Just relax and look at the waves. Don't touch your mouse or keypad for two minutes." If you do, a bright red flashing "FAIL" comes up on the screen—perhaps not the most Zen reminder to go back to your break, but effective nonetheless.

Available at www.donothingfor2minutes.com.

MeditateApp for Android

A comprehensive meditation timer and tracking device, MeditateApp allows you to create plans and schedules, select meditations for particular days and times, and view charts detailing your past activity.

Meditations can be timed and saved in one of three modes: Meditation, Meditation with Affirmation, and Fall Asleep mode, which fades out the sound of the meditation gradually.

Available for Android (free, or $1.99 for the full version) from Google Play.

Mental Workout

The Mental Workout app and website aim to help you cultivate mindfulness, sleep better, reduce your stress levels, and stay focused. Mental Workout's Mindfulness Meditation app, designed by meditation teacher and psychotherapist Stephan Bodian, provides guided meditations and a timer for silent meditations. It also features an eight-week program for beginners, as well as inspirational talks and relaxation instructions.

Beyond the Mindfulness Meditation app, Mental Workout offers several programs for use on Mac, PC, iPhone, iPad, and Android, including apps that use mindfulness-based approaches to help you reduce stress, enhance sleep quality, and quit smoking.

Programs available at varying costs at mentalworkout.com.

Finding the Space to Lead
Meditations and Reflections

Janice Marturano, who brought meditation to General Mills and went on to found the Institute for Mindful Leadership, offers guidance on working and leading with presence and compassion, and audio meditations and reflections to help you tap into the mindful leader within. The recordings include a kindness meditation, desk-chair meditation, reflection on leadership principles, and more.

Available for free from findingthespacetolead.com.

Eckhart Tolle's "Music to Quiet the Mind"

If you'd rather listen to music than sit in silence, try Eckhart Tolle's "Music to Quiet the Mind," available on Spotify. The album is a compilation of Eckhart Tolle's favorite songs to inspire serenity and stillness. Listen to the relaxing songs when you need to calm down at work, or press play when you get home at the end of the day and want to simply experience the "power of now."

Available for free streaming on Spotify.

Appendix C

At Your Service: 12 Sites for Giving and Volunteering

To help you get started volunteering or to take your giving to the next level, here is a list of some of my favorite sites connecting you to opportunities in your community and around the world, put together by our *HuffPost* Impact editor, Jessica Prois:

SmartVolunteer *smartvolunteer.org*

With its motto "Skills-based giving—it's not just for lawyers anymore," SmartVolunteer provides an easy way to donate your skills to nonprofits and other social enterprises looking for pro bono talent. The site emphasizes opportunities in technology, finance, marketing, and human resources. And if you're not able to volunteer on-site, you can search for "virtual" volunteer opportunities, which require only a computer with an Internet connection.

All for Good *allforgood.org*

The largest database of volunteer opportunities online, All for Good is a great platform for finding ways to make a difference. Each month, the site hosts 150,000 local volunteer listings in major cities. All for Good also powers United We Serve and is part of Points of Light, the largest volunteer network in the world.

VolunteerMatch *volunteermatch.org*

With about 77,000 opportunities to give back, VolunteerMatch connects you to causes and lets you tailor your searches according to what you care about most. You can simply type in what matters to you in the "I Care About" box. Besides listing opportunities, the site also offers tools that help organizations—from corporations to colleges—encourage employees and students to volunteer and invite others to participate. Almost 100,000 nonprofits use VolunteerMatch for recruiting.

Catchafire *catchafire.org*

Catchafire connects professionals with nonprofits and social good initiatives for pro bono work. If you love the arts, pitch in to help a nonprofit tell its story with words, pictures, and infographics. If you're a spreadsheet whiz, Catchafire will direct you to an organization in need of help with accounting or everyday administrative tasks. It also helps you track your impact, with a notice that tells you the monetary value of your volunteer work to the organization.

iVolunteer *ivolunteer.org*

As a hub for stories about natural disasters and other events that have left people in desperate need, iVolunteer connects you with nonprofits and relief services in search of volunteers. The site's mission is rooted in the belief that each act of volunteering can inspire others to join the movement.

DonorsChoose *donorschoose.org*

Founded by Charles Best, a former social studies teacher, DonorsChoose helps you make an impact in classrooms around the country. Public school teachers post their requests—from laptops, Kindles, and cameras to jump ropes, art supplies, and storage containers—and you can choose a project that resonates with you and make a donation. Once a project reaches its goal, DonorsChoose ships the materials to the school and then connects you directly with the teacher and students you've helped.

Idealist *idealist.org*

Idealist helps you find a job, an internship, or volunteer opportunity based on where you live, your schedule, and your interests. The site helps you get involved in your own community, updating you on ongoing volunteer opportunities, one-time asks from nonprofits, and events in your area.

UN Volunteers *unv.org*

The United Nations offers volunteer opportunities in two areas: development assistance and humanitarian and peacekeeping operations. If you want to make a difference but aren't able to travel around the world, you can sign up for online-only volunteering projects, from copyediting to drafting proposals for water and sanitation solutions.

DoSomething *dosomething.org*

More than two million young people have found a cause and started their own volunteer projects through DoSomething, one of the most popular giving platforms for millennials. Under the motto "Make the world suck less," DoSomething connects you with the resources you need to launch or join initiatives such as collecting jeans for homeless youth or donating cell phones to domestic-abuse survivors.

Volunteer.gov

If you're a roll-up-your-sleeves type of person, check out Volunteer.gov, a listing of natural and cultural resource service projects with government agencies, including the National Park Service, Geological Survey, and Forest Service. Opportunities range from cleaning debris from beaches to helping the Army Corps of Engineers protect bald eagle nests.

Help from Home *helpfromhome.org*

This UK-based site is committed to helping you "change the world in just your pyjamas." Offering ways to "micro-volunteer," it connects you with ways to give back at a moment's notice in ways that fit into your schedule. Donate unused air miles with a few clicks during your lunch break, proofread a page of text, or knit a blanket for a family in need.

UniversalGiving *universalgiving.org*

If you want to make a difference and travel at the same time, UniversalGiving will connect you with opportunities in more than one hundred countries. Search by category or location to find projects that UniversalGiving has vetted, such as helping to build a health clinic in Kenya, volunteering at an orphanage in Vietnam, or teaching English in Italy.

Acknowledgments

THROUGHOUT 2013, the Third Metric became a bigger and bigger part of my life leading to my commencement speech at Smith, our first Third Metric conference (held in my apartment in New York), and many Third Metric editorial initiatives on *HuffPost* across all of our international editions. But when Richard Pine, my great friend and longtime agent, called me with the idea of writing a book about it, I said no, reminding him of my pledge—to him, myself, my children—never to write another book. And then he called again. And again. And again. Sometimes a good agent has to sell the book to the author first. Finally I said yes (perhaps he caught me on a day when I hadn't had enough sleep), so my first thanks go to Richard. This is our seventh book together and my fourteenth book (it definitely feels like the "surprise baby" you never thought you were going to have) and I'm grateful for all his guidance as well as his absolute refusal to take no for an answer.

Thrive is both deeply personal and based on an enormous amount of research that has resulted in forty-six pages of endnotes. My deep thanks and gratitude go to Zeeshan Aleem, Tom Dan, and Brian Levin for their commitment and dedication to every detail in getting the book to press. Many thanks also to Marcos Saldivar and Anna McGrady for all their help with fact-checking, copyediting, and sourcing.

I'm profoundly grateful to my editor Roger Scholl for his superb editing of the book, including constantly encouraging me to add more of my own personal experiences. Thank you also to Ed Faulkner, my UK editor at Random House, for all his insightful edits, including making sure that my examples and statistics were international and not just United States–centric. My deep thanks go to Tina Constable, the publisher of the Crown Archetype Group, for so passionately believing in the book's central ideas and for her unflagging support in every aspect of its publication; to Maya Mavjee, president of the Crown Publishing Group; editor in chief Mauro DiPreta; director of publicity Tammy Blake; and editorial director of the Harmony imprint, Diana Baroni. I'm also so grateful to Tricia Wygal, senior production editor, who worked tirelessly under a very tight schedule to ensure that the copyediting, proofreading, and voluminous endnotes were held to the highest standards; to Michael Nagin for the book's beautiful design; to Derek Reed, editorial assistant to Roger Scholl, who followed up on every detail and made sure the trains ran on time; and to the entire Crown sales force for all they've done to ensure the book makes it into the hands of readers across the country. And special thanks to Crown's director of marketing, Meredith McGinnis, for all the creativity she brought to the book's publication and to Penny Simon for all her enthusiasm and hard work in ensuring that the book was not only written but read!

My gratitude also goes to Stephen Sherrill and Roy Sekoff, who were indispensable to the writing of this book. Stephen pored over each and every draft and greatly improved all of them, and Roy, despite all the demands of running *HuffPost Live*, found the time—violating *Thrive*'s sleep rules—to do a masterful pass of the final manuscript. And many thanks to Gregory Beyer, John Montorio, and Jimmy Soni for all their great edits and insights; to Carolyn Gregoire and Jessica Prois for compiling the focus, meditation, and volunteering tools, apps, and resources that I have included in the appendix; and to Kerstin Shamberg for helping us with translations from source material in German.

In writing this book, I drew on the wisdom and important research of many academics. I'm particularly grateful to Richard Davidson, professor of psychiatry at the University of Wisconsin; Mark Williams, professor of clinical psychology at Oxford; Jon Kabat-Zinn, founding director of the Stress Reduction Clinic and the Center for Mindfulness at the University of Massachusetts Medical School; and Adam Grant, professor of management at the Wharton School and author of *Give and Take*.

I'm deeply grateful to Sheryl Sandberg for reading an early draft of the manuscript and not only giving me key suggestions but actually sending me line-by-line edits, including a much better structure for the epilogue. I'm also grateful to Howard Schultz for all his feedback, including suggesting I use the story of Icarus as the perfect metaphor for modern burnout! And many thanks to Ellen Goodman, who generously offered her insights on many topics—especially death, which is the subject of the important Conversation Project she has launched—and to Susan Cain for reading the manuscript and giving me her always insightful comments.

Special thanks to Paul Kaye for all his wisdom and unwavering support in helping me live a Third Metric life and to Patricia Fitzgerald for sharing her knowledge about integrative health as well as her enthusiasm and passion for this project.

My love and deep thanks to my friends who read early drafts and offered thoughts: Willow Bay, Faith Bethelard, Nicolas Berggruen, Kimberly Brooks, Mika Brzezinski, Laurie David, Gail Gross, Jacki Kelley, Fran Lasker, Cindi Leive, Kelly Meyer, Jacqueline Novogratz, Heather Reisman, Jan Shepherd, Timothea Stewart, and Joan Witkowski.

Thank you to Jeff Swafford, Paula Kabe, Herbie Ziskend, and Horacio Fabiano for all their support, and a very special thanks to the great team that was responsible for bringing the book to many countries around the world: Amanda Schumacher, Lyndsey Blessing, Jordan Freeman, and Lena Auerbuch.

This is my first book that was read at the manuscript stage by both my daughters, Christina and Isabella. I'm grateful for their suggestions—and corrections—as well as for the incredible source of love and joy they are in my life. Thank you also to my ex-husband, Michael, who read the manuscript while we were on our family Christmas vacation. And finally, I want to thank my sister, Agapi, who read every draft, reminded me of stories I had forgotten, and brought her amazing spirit to the journey of completing this book—as she has always brought it to the journey of our lives together.

The book is dedicated to our mother, Elli, who was its inspiration and who lived a Third Metric life long before it had a name.

Notes

Introduction

4 **40 percent increased risk:** Natalie Slopen, Robert Glynn, Julie Buring, Tené Lewis, David Williams, and Michelle Albert, "Job Strain, Job Insecurity, and Incident Cardiovascular Disease in the Women's Health Study: Results from a 10-Year Prospective Study," *PLoS ONE* 7 (2012): 7.

5 **60 percent greater risk of diabetes:** Alexandros Heraclides, Tarani Chandola, Daniel Witte, and Eric Brunner, "Psychosocial Stress at Work Doubles the Risk of Type 2 Diabetes in Middle-Aged Women: Evidence from the Whitehall II Study," *Diabetes Care* 32 (2009): 2230–35.

5 **In the past thirty years:** Sheldon Cohen and Denise Janicki-Deverts, "Who's Stressed? Distributions of Psychological Stress in the United States in Probability Samples from 1983, 2006, and 2009," *Journal of Applied Social Psychology* 42 (2012): 1320–34.

5 **According to the American Psychological Association:** "Stress by Generations: 2012," American Psychological Association, accessed October 25, 2013, www.apa.org.

5 **The *Exxon Valdez* wreck:** "Sleep, Performance and Public Safety," Division of Sleep Medicine at Harvard Medical School, accessed October 25, 2013, www.healthysleep.med.harvard.edu.

5 **the deadly Metro-North derailment:** Shimon Prokupecz, Mike Ahlers, and Ray Sanchez, "Train Engineer 'Was Nodding Off and Caught Himself Too Late,' Union Rep Says," *CNN*, December 3, 2013, www.cnn.com.

5   **As John Paul Wright:** Kevin Short and Ben Hallman, "Train Engineers Prone to 'Microsleep' Spells, Experts Say," *The Huffington Post*, December 6, 2013, www.huffingtonpost.com.

6   **Over 30 percent of people in the United States:** Centers for Disease Control and Prevention, "Effect of Short Sleep Duration on Daily Activities—United States, 2005–2008," Morbidity and Mortality Weekly Report, March 4, 2011, www.cdc.gov.

6   **and the United Kingdom:** Denis Campbell, "Chronic Lack of Sleep Affects One in Three British Workers," *The Observer*, March 31, 2012, www.theguardian.com.

6   **a study from the Walter Reed Army Institute of Research:** William Killgore, Ellen Kahn-Greene, Erica Lipizzi, Rachel Newman, Gary Kamimori, and Thomas Balkin, "Sleep Deprivation Reduces Perceived Emotional Intelligence and Constructive Thinking Skills," *Sleep Medicine* 9 (2008): 517–26.

7   **"time famine":** Leslie Perlow, "The Time Famine: Toward a Sociology of Work Time," *Administrative Science Quarterly* 44 (1999): 57–81.

7   **Dr. Seuss summed it up beautifully:** *In Search of Dr. Seuss*, directed by Vincent Paterson (1994; Burbank, CA: Warner Home Video, 2010), DVD.

8   **"The kingdom of God is within you":** Luke 17:21, KJV.

8   **Or as Archimedes said:** Peter Schouls, *Descartes and the Enlightenment* (Montreal: McGill-Queen's University Press, 1989), 53.

9   **As Steve Jobs said:** Steve Jobs, Commencement Speech, *Stanford Report*, June 14, 2005, www.news.stanford.edu.

9   **as the poet Rumi put it:** Daniel Ladinsky, trans., *Love Poems from God: Twelve Sacred Voices from the East and West* (New York: Penguin, 2002), 85.

9   **In an op-ed:** Erin Callan, "Is There Life After Work?," *The New York Times*, March 9, 2013, www.nytimes.com.

10   **For *New York Times* food writer Mark Bittman:** Mark Bittman, "I Need a Virtual Break. No Really," *The New York Times*, March 2, 2008, www.nytimes.com.

10   **For Carl Honoré:** Carl Honoré, "The Slow Revolution is Growing . . . Fast," *The Huffington Post*, October 6, 2009, www.huffingtonpost.com.

11   **For Aetna CEO Mark Bertolini:** Katie Little, "Severe Ski Accident Spurs Aetna CEO to Bring Yoga to Work," *CNBC*, March 19, 2013, www.cnbc.com.

11   **For HopeLab president Pat Christen:** Carolyn Gregoire, "How

Technology Is Killing Eye Contact," *The Huffington Post*, September 28, 2013, www.huffingtonpost.com.

11 **For Anna Holmes:** Jessica Bacal, *Mistakes I Made at Work: 25 Influential Women Reflect on What They Got Out of Getting It Wrong* (New York: Plume, 2014), 8–9.

13 **as Gertrude Stein once said:** Linda Simon, *Gertrude Stein Remembered* (Lincoln, NE: University of Nebraska Press, 1994), xi.

14 **Researchers at Carnegie Mellon:** Cohen and Janicki-Deverts, "Who's Stressed?," 1320–34.

14 **higher instances of diabetes:** Masuma Novak, L. Björck, K. W. Giang, C. Heden-Ståhl, L. Wilhelmsen, and A. Rosengren, "Perceived Stress and Incidence of Type 2 Diabetes: A 35-Year Follow-Up Study of Middle-Aged Swedish Men," *Diabetic Medicine* 30 (2013): e8-16.

14 **heart disease:** Laura Manenschijn, L. Schaap, N. M. van Schoor, S. van der Pas, G. M. E. E. Peeters, P. Lips, J. W. Koper, and E. F. C. van Rossum, "High Long-Term Cortisol Levels, Measured in Scalp Hair, Are Associated with a History of Cardiovascular Disease," *The Journal of Clinical Endocrinology & Metabolism* 98 (2013): 2078–83.

14 **obesity:** Susan Melhorn, Eric Krause, Karen Scott, Marie Mooney, Jeffrey Johnson, Stephen Woods, and Randall Sakai, "Meal Patterns and Hypothalamic NPY Expression During Chronic Social Stress and Recovery," *American Journal of Physiology: Regulatory, Integrative and Comparative Physiology* 299 (2010): 813–22.

14 **According to the Centers for Disease Control and Prevention:** "Chronic Diseases: The Power to Prevent, the Call to Control: At a Glance 2009," Centers for Disease Control and Prevention, accessed December 12, 2013, www.cdc.gov.

14 **The Benson-Henry Institute:** "About the Benson-Henry Institute for Mind Body Medicine," Benson-Henry Institute at Massachusetts General Hospital, accessed December 12, 2013, www.massgeneral.org.

14 **While in the United Kingdom:** Jeremy Laurence and Robin Minchom, "Rise in Hospital Admissions for Stress is Blamed on Recession," *The Independent*, September 12, 2012, www.independent.co.uk.

14 **As Tim Straughan:** Graham Smith, "Hospital Admissions for Stress Jump by 7% in Just One Year . . . and More Men Were Treated Than Women," *Daily Mail*, September 11, 2012, www.dailymail.co.uk.

14 **the effects of stress on children:** Andrew Garner, Jack Shonkoff, Benjamin Siegel, Mary Dobbins, Marian Earls, Laura McGuinn, John Pascoe, and David Wood, "Early Childhood Adversity, Toxic Stress,

and the Role of the Pediatrician: Translating Developmental Science into Lifelong Health," *Pediatrics: Official Journal of the American Academy of Pediatrics* 129 (2011): 224–31.

15   **As Nicholas Kristof put it:** Nicholas Kristof, "A Poverty Solution That Begins with a Hug," *The New York Times*, January 7, 2012, www.nytimes.com.

16   **David Brooks wrote:** David Brooks, "The Humanist Vocation," *The New York Times*, June 20, 2013, www.nytimes.com.

17   **But when his sister, Mona Simpson:** Mona Simpson, "A Sister's Eulogy for Steve Jobs," *The New York Times*, October 30, 2011, www.nytimes.com.

18   **In her 1951 novel *Memoirs of Hadrian*:** Marguerite Yourcenar, *Memoirs of Hadrian*, trans. Grace Frick (New York: Farrar, Straus and Giroux, 2005), 25.

18   **Thomas Jefferson's epitaph:** "Jefferson's Gravestone," Thomas Jefferson's Monticello, accessed October 25, 2013, www.monticello.org.

18   **"I'm always relieved":** George Carlin, *Napalm and Silly Putty* (New York: Hyperion, 2002), 170.

18   **Jane Lotter:** Michael Winerip, "Dying with Dignity and the Final Word on Her Life," *The New York Times*, August 5, 2013, www.nytimes.com.

Well-Being

21   **"For a long time":** Marilyn Tam, *The Happiness Choice: The Five Decisions You Will Make That Take You from Where You Are to Where You Want to Be* (Hoboken, N.J.: Wiley, 2013), 9.

23   **as Socrates said:** Thomas Brickhouse and Nicholas Smith, *Plato's Socrates* (Oxford: Oxford University Press, 1994), 201.

24   **Women who have heart attacks:** "Women and Heart Disease Facts," Women's Heart Foundation, accessed November 1, 2013, www.womensheart.org.

24   **women in high-stress jobs:** Jenny Head, Stephen Stansfeld, and Johannes Siegrist, "The Psychosocial Work Environment and Alcohol Dependence: A Prospective Study," *Occupational and Environmental Medicine* 61 (2004): 219–24.

24   **Stress and pressure:** (1) Linda Carroll, "Eating Disorders Stalk Women into Adulthood," *Today News*, July 6, 2011, www.today.com; (2) "Midlife," The Renfrew Center, accessed December 1, 2013, www.renfrewcenter.com.

25   **Caroline Turner:** Caroline Turner, "Why We Women Leave Our

Jobs, and What Business Can Do to Keep Us," *Diversity MBA Magazine*, August 15, 2012, www.diversitymbamagazine.com.

25   **In fact, 43 percent of women:** Paulette Light, "Why 43% of Women with Children Leave Their Jobs, and How to Get Them Back," *The Atlantic*, April 19, 2013, www.theatlantic.com.

26   **"I'm at the table. I've made it":** Margo Eprecht, "The Real Reason Women Are Leaving Wall Street," *Quartz*, September 5, 2013, www.qz.com.

26   **"You are not your bank account":** Anne Lamott, "Let Us Commence," *Salon*, June 6, 2003, www.salon.com.

26   **"I was an exhausted, nervous wreck":** Paulette Light, "Why 43% of Women with Children Leave Their Jobs, and How to Get Them Back."

27   **Light writes:** Ibid.

27   **"It's not 'What do I want to do?'":** Catherine Pearson, "Women and Stress: The Moment Kate Knew She Had to Change Her Life," *The Huffington Post*, May 22, 2013, www.huffingtonpost.com.

28   **"I do not try to dance better":** "City Ballet School–San Francisco," City Ballet School–San Francisco, accessed December 1, 2013, www.cityballetschool.org.

28   **According to a *ForbesWoman* survey:** Meghan Casserly, ForbesWoman, and TheBump.com, "Parenthood and the Economy 2012 Survey Results," *Forbes*, September 12, 2012, www.forbes.com.

28   **Belgian philosopher Pascal Chabot:** Pascal Chabot, "Burnout Is Global," *Le Huffington Post*, January 20, 2013, www.huffingtonpost.fr.

29   **Marie Asberg:** Mark Williams and Danny Penman, *Mindfulness: An Eight-Week Plan for Finding Peace in a Frantic World* (Emmaus, PA: Rodale, 2011), Kindle edition, 213.

29   **"Often, the very first things":** Ibid., 214.

29   **"If I were called upon":** James Woelfel, "Frederick Buechner: The Novelist as Theologian," *Theology Today* 40 (1983).

29   **using illegal drugs:** "Results from the 2010 National Survey on Drug Use and Health: Summary of National Findings," U.S. Department of Health and Human Services, accessed December 1, 2013, www.oas.samhsa.gov.

29   **twelve million are using prescription painkillers:** "Policy Impact: Prescription Painkiller Overdoses," Centers for Disease Control and Prevention, accessed December 1, 2013, www.cdc.gov.

30   **prescription sleep aids to go to sleep:** "CDC: Nearly 9 Million Americans Use Prescription Sleep Aids," *CBS News*, August 29, 2013, www.cbsnews.com.

30   **400 percent since 1988:** Maia Szalavitz, "What Does a 400% Increase in Antidepressant Use Really Mean?," *Time*, October 20, 2011, www.healthland.time.com.

30   **In the United Kingdom, prescriptions:** (1) Ricardo Gusmão, Sónia Quintão, David McDaid, Ella Arensman, Chantal Van Audenhove, Claire Coffey, Airi Värnik, Peeter Värnik, James Coyne, and Ulrich Hegerl, "Antidepressant Utilization and Suicide in Europe: An Ecological Multi-National Study," *PLoS ONE* 8 (2013): e66455; (2) Rachel Reilly, "Prozac Nation: Use of Antidepressants in the UK Has Soared by 500% in the Past 20 Years," *Daily Mail*, July 5, 2013, www.dailymail.co.uk.

30   **According to a Danish study:** Rebecca Smith, "Highflying Women 'More Likely to Develop Heart Disease,'" *The Telegraph*, May 6, 2010, www.telegraph.co.uk.

30   **In Germany:** "Workplace Stress is Costing Germany Time, Money, Health," *Deutsche Welle*, January 29, 2013, www.dw.de.

30   **When she was the German Labour Minister:** Aurelia End, "Germany Wages War Against Burnout," Agence France-Presse, February 4, 2012.

31   **In China, according to a 2012 survey:** Chen Xin, "Survey Shows Chinese Workers Stressed Out," *China Daily*, October 19, 2012, www.chinadaily.com.cn.

31   **According to a Harvard Medical School study:** Leslie Kwoh, "When the CEO Burns Out," *The Wall Street Journal*, May 7, 2013, www.online.wsj.com.

31   **a record $1.2 billion fine:** Peter Lattman and Ben Protess, "SAC Capital to Plead Guilty to Insider Trading," *The New York Times*, November 4, 2013, www.dealbook.nytimes.com.

31   **one thousand emails he gets every day:** Jennifer Senior, "How Email Is Swallowing Our Lives," *New York*, July 31, 2013, www.nymag.com.

31   **Lloyds's chairman Sir Winfried Bischoff:** Dan Milmo, "Lloyds Bank Boss Horta-Osório Returning to Work After Sick Leave," *The Guardian*, December 14, 2011, www.theguardian.com.

31   **Upon his return, Horta-Osório said:** Jill Treanor, "Lloyds Chief 'Did Not Sleep for Five Days,'" *The Guardian*, December 15, 2011, www.theguardian.com.

31   **And in October 2013, Hector Sants:** Julia Werdigier, "Hector Sants Resigns From Barclays," *The New York Times*, November 13, 2013, www.dealbook.nytimes.com.

31   **The word "stress" was first used:** Esther Sternberg, *Healing Spaces:*

The Science of Place and Well-Being (Cambridge, MA: Harvard University Press, 2009), 95–96.

32 **"The greatest weapon against stress":** Winifred Gallagher, *Rapt: Attention and the Focused Life* (New York: Penguin, 2009), 6.

34 **Lee Kai-Fu:** Josh Chin and Paul Mozur, "Gloom Falls Over Chinese Web as Lee Kai-Fu Reveals Cancer Diagnosis," *The Wall Street Journal*, September 6, 2013, www.blogs.wsj.com.

34 **"And every day, the world will drag you":** Iain Thomas, "The Grand Distraction," *I Wrote This For You Blog*, June 19, 2012, www.iwrotethisforyou.me.

35 **what's good for us as individuals:** "Healthy Employees, Healthy Profits: A Stronger Business Case for Employee Health Management Programs," OptumHealth Resource Center for Health and Wellbeing Position Paper, accessed December 12, 2013, www.optumhealth.com.

35 **Studies show that U.S. employers:** Michael Porter, Elizabeth Teisberg, and Scott Wallace, "What Should Employers do about Healthcare?" Harvard Business School Working Knowledge Forum, July 16, 2008, www.hbswk.hbs.edu.

36 **In the United Kingdom:** Laurence and Minchom, "Rise in Hospital Admissions for Stress is Blamed on Recession."

36 **Michael Porter recommends:** Porter, Teisberg, and Wallace, "What Should Employers do about Healthcare?"

36 **Howard Schultz, the CEO of Starbucks:** David A. Kaplan, "Howard Schultz Brews Strong Coffee at Starbucks," *CNN Money*, November 17, 2011, www.management.fortune.cnn.com.

36 **During Starbucks' earlier years:** Howard Schultz and Dori Jones Yang, *Pour Your Heart Into It: How Starbucks Built a Company One Cup at a Time* (New York: Hyperion, 1997), 127–135.

36 **"The lack of attention":** Marguerite Rigoglioso, "Time to Detox the Work Environment," Stanford Graduate School of Business press release, April 1, 2009, on the Stanford Graduate School of Business News website, www.gsb.stanford.edu.

37 **The supermarket chain's former CEO Steve Burd recounts:** "Escape Fire: The Fight to Save America's Health Care," *CNN*, March 10, 2013, www.transcripts.cnn.com.

37 **So Safeway offered incentives:** Ibid.

37 **Esther Sternberg explains:** Esther Sternberg, interview with Krista Tippett, "The Science of Healing Places with Esther Sternberg," *On Being*, American Public Media, September 27, 2012, www.onbeing.org.

38 **"In Asian languages":** Jon Kabat-Zinn, *Arriving at Your Own Door: 108 Lessons in Mindfulness* (New York: Hyperion, 2007), 3.

39 **"What was the very best moment":** Nicholson Baker, *The Anthologist* (New York: Simon & Schuster, 2009), 237.

39 **Mark Williams and Danny Penman:** Williams and Penman, *Mindfulness*, 55, 77.

40 **"You wander from room":** Andrew Harvey, *The Direct Path: Creating a Personal Journey to the Divine Using the World's Spiritual Traditions* (New York: Harmony, 2001).

42 **"Science—the same reductionistic science":** Herbert Benson and William Proctor, *Relaxation Revolution: The Science and Genetics of Mind Body Healing* (New York: Scribner, 2011), 59.

42 **the authors recommend:** Ibid., 16.

43 **A study funded by the National Institutes of Health:** Robert Schneider, Charles Alexander, Frank Staggers, Maxwell Rainforth, John Salerno, Arthur Hartz, Stephen Arndt, Vernon Barnes, and Sanford Nidich, "Long-term Effects of Stress Reduction on Mortality in Persons > or = 55 Years of Age with Systemic Hypertension," *American Journal of Cardiology* 95 (2005): 1060–64.

43 **observe Mark Williams and Danny Penman:** Williams and Penman, *Mindfulness*, 51.

43 **levels of antibodies to the flu vaccine:** Richard Davidson, Jon Kabat-Zinn, Jessica Schumacher, Melissa Rosenkranz, Daniel Muller, Saki F. Santorelli, Ferris Urbanowski, Anne Harrington, Katherine Bonus, and John F. Sheridan, "Alterations in Brain and Immune Function Produced by Mindfulness Meditation," *Psychosomatic Medicine: Journal of Behavioral Medicine* 65 (2003): 564–70.

43 **severity and length of colds:** Bruce Barrett, Mary S. Hayney, Daniel Muller, David Rakel, Ann Ward, Chidi N. Obasi, Roger Brown, Zhengjun Zhang, Aleksandra Zgierska, James Gern, Rebecca West, Tola Ewers, Shari Barlow, Michele Gassman, and Christopher L. Coe, "Meditation or Exercise for Preventing Acute Respiratory Infection: A Randomized Trial," *Annals of Family Medicine* 10 (2012): 337–46.

43 **researchers at Wake Forest University found:** Fadel Zeidan, Katherine T. Martucci, Robert A. Kraft, Nakia S. Gordon, John G. McHaffie, and Robert C. Coghill, "Brain Mechanisms Supporting the Modulation of Pain by Mindfulness Meditation," *The Journal of Neuroscience* 31 (2011): 5540–48.

43 **Researchers at Massachusetts General Hospital:** Manoj K. Bhasin, Jeffery A. Dusek, Bei-Hung Chang, Marie G. Joseph, John W.

Denninger, Gregory L. Fricchione, Herbert Benson, and Towia A. Libermann, "Relaxation Response Induces Temporal Transcriptome Changes in Energy Metabolism, Insulin Secretion and Inflammatory Pathways," *PLoS ONE* 8 (2013): e62817.

43 **reduced yearly medical costs:** Robert E. Herron, "Changes in Physician Costs Among High-Cost Transcendental Meditation Practitioners Compared With High-Cost Nonpractitioners Over 5 Years," *American Journal of Health Promotion* 26 (2011): 56–60.

43 **One study found:** Sara W. Lazar, Catherine E. Kerr, Rachel H. Wasserman, Jeremy R. Gray, Douglas N. Greve, Michael T. Treadway, Metta McGarvey, Brian T. Quinn, Jeffery A. Dusek, Herbert Benson, Scott L. Rauch, Christopher I. Moore, and Bruce Fischl, "Meditation Experience is Associated with Increased Cortical Thickness," *NeuroReport* 16 (2005): 1893–97.

43 **Dr. Richard Davidson:** Antoine Lutz, Lawrence Greischar, Nancy Rawlings, Matthieu Ricard, and Richard Davidson, "Long-Term Meditators Self-Induce High-Amplitude Gamma Synchrony During Mental Practice," *Proceedings of the National Academy of Sciences* 101 (2004): 16369–373.

44 **"further reaches of human plasticity":** Richard Davidson, interview with Krista Tippett, *On Being*, American Public Media, June 23, 2011, www.onbeing.org.

44 **He calls meditation:** Marc Kaufman, "Meditation Gives Brain a Charge, Study Finds," *The Washington Post*, January 3, 2005, www.washingtonpost.com.

44 **"Meditation is not just blissing out":** Frankie Taggart, "Buddhist Monk Is World's Happiest Man," *Agence France-Presse*, October 29, 2012.

44 **"You don't learn to sail":** Matthieu Ricard, "Buddhist Perspective" (panel at Mind and Life XXVII: Craving, Desire and Addiction, Dharamsala, India, October 31, 2013).

44 **After placing more than 250 sensors:** Taggart, "Buddhist Monk Is World's Happiest Man."

44 **As Ricard explains:** Matthieu Ricard, interview with Krista Tippett, *On Being*, American Public Media, October 27, 2011, www.onbeing.org.

45 **"People look for retreats":** Christopher Gill, trans., *Marcus Aurelius: Meditations, Books 1–6* (New York: Oxford University Press, 2013), 20.

45 **Researchers at UCLA found:** J. David Creswell, Michael R. Irwin, Lisa J. Burklund, Matthew D. Lieberman, Jesusa M. G. Arevalo, Jeffrey

Ma, Elizabeth Crabb Breen, and Steven W. Cole, "Mindfulness-Based Stress Reduction Training Reduces Loneliness and Pro-Inflammatory Gene Expression in Older Adults: A Small Randomized Controlled Trial," *Brain, Behavior, and Immunity* 26 (2012): 1095–101.

45   **researchers from the University of Michigan documented:** Anthony P. King, Thane M. Erickson, Nicholas D. Giardino, Todd Favorite, Sheila A. H. Rauch, Elizabeth Robinson, Madhul Kulkarni, and Israel Liberzon, "A Pilot Study of Group Mindfulness-Based Cognitive Therapy (MBCT) for Combat Veterans with Post-Traumatic Stress Disorder (PTSD)," *Depression and Anxiety* 30 (2013): 638–45.

45   **reduce depression among pregnant women:** Cassandra Vieten and John Astin, "Effects of a Mindfulness-Based Intervention During Pregnancy on Prenatal Stress and Mood: Results of a Pilot Study," *Archives of Women's Mental Health* 11 (2008): 67–74.

45   **teens:** Filip Raes, James W. Griffith, Kathleen Van Der Gucht, and J. Mark G. Williams, "School-Based Prevention and Reduction of Depression in Adolescents: A Cluster-Randomized Controlled Trial of a Mindfulness Group Program," *Mindfulness* (2013).

45   **A study led by University of North Carolina:** Barbara L. Fredrickson, Michael A. Cohn, Kimberly A. Coffey, Jolynn Pek, and Sandra M. Finkel, "Open Hearts Build Lives: Positive Emotions, Induced Through Loving-Kindness Meditation, Build Consequential Personal Resources," *Journal of Personal and Social Psychology* 95 (2008): 1045–62.

45   **A study of patients:** "Mindfulness Based Cognitive Therapy and the Prevention of Relapse in Depression," University of Oxford Centre for Suicide Research, accessed December 1, 2013, www.cebmh.warne.ox.ac.uk.

46   **Richard Davidson has come to view:** Penelope Green, "This is Your Brain on Happiness," *O, The Oprah Magazine*, March 2008, www.oprah.com.

46   **"We can actually practice to enhance our well-being":** Peter S. Goodman, "Why Companies Are Turning to Meditations and Yoga to Boost the Bottom Line," *The Huffington Post*, July 26, 2013, www.huffingtonpost.com.

46   **Davidson found "remarkable results":** Taggart, "Buddhist Monk Named Happiest Man in the World."

46   **Scientists from Harvard and Northeastern Universities:** (1) "Can Meditation Make You a More Compassionate Person?" Northwestern University press release, April 1, 2013, www.northeastern.edu; (2) Paul Condon, Gaëlle Desbordes, Willa Miller, and David DeSteno, "Medi-

tation Increases Compassionate Responses to Suffering," *Psychological Science* 24 (2013): 2125–27.

46   **"Ideas are like fish":** David Lynch, *Catching Big Fish: Meditation, Consciousness, and Creativity* (New York: Tarcher, 2007), 1.

47   **Steve Jobs:** Walter Isaacson, *Steve Jobs* (New York: Simon & Schuster, 2011), 9.

47   **Giuseppe Pagnoni:** Giuseppe Pagnoni, Milos Cekic, and Ying Guo, "'Thinking About Not-Thinking': Neural Correlates of Conceptual Processing During Zen Meditation," *PLoS ONE* 3 (2008): e3083.

47   **"The regular practice of meditation":** "Zen Training Speeds the Mind's Return After Distraction, Brain Scans Reveal," Woodruff Health Sciences Center News press release, September 9, 2008, www.shared.web.emory.edu.

47   **The Bank of England:** Asa Bennett, "Bank of England Runs Meditation Classes for Staff Mindfulness," *The Huffington Post*, November 20, 2013, www.huffingtonpost.com.

47   **And in the military:** Julie Watson, "Marines Studying Mindfulness-based Training Can Benefit Troops," Associated Press, January 19, 2013, www.bigstory.ap.org.

47   **the David Lynch Foundation's Operation Warrior Wellness:** "Operation Warrior Wellness: Building Resilience and Healing the Hidden Wounds of War," David Lynch Foundation for Consciousness-Based Education and World Peace, accessed December 10, 2013, www.davidlynchfoundation.org.

48   **Bill Ford:** Tatiana Serafin, "Sit. Breathe. Be a Better Leader." *Inc.*, October 18, 2011, www.inc.com.

48   **Jeff Weiner:** Megan Rose Dickey, "The Secret Behind the Silicon Valley Elite's Success: Meditation," *Business Insider*, June 25, 2013, www.businessinsider.com.

48   **Mark Bertolini:** Mark Bertolini, interview with Arianna Huffington, "Squawk Newsmaker," *Squawk Box*, CNBC, March 12, 2013, www.huffingtonpost.com.

48   **Marc Benioff:** Sarah Perez and Anthony Ha, "Marc Benioff Says, 'There Would Be No Salesforce.com Without Steve Jobs,'" *Tech Crunch*, September 10, 2013, www.techcrunch.com.

48   **Evan Williams:** Megan Rose Dickey, "The Secret Behind the Silicon Valley Elite's Success: Meditation."

48   **George Stephanopoulos:** "George Stephanopoulos Talks Benefits of Meditation at the Third Metric Women's Conference," *The Huffington Post*, June 7, 2013, www.huffingtonpost.com.

48 **Andrew Ross Sorkin:** Marcus Baram, "Ray Dalio, Hedge Fund Genius, Says Meditation Is Secret to His Success," *International Business Times*, November 12, 2013, www.ibtimes.com.

48 **Jerry Seinfeld:** Jerry Seinfeld, interview with George Stephanopoulos, *Good Morning America*, December 13, 2012, www.abcnews.go.com.

48 **Kenneth Branagh:** Crystal G. Martin, "Kenneth Branagh's Aha! Moment: How I Learned to Meditate," *O, The Oprah Magazine*, May 2011, www.oprah.com.

48 **Oprah Winfrey:** "Oprah Winfrey and Deepak Chopra Launch 21-Day Meditation Experience on Desire and Destiny," OWN: Oprah Winfrey Network press release, October 28, 2008, www.press.discovery .com.

48 **Rupert Murdoch:** "Rupert Murdoch is Giving Transcendental Meditation a Try," *The Huffington Post*, April 23, 2013, www.huffington post.com.

48 **As Bob Roth:** Bob Roth (Executive Director, David Lynch Foundation), conversation with the author, New York City, December 3, 2013.

48 **Lena Dunham, the creator:** Carolyn Gregoire, "Lena Dunham: 'I've Been Meditating Since I Was 9 Years Old,'" *The Huffington Post*, October 9, 2013, www.huffingtonpost.com.

49 **Padmasree Warrior:** Matt Richtel, "Silicon Valley Says Step Away from the Device," *The New York Times*, July 23, 2012, www.nytimes .com.

49 **"Vanquishing infectious disease has":** Penny George, "What Is Integrative Medicine and Why Is It Critical to Today's Healthcare Discussion?" *The Huffington Post*, May 14, 2013, www.huffingtonpost.com.

49 **According to Taoist philosophy:** Bernard Down, "Death in Classical Daoist Thought," *Philosophy Now*, 2000, www.philosophynow.org.

49 **Lectio Divina:** Lawrence S. Cunningham and Keith J. Egan, *Christian Spirituality: Themes from the Tradition* (Mahwah, NJ: Paulist, 1996), 38.

49 **The Quakers built:** "Quakers," BBC Religions, last updated July 3, 2009, www.bbc.co.uk.

50 **"If pressed to say":** Ibid.

50 **In the 1970s, Basil Pennington:** Mark Finley, "Biblical Spirituality: Rediscovering Our Biblical Roots or Embracing the East?" *Ministry: International Journal for Pastors*, August 2012, www.ministry magazine.org.

51 **As the Prophet Muhammad himself said:** Al-Mamum Al-Suhrawardy, *The Wisdom of Muhammad* (New York: Citadel, 2001), 81.

51 **Judaism also has a long mystical tradition:** Les Lancaster, "The Essence of Jewish Meditation," BBC Religions, August 13, 2009, www.bbc.co.uk.

52 **Torah coach Frumma Rosenberg-Gottlieb:** Frumma Rosenberg-Gottlieb, "On Mindfulness and Jewish Meditation, Part I," Chabad.org, 2013, www.chabad.org.

52 **as Genesis 24 tells us:** Genesis 24:63, KJV.

53 **In her forthcoming book:** Tessa Watt, *Mindful London* (London: Virgin, 2014).

53 **"Have patience":** P. C. Mozoomdar, ed., *The Interpreter* (1885): 76.

55 **At Facebook:** Jessica Stillman, "Sheryl Sandberg Leaves Work at 5:30. Why Can't You?," *Inc.*, April 9, 2012, www.inc.com.

55 **According to 2012 numbers:** Charlotte McDonald, "Are Greeks the Hardest Workers in Europe?" *BBC News Magazine*, February 25, 2012, www.bbc.co.uk.

55 **One of the most:** Caitlin Kelly, "O.K., Google, Take a Deep Breath," *The New York Times*, April 28, 2012, www.nytimes.com.

56 **Janice Marturano set up:** David Gelles, "The Mind Business," *Financial Times*, August 24, 2012, www.ft.com.

56 **"The main business case for meditation":** Ibid.

57 **35 percent of large and midsize U.S. employers:** "Aon Hewitt 2013 Health Care Survey," Aon, accessed November 22, 2013, www.aon.com.

57 **Target:** Gelles, "Mind Business."

57 **Apple:** Wallace Immen, "Meditation Finds an Ommm in the Office," *The Globe and Mail*, November 27, 2012, www.theglobeandmail.com.

57 **Nike:** "Nike Tennessee Recognized For Employment Practices," Nike, Inc. press release, March 10, 2008, www.nikeinc.com.

57 **Procter and Gamble:** Scott Thompson, "The Advantages of a Meditative Space in the Workplace," *Demand Media: Work*, accessed November 20, 2013, www.work.chron.com.

57 **"Companies that make sincere efforts":** Jacquelyn Smith, "The Top 25 Companies for Work-Life Balance," *Forbes*, August 10, 2012, www.forbes.com.

57 *Fortune*'s **"100 Best Companies to Work For":** "100 Best Companies to Work For," *Fortune*, 2013, www.money.cnn.com.

57 **At Promega:** Goodman, "Why Companies Are Turning to Meditation and Yoga to Boost the Bottom Line."

58 **The Minneapolis staffing company Salo:** Sarah McKenzie, "Transforming the Workplace into a Blue Zone," *Southwest Journal*, January 14, 2013, www.southwestjournal.com.

58 **"Blue Zones":** "Blue Zone Communities—Creating Environments of Health," Blue Zones, accessed December 1, 2013, www.bluezones.com.

58 **Now Buettner is helping:** McKenzie, "Transforming the Workplace into a Blue Zone."

58 **Danny Wegman:** Jillian Berman, "Wegmans Improves its Bottom Line by Helping Employees Shrink Their Waistlines," *The Huffington Post*, August 5, 2013, www.huffingtonpost.com.

58 **At Aetna:** Russ Britt, "Aetna Completes Coventry Buyout, Raises Full-year Outlook," *The Wall Street Journal*, May 7, 2013, www.blogs.marketwatch.com.

58 **Mark Bertolini discovered:** Jeffrey Young, "Company Wellness Programs May Boost Bottom Lines, Aetna CEO Mark Bertolini Says," *The Huffington Post*, June 6, 2013, www.huffingtonpost.com.

59 **brought in Duke University:** "Aetna Delivers Evidence-based Mind-Body Stress Management Programs," Aetna News Hub press release, February 23, 2012, www.newshub.aetna.com.

59 **A 7 percent drop:** Young, "Company Wellness Programs May Boost Bottom Lines, Aetna CEO Mark Bertolini Says."

59 **doing yoga one:** "Aetna Delivers Evidence-Based Mind-Body Stress Management Programs."

59 **Ray Dalio:** Courtney Comstock, "Ray Dalio is Too Modest to Admit He Returned 38% YTD Using Transcendental Meditation," *Business Insider*, October 25, 2010, www.businessinsider.com.

59 **"No one in our time":** Aleksandr Isaevich Solzhenitsyn, *The Solzhenitsyn Reader: New and Essential Writings, 1947–2005*, eds. Edward E. Ericson and Daniel J. Mahoney (Wilmington, DE: Intercollegiate Studies Institute, 2009), 623.

59 **LinkedIn CEO Jeff Weiner coined:** Jeff Weiner, "Managing Compassionately," LinkedIn, October 15, 2012, www.linkedin.com.

60 **John Mackey, the CEO of Whole Foods:** Arianna Huffington, "Redefining Success: Takeaways from Our Third Metric Conference," *The Huffington Post*, June 14, 2013, www.huffingtonpost.com.

60 **Farhad Chowdhury:** Ben Weiss, "The Four Cool Ways the Top Employers Create Work-Life Balance," *U.S. News and World Report*, June 19, 2013, www.money.usnews.com.

60 **As Gregory Berns:** Gregory Berns, "Neuroscience Sheds New Light on Creativity," *Fast Company*, October 1, 2008, www.fastcompany.com.

61   **As Mark Williams explains:** Williams and Penman, *Mindfulness*, 26-27.

61   **summed up by Montaigne:** Rolf Dobelli, *Arrêtez de vous tromper: 52 erreurs de jugement qu'il vaut mieux laisser aux autres* (Paris: Eyrolles, 2012), 171.

62   **150 times a day:** James Roberts and Stephen Pirog, "A Preliminary Investigation of Materialism and Impulsiveness as Predictors of Technological Addictions Among Young Adults," *Journal of Behavioral Addictions* 2 (2012): 56–62.

62   **Worse, there is evidence:** Gary Small and Gigi Vorgan, *iBrain: Surviving the Technological Alteration of the Modern Mind* (New York: William Morrow, 2009), 2, 20.

62   **David Roberts:** David Roberts, "Goodbye for Now," *Grist*, August 19, 2013, www.grist.org.

63   **A 2012 McKinsey Global Institute study:** Michael Chui, James Manyika, Jacques Bughin, Richard Dobbs, Charles Roxburgh, Hugo Sarrazin, Geoffrey Sands, and Magdalena Westergren, "The Social Economy: Unlocking Value and Productivity Through Social Technologies," McKinsey Global Institute Report, July 2012, www.mckinsey.com.

63   **According to SaneBox:** Jennifer Senior, "How Email is Swallowing Our Lives," *New York*, July 31, 2013, www.nymag.com.

63   **she coined the term "continuous partial attention":** Linda Stone, email to the author, December 17, 2013.

63   **"email apnea":** Linda Stone, "Just Breathe: Building the Case for Email Apnea," *The Huffington Post*, February 8, 2008, www.huffington post.com.

64   **Disrupting your body's breathing pattern:** Ibid.

64   **"Email is your servant":** Tim Harford, "Ten Email Commandments," *Financial Times*, September 13, 2013, www.ft.com.

64   **Kimberly Brooks:** Kimberly Brooks, "Let's Take the Phone Stacking Game One Step Further: Ban the Meal Shot," *The Huffington Post*, September 24, 2013, www.huffingtonpost.com.

65   **The editor of *Scene* magazine Peter Davis:** Caroline Tell, "Step Away From the Phone!," *The New York Times*, September 20, 2013, www.nytimes.com.

65   **Leslie Perlow:** Leslie A. Perlow and Jessica L. Porter, "Making Time Off Predictable—And Required," *Harvard Business Review*, October 2009, www.hbr.org.

65   **company-wide program:** "Sustainable Intensity," The Boston Consulting Group, accessed December 1, 2013, www.bcg.com.

65 **And after noticing that engineers:** Chuck Leddy, "Slowing the Work Treadmill," *Harvard Gazette*, August 27, 2013, www.news.harvard.edu.

65 **A study by researchers:** Gloria Mark, Stephen Voida, and Armand Cardello, "A Pace Not Dictated by Electrons: An Empirical Study of Work Without Email" (Computer-Human Interaction Conference 2012, Proceedings of the SIGCHI Conference on Human Factors in Computing Systems, May 5–10, 2012), 555–64.

66 **That's what Shayne Hughes:** Shayne Hughes, "I Banned All Internal Emails at My Company for a Week," *Forbes*, October 25, 2012, www.forbes.com.

66 **Volkswagen has a special policy:** (1) David Burkus, "Sleepless in Senior Leadership: The Workplace Effects of Sleep Deprivation," *SmartBlog on Leadership*, July 2, 2012, www.smartblogs.com; (2) Volkswagen communication personnel, phone conversation with the author, December 19, 2013.

66 **FullContact:** Bart Lorang, "Paid Vacation? That's Not Cool. You Know What's Cool? Paid PAID Vacation," *FullContact Blog*, July 10, 2012, www.fullcontact.com.

67 **The good news, as immunologist Esther Sternberg explained:** Esther Sternberg, interview with Krista Tippett, "The Science of Healing Places with Esther Sternberg," *On Being*, American Public Media, September 27, 2012, www.onbeing.org.

67 **increased power lowers an executive's ability to be empathic:** Jeremy Hogeveen, Michael Inzlicht, and Sukhvinder Obhi, "Power Changes How the Brain Responds to Others," *Journal of Experimental Psychology: General* (2013).

67 **Another study on leadership and perspective:** (1) Adam Galinsky, Joe Magee, M. Ena Inesi, and Deborah Gruenfeld, "Power and Perspectives Not Taken," *Psychological Science* 17 (2006): 1068–74; (2) Vivek K. Wadhera, "Losing Touch," *Kellogg Insight*, November 1, 2009, www.insight.kellogg.northwestern.edu.

68 **As Sheryl Sandberg told me:** Sheryl Sandberg, email to the author, December 2013.

68 **The Huffington Post decided:** "*The Huffington Post*'s Oasis 2012: First Looks at Our DNC Retreat Center," *The Huffington Post*, September 2, 2012, www.huffingtonpost.com.

69 **As Aleksandr Solzhenitsyn asked:** Aleksandr Solzhenitsyn, *In the First Circle* (New York: Harper Perennial, 2009).

69 **"Remember the Sabbath day":** Exodus 20:8–10, ESV.

69 **For observant Jews:** "The Thirty-Nine Categories of Sabbath Work," *Orthodox Union*, accessed December 1, 2013, www.ou.org.

69 **Shabbat ends:** "Shabbat Conclusion Worship Service: Havdallah Blessings," *Reform Judaism*, accessed December 1, 2013, www.reformjudaism.org.

70 **According to a 2009 study from Brigham Young University:** Julianne Holt-Lunstad, Wendy Birmingham, Adam M. Howard, and Dustin Thoman, "Married with Children: The Influence of Parental Status and Gender on Ambulatory Blood Pressure," *Annals of Behavioral Medicine* 38 (2009): 170–79.

71 **A study commissioned by the American Psychological Association:** "Stress by Generations: 2012."

71 **Moreover, the findings:** Ibid.

71 **In the United Kingdom:** Eleanor Bradford, "Half of Teenagers Sleep Deprived, Study Says," *BBC News*, August 25, 2013, www.bbc.co.uk.

72 **heart disease:** Laura Manenschijn, L. Schaap, N. M. van Schoor, S. van der Pas, G. M. E. E. Peeters, P. Lips, J. W. Koper, and E. F. C. van Rossum, "High Long-Term Cortisol Levels, Measured in Scalp Hair, Are Associated with a History of Cardiovascular Disease," *The Journal of Clinical Endocrinology & Metabolism* 98 (2013): 2078–83.

72 **diabetes:** Masuma Novak, Lena Björck, Kok Wai Giang, Christina Heden-Ståhl, Lars Wilhelmsen, and Annika Rosengren, "Perceived Stress and Incidence of Type 2 Diabetes: A 35-Year Follow-up Study of Middle-Aged Swedish Men," *Diabetic Medicine* 30 (2013): e8–e16.

72 **obesity:** Susan Melhorn, Eric Krause, Karen Scott, Marie Mooney, Jeffrey Johnson, Stephen Woods, and Randall Sakai, "Meal Patterns and Hypothalamic NPY Expression During Chronic Social Stress and Recovery," *American Journal of Physiology: Regulatory, Integrative and Comparative Physiology* 299 (2010): 813–22.

72 **already, 19 percent of millennials:** Sharon Jayson, "Who's Feeling Stressed? Young Adults, New Survey Shows," *USA Today*, February 7, 2013, www.usatoday.com.

72 **Not surprisingly:** "Stress by Generations: 2012."

73 **Writing in *The New York Times*:** Anand Giridharadas, "Women Are at the Table, So Now What?" *The New York Times*, June 14, 2013, www.nytimes.com.

74 **As Dr. Michael Roizen:** Cheryl Powell, "Latest Cleveland Clinic Venture a Real Sleeper," *Akron Beacon Journal Online*, August 8, 2011, www.ohio.com.

74 **Bill Clinton:** Weston Kosova, "Running on Fumes: Pulling All-Nighters, Bill Clinton Spent His Last Days Obsessing Over Details and Pardons," *Newsweek*, February 26, 2001, www.newsweek.com.

74 **And in 2013, when the European Union:** Antonis Polemitis and Andreas Kitsios, "Cyprus Bailout: Stupidity, Short-Sightedness, Something Else?," *Cyprus.com*, accessed December 1, 2013, www.cyprus.com.

74 **The financial journalist Felix Salmon:** Felix Salmon, "The Cyprus Precedent," *Reuters*, March 17, 2013, www.blogs.reuters.com.

75 **"Sleep deprivation negatively impacts":** Arianna Huffington, "Why We All Need More Sleep," *The Telegraph*, January 28, 2013, www.telegraph.co.uk.

75 **A study at Duke University:** Edward Suarez, "Self-Reported Symptoms of Sleep Disturbance and Inflammation, Coagulation, Insulin Resistance and Psychosocial Distress: Evidence for Gender Disparity," *Brain, Behavior and Immunity* 22 (2008): 960–68.

75 **Till Roenneberg:** Till Roenneberg, "Five Myths About Sleep," *The Washington Post*, November 21, 2012, www.articles.washingtonpost.com.

76 **A study conducted at Harvard Medical School:** Mareen Weber, Christian Webb, Sophie Deldonno, Maia Kipman, Zachary Schwab, Melissa Weiner, and William Killgore, "Habitual 'Sleep Credit' Is Associated with Greater Grey Matter Volume of the Medial Prefrontal Cortex, Higher Emotional Intelligence and Better Mental Health," *Journal of Sleep Research* 22 (2013): 527–34.

76 **"It's like a dishwasher":** Maiken Nedergaard, interview with Jon Hamilton, "Brains Sweep Themselves Clean of Toxins During Sleep," *All Things Considered*, NPR, October 17, 2013, www.npr.org.

76 **Professor Nedergaard made an analogy:** James Gallagher, "Sleep 'Cleans' the Brain of Toxins," *BBC News*, October 17, 2013, www.bbc.co.uk.

76 **As the Great British Sleep Survey found:** "The Great British Sleep Survey 2012," *Sleepio*, accessed November 1, 2013. www.greatbritishsleepsurvey.com.

76 **A 2011 Harvard Medical School study:** Ronald Kessler, Patricia Berglund, Catherine Coulouvrat, Goeran Hajak, Thomas Roth, Victoria Shahly, Alicia Shillington, Judith Stephenson, and James Walsh, "Insomnia and the Performance of US Workers: Results from the America Insomnia Survey," *SLEEP* 34 (2011): 1161–71.

77 **A study published in *Science*:** Daniel Kahneman, Alan Krueger,

David Schkade, Norbert Schwarz, and Arthur Stone, "A Survey Method for Characterizing Daily Life Experience: The Day Reconstruction Method (DRM)," *Science* 306 (2004): 1776–80.

77 **Richard Easterlin conducted:** Richard Easterlin, "Will Raising the Incomes of All Increase the Happiness of All?" *Journal of Economic Behavior and Organization* 27 (1997): 35–47.

77 **"I have a nap":** Charlie Rose, conversation with the author, January 9, 2014.

77 **According to David Randall:** David K. Randall, "Rethinking Sleep," *The New York Times*, September 22, 2012, www.nytimes.com.

78 **Researchers at Rensselaer Polytechnic Institute:** Brittany Wood, Mark Rea, Barbara Plitnick, and Mariana Figueiro, "Light Level and Duration of Exposure Determine the Impact of Self-Luminous Tablets on Melatonin Suppression," *Applied Ergonomics* 44 (2013): 237–40.

78 **We desperately need to purge our lives:** Anne-Marie Slaughter, "Why Women Still Can't Have It All," *The Atlantic*, June 13, 2012, www .theatlantic.com.

78 **women are the most fatigued:** "Women and Sleep," National Sleep Foundation, accessed December 1, 2013, www.sleepfoundation .org.

78 **Working moms get the least sleep:** "Yawn! Most Mothers Don't Get Enough Sleep," *Reuters/NBC News*, October 20, 2006, www.nbc news.com.

78 **"Women are significantly":** Michael Breus, conversation with the author, July 23, 2010.

79 **Dr. Breus swears that:** Jenny Stamos Kovacs, "Lose Weight While You Sleep!," *Glamour*, February 2, 2009, www.glamour.com.

79 **"Everything you do":** Michael Breus, conversation with the author, July 23, 2010.

79 **There's a reason why:** Robert L. Snow, *Deadly Cults: The Crimes of True Believers* (Westport, Conn.: Praeger, 2003), 161.

82 **Professor Roenneberg explains:** Roenneberg, "Five Myths About Sleep."

82 **He goes on:** Ibid.

82 **According to a recent study:** Kelly Glazer Baron, Kathryn Reid, and Phyllis Zee, "Exercise to Improve Sleep in Insomnia: Exploration of the Bidirectional Effects," *Journal of Clinical Sleep Medicine* 9 (2013): 819–84.

83 **getting more sleep can lead to weight loss:** Kovacs, "Lose Weight While You Sleep!"

84   **And to help keep her appointment:** Cindi Leive, "Sleep Challenge 2010: Three Tiny Things I Wish I Had Known Years Ago," *Glamour*, January 7, 2010, www.glamour.com.

86   **Dr. Breus explains:** Michael J. Breus, January 20, 2010 (12:51 p.m.), comment on "Sleep Challenge 2010: Perchance to Dream," *The Huffington Post*, January 19, 2010, www.huffingtonpost.com.

86   **summed up by Rumi:** Jalal al-Din Rumi, *The Essential Rumi: New Expanded Edition*, trans. Coleman Barks and John Moyne (New York: HarperOne, 2004), 255.

86   **Banish all LCD screens:** Stephani Sutherland, "Bright Screens Could Delay Bedtime," *Scientific American*, February 1, 2013, www.scientific american.com.

87   **"Try unplugging":** Mika Brzezinski, "Unplugging Is Easier Said Than Done," *The Huffington Post*, January 7, 2014, www.huffington post.com.

88   **As for Cindi:** Cindi Leive, "My Digital Detox: How I Ditched My Email and Social Media for a Week . . . and the Cold Sweats Weren't So Bad," *The Huffington Post*, January 8, 2014, www.huffingtonpost.com.

89   **ten years ago, Cheri Mah:** Peter Keating, "Sleeping Giants," *ESPN The Magazine*, April 5, 2012, www.espn.go.com.

89   **Some early studies:** Ibid.

89   **Over three seasons:** Ibid.

90   **Not only did on-court performance improve:** Erin Allday, "Stanford Athletes Sleep for Better Performance," *San Fransisco Chronicle*, July 4, 2011, www.sfgate.com.

90   **In 2005, the U.S. Olympic Committee:** Keating, "Sleeping Giants."

90   **And many have taken the advice to heart:** Kimberly Boyd, "3 Sleep Lessons We Can Learn from Olympians," One Medical Group, August 10, 2012, www.onemedical.com.

90   **The Dallas Mavericks:** Jeff Caplan, "Mavs First to Dive into Fatigue Analysis," *Hang Time Blog*, October 16, 2013, www.hangtime.blogs.nba .com.

91   **Los Angeles Lakers superstar Kobe Bryant:** Keating, "Sleeping Giants."

91   **He's also done meditation:** "Athletes Who Meditate: Kobe Bryant and Other Sports Stars Who Practice Mindfulness," *The Huffington Post*, May 30, 2013, www.huffingtonpost.com.

91   **Jackson also taught the concept:** Phil Jackson, interview with Oprah Winfrey, *Super Soul Sunday*, Oprah Winfrey Network, June 16, 2013.

91   **When Michael Jordan was the star:** George Mumford, interview

with Lineage Project, accessed December 1, 2013, www.lineageproject
.org.

91   **And a video of:** "Athletes Who Meditate."

91   **Former Miami Dolphins running back:** Ibid.

92   **Tennis great Ivan Lendl:** Jim Loehr and Tony Schwartz, *The Power
      of Full Engagement: Managing Energy, Not Time, Is the Key to High Per-
      formance and Personal Renewal* (New York: Free Press, 2003), Kindle
      edition, 2731–36.

92   **Charlie Rose, in an interview with Murray:** Charlie Rose, interview
      with Andy Murray, *Charlie Rose*, Public Broadcasting Service, Septem-
      ber 11, 2012.

92   **As Tony Schwartz:** Tony Schwartz, "How to Recover Your Core
      Rhythm," *Harvard Business Review*, October 26, 2011, www.blogs.hbr
      .org.

92   **"The same rhythmic movement":** Ibid.

93   **In a study last year at the University of Washington:** David Levy,
      Jacob Wobbrock, Alfred Kaszniak, and Marilyn Ostergren, "The Ef-
      fects of Mindfulness Meditation Training on Multitasking in a High-
      Stress Information Environment," *Proceedings of Graphics Interface*
      (2012): 45–52, www.faculty.washington.edu.

93   **"Meditation is a lot like":** Anita Bruzzese, "Meditation Can Keep You
      More Focused at Work, Study Says," *USA Today*, July 10, 2012, www
      .usatoday30.usatoday.com.

94   **Silicon Valley executive Nilofer Merchant:** David Hochman, "Hol-
      lywood's New Stars: Pedestrians," *The New York Times*, August 16,
      2013, www.nytimes.com.

94   **One of my favorite phrases:** "Solvitur ambulando," *Online Etymology
      Dictionary*, www.dictionary.reference.com.

95   **Indeed, doctors are discovering:** Judith Lothian, "Safe, Healthy
      Birth: What Every Pregnant Woman Needs to Know," *The Journal of
      Perinatal Education* 18 (2009): 48–54.

95   **"Ithaka" by the Greek poet Constantine Cavafy:** C. P. Cavafy, *Col-
      lected Poems*, trans. Edmund Keeley, Philip Sherrard, ed., and George
      Savidis, rev. ed. (Princeton, NJ: Princeton University Press, 1992), 36.

96   **Thomas Jefferson claimed:** Thomas Jefferson to Peter Carr, August
      19, 1785, in *The Avalon Project: Documents in Law, History and Diplo-
      macy*, accessed December 1, 2013, www.avalon.law.yale.edu.

96   **For Ernest Hemingway:** Ernest Hemingway, *A Moveable Feast: The
      Restored Edition* (New York: Scribner, 2009), 37.

96   **Nietzsche went even further and proclaimed:** Friedrich Nietzsche,

Sämtliche Werke: kritische Studienausgabe in 15 Bänden / 6 Der Fall Wagner. Götzen-Dämmerung. Der Antichrist. Ecce home. Dionysos-Dithyramben. Nietzsche contra Wagner, eds. Giorgio Colli and Mazzino Montinari (Munich: Deutscher Taschenbuch Verlag, 1988), 64.

96 **For Henry David Thoreau:** Henry David Thoreau, "Walking," *The Atlantic,* June 1, 1862, www.theatlantic.com.

96 **Scientific studies increasingly show:** Kim Painter, "Exercise Helps Fight Anxiety, Depression," *USA Today,* April 26, 2010, www.usatoday30 .usatoday.com.

97 **University of Essex:** "Ecotherapy: The Green Agenda for Mental Health," *Mind Week Report,* May 2007, www.mind.org.uk.

97 **Psychologist Laurel Lippert Fox:** Hochman, "Hollywood's New Stars: Pedestrians."

97 **according to the World Health Organization:** "Depression," World Health Organization Fact Sheet, October 2012, www.who.int.

97 **Research has shown:** Amanda Gardner, "Being Near Nature Improves Physical, Mental Health," *USA Today,* October 15, 2009, www .usatoday30.usatoday.com.

97 **He coauthored a study:** Netta Weinstein, Andrew Przybylski, and Richard Ryan, "Can Nature Make Us More Caring? Effects of Immersion in Nature on Intrinsic Aspirations and Generosity," *Personality and Social Psychology Bulletin* 35 (2009): 1315–29.

97 **Another study, this one by Dutch researchers:** Jolana Maas, Robert Verheij, Peter Groenewegen, Sjerp de Vries, and Peter Spreeuwenberg, "Green Space, Urbanity, and Health: How Strong is the Relation?," *Journal of Epidemiology and Community Health* 60 (2006): 587–92.

98 **"As health-care costs spiral":** Gardner, "Being Near Nature Improves Physical, Mental Health."

98 **According to an American Cancer Society study:** (1) Alpa Patel, Leslie Bernstein, Anusila Deka, Heather Spencer Feigelson, Peter T. Campbell, Susan M. Gapstur, Graham A. Colditz, and Michael J. Thun, "Leisure Time Spent Sitting in Relation to Total Mortality in a Prospective Cohort of US Adults," *American Journal of Epidemiology* 172 (2010): 419-29; (2) James A. Levine, "What Are the Risks of Sitting Too Much?" Mayo Clinic: Adult Health, accessed December 1, 2013, www.mayoclinic.com.

98 **A 1950s study:** William Hudson, "Sitting for Hours Can Shave Years off Life," *CNN,* June 24, 2011, www.cnn.com.

98 **A study led by University of Illinois:** (1) Michelle Voss, Ruchika Prakash, Kirk Erickson, Chandramallika Basak, Laura Chaddock,

Jennifer S. Kim, Heloisa Alves, Susie Heo, Amanda Szabo, Siobhan White, Thomas Wójcicki, Emily Mailey, Neha Gothe, Erin Olson, Edward McAuley, and Arthur F. Kramer, "Plasticity of Brain Networks in a Randomized Intervention Trial of Exercise Training in Older Adults," *Frontiers in Aging Neuroscience* 2 (2010): 32; (2) "Attention, Couch Potatoes! Walking Boosts Brain Connectivity, Function," University of Illinois at Urbana-Champaign press release, August 27, 2010, on *Science Daily*, www.sciencedaily.com.

98 **Though he didn't have the science:** Henry David Thoreau, *Thoreau: A Book of Quotations*, ed. Bob Blaisdell (Mineola, N.Y.: Dover, 2000), 26.

98 **In her book *Wanderlust*:** Rebecca Solnit, *Wanderlust: A History of Walking* (New York: Penguin, 2001), 29.

99 **the concept of Ma:** Isao Tsujimoto, "The Concept of 'Ma' in Japanese Life and Culture," video lecture, JapanNYC from Carnegie Hall, New York, NY, April 27, 2011.

99 **"Except for the point":** Manmohan K. Bhatnagar, ed., *Twentieth Century Literature in English, Volume 2* (New Delhi: Atlantic Publishers and Distributors, 2000), 56.

99 **"Space is substance":** Alan Fletcher, *The Art of Looking Sideways* (London: Phaidon, 2001), 370.

100 **"Words inscribe a text":** Geoff Nicholson, *The Lost Art of Walking: The History, Science, and Literature of Pedestrianism* (New York: Riverhead Books, 2008), 27.

100 **Even the supremely focused Thoreau:** Thoreau, "Walking."

101 **Journalist Wayne Curtis:** Wayne Curtis, "The Walking Dead," *The Smart Set*, August 19, 2013, www.thesmartset.com.

101 **He cites a University of Washington study:** Leah Thompson, Frederick Rivara, Rajiv Ayyagari, and Beth Ebel, "Impact of Social and Technological Distraction on Pedestrian Crossing Behaviour: An Observational Study," *Injury Prevention* 19 (2012): 232–37.

101 **Another study found:** Eric Lamberg and Lisa Muratori, "Cell Phones Change the Way We Walk," *Gait and Posture* 35 (2012): 688–90.

101 **As *Guardian* columnist Oliver Burkeman:** Oliver Burkeman, "Together We Can Fight the Scourge of Texting While Walking," *The Guardian*, October 28, 2013, www.theguardian.com.

101 **In December 2013:** "Tourist Walks off Australia Pier While Checking Facebook," *BBC News*, December 19, 2013, www.bbc.co.uk.

101 **According to an Ohio State University:** "Distracted Walking: Injuries Soar for Pedestrians on Phones," Ohio State Research and Communications press release, June 19, 2013, www.researchnews.osu.edu.

102 **"I suspect the greatest mental benefits":** Oliver Burkeman, "This Column Will Change Your Life: A Step in the Right Direction," *The Guardian*, July 23, 2010, www.theguardian.com.

102 **Gregory Berns:** Gregory Berns, "Neuroscience Sheds New Light on Creativity," *Fast Company*, October 1, 2008, www.fastcompany.com.

103 **Allen McConnell, professor of psychology at Miami University:** Allen McConnell, "Friends with Benefits: Pets Make Us Happier, Healthier," *Psychology Today*, July, 11, 2011, www.psychologytoday .com.

103 **In another study:** Allen McConnell, Christina Brown, Tony Shoda, Laura Stayton, and Colleen Martin, "Friends with Benefits: On the Positive Consequences of Pet Ownership," *Journal of Personality and Social Psychology* 101 (2011): 1239–52.

103 **Interestingly, the studies:** McConnell, "Friends with Benefits."

103 **Like spouses and close friends:** Ibid.

103 **But the benefits of pets:** Kathleen Doheny, "Pets for Depression and Health," WebMD, accessed December 1, 2103, www.webmd.com.

104 **reduced risk of heart disease:** Glenn N. Levine, Karen Allen, Lynne T. Braun, Hayley E. Christian, Erika Friedmann, Kathryn A. Taubert, Sue Ann Thomas, Deborah L. Wells, and Richard A. Lange, "Pet Ownership and Cardiovascular Risk: A Scientific Statement from the American Heart Association," *Circulation* 127 (2013): 2353–63.

104 **lower levels of stress:** "Dog's Best Friend? You!," *Daily Mail*, accessed December 1, 2013, www.dailymail.co.uk.

104 **decreased for workers:** Randolph Barker, Janet Knisely, Sandra Barker, Rachel Cobb, and Christine Schubert, "Preliminary Investigation of Employee's Dog Presence on Stress and Organizational Perceptions," *International Journal of Workplace Health Management* 5 (2012): 15–30.

104 **said Randolph Barker:** Sathya Abraham, "Benefits of Taking Fido to Work May Not Be Far-Fetched," VCU Medical Center press release, March 30, 2012, www.news.vcu.edu.

104 **Barker also found:** Ibid.

104 **Today, only 17 percent:** Claire Suddath, "The Shaggy, Slobbery World of Pet-Friendly Offices," *Businessweek*, June 1, 2012, www.busi nessweek.com.

104 **Google takes it so seriously:** "Google Code of Conduct," Google Investor Relations, last modified April 25, 2012, www.investor.google .com.

105 **After the tragic massacre in Newtown:** "Newtown Says Thank You

to Therapy Dogs," *The Huffington Post*, June 25, 2013, www.huffington post.com.

105 **Another young girl and a therapy dog:** Jane Teeling and Aine Pennello, "Sandy Hook Student, Rescue Dog Bond: 'She Just Feels Safe,'" *Today News*, August 25, 2013, www.today.com.

106 **In her book:** *On Looking: Eleven Walks with Expert Eyes*, Simon & Schuster, accessed December 1, 2013, www.pages.simonandschuster .com.

106 **"A person can learn":** John Grogan, *Marley and Me* (New York: William Morrow, 2005), 279.

106 **Novelist Jonathan Carroll:** "FAQ," JonathanCarroll.com, accessed November 13, 2013, www.jonathancarroll.com.

107 **Peter Whoriskey:** Peter Whoriskey, "If You're Happy and You Know It . . . Let Your Government Know," *The Washington Post*, March 29, 2012, www.articles.washingtonpost.com.

107 **articulated by Robert F. Kennedy in 1968:** Robert F. Kennedy, "Remarks at the University of Kansas" (speech, Lawrence, Kansas, March 18, 1968), John F. Kennedy Presidential Library and Museum, www .jfklibrary.org.

108 **In France in 2008:** (1) Joseph E. Stiglitz, Amartya Sen, and Jean-Paul Fitoussi, "Report by the Commission on the Measurement of Economic Performance and Social Progress," September 14, 2009, www .stiglitz-sen-fitoussi.fr; (2) Peter Whoriskey, "If You're Happy and You Know It . . . Let Your Government Know."

108 **David Cameron:** Allegra Stratton, "David Cameron Aims to Make Happiness a New GDP," *The Guardian*, November 14, 2010, www .theguardian.com.

108 **Four years later, he announced:** Hélène Mulholland and Nicholas Watt, "David Cameron Defends Plans for Wellbeing Index," *The Guardian*, November 25, 2010, www.theguardian.com.

109 **"Better Life Index":** Irene Chapple, "Survey: Australia the 'Lucky Country' for a Better Life," *CNN*, May 31, 2013, www.cnn.com.

109 **And the United Nations:** "Report Calls on Policymakers to Make Happiness a Key Measure and Target of Development," United Nations Sustainable Development Solutions Network press release, accessed December 1, 2013, UNSDSN website, www.unsdsn.org.

109 **"subjective well-being":** Whoriskey, "If You're Happy and You Know It . . . Let the Government Know."

109 **In fact, the idea of measuring our well-being:** "No Longer the Dismal Science?" *The Economist*, April 6, 2012, www.economist.com.

110 **In the United Kingdom, for instance:** "Personal Well-being Across the UK, 2012/13," Office of National Statistics, accessed December 1, 2013, www.ons.gov.uk.

110 **as some papers trumpeted:** Patrick Collinson, "UK Population's Happiness is on the Up," *The Guardian*, July 30, 2013, www.theguardian.com.

110 **In 2011, there were:** Mark Easton, "The North/South Divide on Antidepressants," *BBC News*, August 2, 2012, www.bbc.co.uk.

Wisdom

115 **"The endless cycle":** Cleanth Brooks, *The Hidden God: Hemingway, Faulkner, Yeats, Eliot, and Warren* (New Haven, CT: Yale University Press, 1963), 84.

117 **like rats in the famous experiment:** B. F. Skinner, *The Behavior of Organisms: an Experimental Analysis* (New York: Appleton-Century-Crofts, 1938).

117 **"Puffed up by his":** Christopher Booker, *The Seven Basic Plots: Why We Tell Stories* (New York: Continuum, 2004), 330.

118 **"Not a single sparrow":** Matt. 10:29, NLT.

118 **"Perhaps all the dragons":** Rainer Maria Rilke, *Letters to a Young Poet*, trans. Reginald Snell (New York: Start Publishing, 2013), Kindle edition, 623–24.

118 **Marcus Aurelius:** Jonathan Star, *Two Suns Rising: A Collection of Sacred Writings* (New York: Bantam Books, 1991), 105.

121 **"Resentment is like drinking poison":** Carrie Fisher, *Wishful Drinking* (New York: Simon & Schuster, 2008), 153.

122 **"all of humanity's problems":** Blaise Pascal, *Pensées* (Paris: Société Française d'imprimerie et de Librairie, 1907), 345.

124 **write about her struggle:** Christina Huffington, "Addiction Recovery: Getting Clean At 22," *The Huffington Post*, April 13, 2013, www.huffingtonpost.com.

125 **"Here's what no one tells you":** Christina Huffington, "Cocaine Almost Killed Me," *Glamour*, September 2013, 290.

125 **"The harder we press":** Stephen Nachmanovitch, *Free Play: Improvisation in Life and Art* (New York: Tarcher, 1991), 64.

127 **"intentionally bringing into awareness":** Williams and Penman, *Mindfulness*, 109.

127 **Gratitude exercises have been:** Joyne Bono, Theresa Glomb, Winny Shen, Eugene Kim, and Amanda Koch, "Building Positive Resources:

Effects of Positive Events and Positive Reflection on Work-Stress and Health," *Academy of Management Journal* 56 (2012): 1601.

129 **"Grace isn't something":** John-Roger and Paul Kaye, *The Rest of Your Life: Finding Repose in the Beloved* (Los Angeles: Mandeville, 2007), Kindle edition, 1983–85.

129 **"On a day when":** Daniel Ladinsky, trans., *Love Poems from God: Twelve Sacred Voices from the East and West* (New York: Penguin, 2002), 79.

129 **"It is a glorious destiny":** Thomas Merton, *Conjectures of a Guilty Bystander* (New York: Doubleday, 1966), 154.

130 **"a life oriented around gratefulness":** Robert A. Emmons and Michael E. McCullough, eds., *The Psychology of Gratitude* (Oxford: Oxford University Press, 2004), Kindle edition, 152–73.

130 **There had been many warning signs:** Andrew Wallace-Hadrill, "Pompeii: Portents of Disaster," BBC History, March 29, 2011, www .bbc.co.uk.

132 **Intuition, not intellect:** William Hermans, *Einstein and the Poet: In Search of the Cosmic Man* (Wellesley, MA: Branden Books, 2013), 17.

132 **The third-century philosopher Plotinus:** Caroline Spurgeon, *Mysticism in English Literature* (Cambridge, Eng.: Cambridge University Press, 2011), 154.

132 **Science has confirmed:** Gary Klein, *Sources of Power: How People Make Decisions* (Cambridge, MA: MIT Press, 1999), 3.

132 **"It has long been realized":** Martin Seligman and Michael Kahana, "Unpacking Intuition: A Conjecture," *Perspectives on Psychological Science* 4 (2009): 399–402.

133 **Malcolm Gladwell:** Malcolm Gladwell, *Blink: The Power of Thinking Without Thinking* (New York: Little, Brown, and Company, 2005), 11.

133 **But a few art historians:** Ibid., 8.

133 **In his book *Sources of Power*:** Gary Klein, *Sources of Power*, 32.

134 **When he asked them how:** Ibid., 40.

135 **"The longer we wait":** Gary Klein, *Intuition at Work: Why Developing Your Gut Instinct Will Make You Better at What You Do* (New York: Doubleday Business, 2002), 35.

136 **sleep deprivation lowers:** Killgore, Kahn-Greene, Lipizzi, Newman, Kamimori, and Balkin, "Sleep Deprivation Reduces Perceived Emotional Intelligence and Constructive Thinking Skills."

136 **And when we're sleep deprived:** Christopher M. Barnes, John Schaubroeck, Megan Huth, and Sonia Ghumman, "Lack of Sleep and Unethical Conduct," *Organizational Behavior and Human Decision Processes* 115 (2011): 169–80.

136 **"Intuition is soul guidance"**: Paramhansa Yogananda, *Autobiography of a Yogi* (Nevada City, CA: Crystal Clarity Publishers, 2003), Kindle edition, 2348–50.

137 **"The people in the Indian countryside"**: Isaacson, *Steve Jobs*, 48.

137 **It helps us live:** Pierre Hadot, *The Inner Citadel: The Meditations of Marcus Aurelius*, trans. Michael Chase (Cambridge, MA: Harvard University Press, 2002).

138 **"You learn to speak"**: Jean Pierre Camus, *The Spirit of S. Francis de Sales: Bishop and Prince of Geneva* (London: Rivingtons, 1880), 3.

139 **"People have a pathological"**: Matt Richtel, "Silicon Valley Says Step Away from the Device," *The New York Times*, July 23, 2012, www .nytimes.com.

139 **"What we know from the neuroscience"**: Mark Williams, "Stress and Mindfulness," *Mindful*, accessed December 1, 2013, www .mindful.org.

140 **"cultivates our ability"**: Ibid.

140 **As Nassim Taleb:** Nassim N. Taleb, "Beware the Big Errors of 'Big Data,'" *Wired*, February 8, 2013, www.wired.com.

140 **"There are many things"**: David Brooks, "What Data Can't Do," *The New York Times*, February 18, 2013, www.nytimes.com.

140 **Harvard Business School professor Nancy Koehn:** Nancy F. Koehn, "Crisis Leadership: Lessons from Here and Now," presentation, Aspen Ideas Festival, Aspen, June 28, 2013, www.aspenideas.org.

141 **More than three thousand:** "What is Distracted Driving?," Distraction.gov, accessed December 1, 2013, www.distraction.gov.

141 **Lori Leibovich:** Lori Leibovich, "Mom's Digital Diet," *The Huffington Post*, October 24, 2012, www.huffingtonpost.com.

141 **Caroline Knorr from Common Sense Media:** (1) Caroline Knorr, "Study Reveals Just How Much Our Kids Love Digital Devices," *The Huffington Post*, October 30, 2013, www.huffingtonpost.com; (2) "Zero to Eight: Children's Media Use in America 2013," Common Sense Media, October 28, 2013, www.commonsensemedia.org.

141 **According to Stephanie Donaldson-Pressman:** Rebecca Jackson, "How Changes in Media Habits Could Transform Your Child's Mental Health," *The Huffington Post*, October 9, 2013, www.huffington post.com.

142 **"the average eight- to ten-year-old"**: "Policy Statement: Children, Adolescents, and the Media," *Pediatrics: Official Journal of the American Academy of Pediatrics* 132 (2013): 959.

142 **Louis C.K. has put:** Louis C.K., *Oh My God: An HBO Comedy Special* (2013; Phoenix, AZ: HBO).

143 **"The Day I Stopped Saying 'Hurry Up'":** Rachel Macy Stafford, "The Day I Stopped Saying 'Hurry Up,'" *The Huffington Post*, August 6, 2013, www.huffingtonpost.com.

143 **"My heart leaps":** William Wordsworth, *The Collected Poems of William Wordsworth* (Hertfordshire: Wordsworth Editions, 1998), 91.

144 **A study led by Lijing L. Yan:** Lijing L. Yan, Kiang Liu, Karen A. Matthews, Martha L. Daviglus, T. Freeman Ferguson, and Catarina I. Kiefe, "Psychosocial Factors and Risk of Hypertension: The Coronary Artery Risk Development in Young Adults (CARDIA) Study," *The Journal of the American Medical Association* 290 (2003): 2138–48.

144 **As nutrition expert Kathleen M. Zelman says:** Kathleen M. Zelman, "Slow Down, You Eat Too Fast," *WebMD*, accessed December 1, 2013, www.webmd.com.

144 **Even sex is better:** Janis Graham, "8 Reasons to Slooow Down," *WebMD*, accessed December 10, 2013, www.webmd.com.

144 **Research published in the *Harvard Business Review*:** Teresa M. Amabile, Constance N. Hadley, and Steven J. Kramer, "Creativity Under the Gun," *Harvard Business Review*, August 2002, www.hbr.org.

145 **"Our computers, our movies":** *Faster: The Acceleration of Just About Everything*, Random House, accessed December 1, 2013, www.randomhouse.com.

145 **"time famine":** Perlow, "The Time Famine: Toward a Sociology of Work Time."

146 **"Her heart sat silent":** Christina Rossetti, *Selected Poems*, ed. C. H. Sisson (New York: Routledge, 2002), 106.

147 **As physicist Paul Davies wrote:** Paul Davies, "That Mysterious Flow," *Scientific American*, September 2002, 42.

147 **Studies have shown that:** Keith O'Brien, "How to Make Time Expand," *The Boston Globe*, September 9, 2012, www.bostonglobe.com.

147 **According to a 2011 Gallup poll:** Magali Rheault, "In U.S., 3 in 10 Working Adults Are Strapped for Time," Gallup, July 20, 2011, www.gallup.com.

148 **According to a 2008 Pew report:** "Free Time: Middle America's Top Priority," *Pew Research Center*, July 9, 2008, www.pewresearch.org.

148 **Vatsal Thakkar, a psychiatry professor:** Vatsal G. Thakkar, "Diagnosing the Wrong Deficit," *The New York Times*, April 27, 2013, www.nytimes.com.

149 **"I give it to you":** William Faulkner, *The Sound and the Fury* (New York: Vintage Books, 1990), 76.

149 **As Carl Honoré:** Carl Honoré, *In Praise of Slowness: How a Worldwide Movement Is Challenging the Cult of Speed* (New York: HarperOne, 2004), 275.

150 **"Scrooge with a stopwatch":** Ibid., 3.

150 **"Have I gone":** Ibid.

150 **The Slow Food movement:** "Our History," Slow Food International, accessed December 1, 2013, www.slowfood.com.

150 **"Slow Thinking is intuitive":** Carl Honoré, "In Praise of Slow Thinking," *The Huffington Post*, October 23, 2009, www.huffington post.com.

151 **We are not going to eliminate:** (1) United States War Department, Henry Martyn Lazelle, and Leslie J. Perry, *The War of the Rebellion: A Compilation of the Official Records of the Union and Confederate Armies* (Washington: Government Printing Office, 1899), 786. (2) "deadline," *Online Etymology Dictionary*, www.etymonline.com.

151 **"Everything changed the day":** Brian Andreas, *Enough Time (Female)*, print.

151 **During natural disasters:** Department of Homeland Security: Science and Technology, "Lessons Learned—Social Media and Hurricane Sandy: Virtual Social Media Working Group," www.naseo.org.

151 **as Eric Schmidt:** Eric Schmidt and Jared Cohen, *The New Digital Age: Reshaping the Future of People, Nations and Business* (New York: Alfred A. Knopf, 2013), 230.

152 **Whether it's CollegeHumor:** Zachary Sniderman, "Do Celebrities Really Help Online Causes?," *Mashable*, June 29, 2011, www.mashable .com.

152 **"It Gets Better":** Tara Parker-Pope, "Showing Gay Teenagers a Happy Future," *The New York Times*, September 22, 2010, www.well.blogs .nytimes.com.

152 **Glen James:** Steve Annear, "Fundraiser Started for Homeless Man Who Turned in $40,000, Passport," *Boston Magazine*, September 16, 2013, www.bostonmagazine.com.

152 **"Nothing is too inconsequential":** Michael Calderone, "GOP Primary Show: Non-Stop News and Noise in the Age of Twitter," *The Huffington Post*, February 7, 2012, www.huffingtonpost.com.

152 **"We are in great haste":** Henry David Thoreau, *Walden (Or Life in the Woods)* (Radford, VA: Wilder Publications, 2008), 34.

153 **24.1 million tweets:** Omid Ashtari, "The Super Tweets of #SB47," *Twitter Blog*, February 4, 2013, www.blog.twitter.com.

153 **10,901 tweets:** "Twitter Recap: Grammys 2012," *Twitter Blog*, February 15, 2012, www.blog.twitter.com.

153 **But as Twitter's Rachael Horwitz:** Rachael Horwitz (Senior Manager, Twitter Communications), email to the author.

153 **there were an astounding:** Fred Graver, "#VMAs 2013," *Twitter Blog*, August 26, 2013, www.blog.twitter.com.

154 **poverty is on the rise:** Robert Reich, "The Downward Mobility of the American Middle Class," *Christian Science Monitor*, February 7, 2012, www.csmonitor.com.

154 **fallen into chronic unemployment:** Yuki Noguchi, "Economists, Unemployed Fret Over Long-Term Jobless Aid Lapse," NPR, December 17, 2013, www.npr.org.

154 **And that 400 million:** "Report Finds 400 Million Children Living in Extreme Poverty," World Bank Group press release, October 10, 2013, on the World Bank website, www.worldbank.org.

155 **Or as Viral Mehta:** Viral Mehta, "Lessons in Living on the Edge from Mahatma Gandhi," *The Huffington Post*, August 31, 2012, www .huffingtonpost.com.

155 **"life audit":** It is easy to become prey to what business writer Greg McKeown calls "the undisciplined pursuit of more." He recommends conducting a regular life audit. Greg McKeown, "The Disciplined Pursuit of Less," *Harvard Business Review*, August 8, 2012, www.blogs .hbr.org.

156 **Once when I was on:** Stephen Colbert, interview with the author, *Colbert Report*, Comedy Central, September 25, 2006, www.colbert nation.com.

157 **quoting G. K. Chesterton:** Dale Ahlquist, *G. K. Chesterton: The Apostle of Common Sense* (San Francisco, CA: Ignatius, 2003), 30.

157 **Or as Julian of Norwich:** Julian of Norwich, *Revelations of Divine Love*, ed. Roger Hudleston (Mineola, NY: Dover, 2006), XXII.

157 **Or as Sophocles' Oedipus cried:** as described in Albert Camus, *The Myth of Sisyphus: And Other Essays*, trans. Justin O'Brien (New York: Random House, 1991), 122.

157 **"If you walk in with fear":** "Loving Each Day: Reflections on the Spirit Within," Movement of Spiritual Inner Awareness, November 21, 2012, www.msia.org.

157 **"When you worry":** John-Roger, *Timeless Wisdom* (Los Angeles: Mandeville, 2008), 155.

159 **"After all, computers crash":** "My Motherboard, My Self," *Sex and the City*, HBO (July 15, 2001).

159　**Karen Horneffer-Ginter asks:** Karen Horneffer-Ginter, "Full Cup, Thirsty Spirit: Why We Stink at Taking Breaks," *The Huffington Post*, April 2, 2012, www.huffingtonpost.com.

159　**As mathematician Alfred North Whitehead:** Alfred North Whitehead, *An Introduction to Mathematics* (Whitefish, MT: Kessinger, 2010), 61.

160　**Indeed, research by John Bargh:** John A. Bargh and Tanya L. Chartrand, "The Unbearable Automaticity of Being," *Social Cognition: Key Readings*, ed. David Hamilton (New York: Psychology Press, 2005), 228–49.

160　**"An old Cherokee is teaching":** C. C. Wills, *A Cherokee Wish* (Victoria, BC: FriesenPress, 2013), Kindle edition, 33–43.

161　**To Aristotle:** Aristotle, *The Nicomachean Ethics*, trans. David Ross (Oxford: Oxford University Press, 2009), Kindle edition, 3375–76.

161　**To Ovid:** John Bartlett and Geoffrey O'Brien, *Bartlett's Familiar Quotations, 18th ed.* (New York: Little, Brown and Company, 2012), 102.

161　**And as Benjamin Franklin put it:** Benjamin Franklin, *Poor Richard's Almanack* (Waterloo, IA: U.S.C. Publishing Co., 1914), 54.

161　**Charles Duhigg:** Charles Duhigg, "The Habit Loop," *The Power of Habit: Why We Do What We Do in Life and Business* (New York: Random House, 2012), 3–10.

161　**The poet Mark Nepo:** Mark Nepo, *The Book of Awakening: Having the Life You Want by Being Present to the Life You Have* (San Francisco: Conari Press, 2011), Kindle edition, 3329–30.

162　**"Keystone habits":** Duhigg, *The Power of Habit*, 100–01.

162　**As a number of psychological studies:** Ibid., 137.

162　**Dr. Judson Brewer of Yale:** Judson Brewer, "Self-Control Is a Non-Renewable Resource," *The Huffington Post*, April 15, 2013, www.huffingtonpost.com.

163　**"We get a sense of belonging":** Bev Betkowski, "Risks Hold Little Weight When It Comes to Bad Behaviour," *Folio*, December 1, 2006, www.folio.ualberta.ca.

163　**And given that we're social creatures:** Charles Duhigg, *The Power of Habit*, 124–25.

163　**This is why Alcoholics Anonymous:** Ibid., 68.

163　**In 1984:** National Highway Traffic Safety Administration, "America's Experience with Seat Belt and Child Seat Use," *Presidential Initiative for Increasing Seat Belt Use Nationwide* (1997), www.nhtsa.gov.

163　**By 2012 that number was flipped:** National Highway Traffic Safety

Administration, "Seatbelt Use in 2012—Use Rates in the States and Territories," *Traffic Safety Facts* (July 2013), www.nrd.nhtsa.dot.gov.

164 **"upstream" intervention:** Bas Verplanken and Wendy Wood, "Interventions to Break and Create Consumer Habits," *Journal of Public Policy & Marketing* 25 (2006): 90–103.

164 **Stoicism is a school of philosophy:** Dirk Baltzly, "Stoicism," *The Stanford Encyclopedia of Philosophy*, ed. Edward N. Zalta (2013), www.plato.stanford.edu.

164 **"Stoicism took off":** Rob Goodman and Jimmy Soni, "Five Reasons Why Stoicism Matters Today," *The Huffington Post*, September 29, 2012, www.huffingtonpost.com.

165 **In the W. C. Fields movie:** Wes D. Gehring, *Groucho and W. C. Fields: Huckster Comedians* (Jackson, Miss.: University Press of Mississippi, 1994), 49.

165 **In his *Meditations*:** Marcus Aurelius, *Meditations*, trans. Gregory Hays (New York: Modern Library, 2012), Kindle edition, 926–29.

166 **"a hindrance to myself":** George Long, trans., *The Discourses of Epictetus: With the Encheiridion and Fragments* (London: Long Press, 2007), 7.

166 **Or, in the classic comic strip:** Walt Kelly, *Pogo: We Have Met the Enemy and He Is Us* (New York: Simon & Schuster, 1972).

166 **As Seneca said:** Jan Nicolaas Sevenster, *Paul and Seneca* (Leiden, Netherlands: E.J. Brill, 1961), 117.

166 **"Sometimes people let":** Andy Warhol, *The Philosophy of Andy Warhol (From A to B and Back Again)* (San Diego: Harvest, 1977), 112.

167 **Viktor Frankl:** Viktor Frankl, *Man's Search for Meaning* (Boston: Beacon, 2000), 66.

167 **And what Frankl did:** Ibid., 67.

168 **"Naked I came":** Job 1:21, NASV.

168 **As Francine and David Wheeler:** "Oprah and Sandy Hook Parents Francine and David Wheeler: Ben's Light," *Super Soul Sunday*, Oprah Winfrey Network, November 24, 2013, www.oprah.com.

169 **Nelson Mandela:** Arwa Damon and Faith Karimi, "Nelson Mandela Death: World Mourns South Africa's First Black President," *CNN*, December 6, 2013, www.cnn.com.

169 **Psychologist Salvatore Maddi:** Salvatore R. Maddi and Deborah M. Khoshaba, *Resilience at Work: How to Succeed No Matter What Life Throws at You* (New York: AMACOM, 2005), 17.

170 **finding ways to use the crisis:** Ibid., 50–65.

170 **10 percent of us:** Laurence Gonzales, *Deep Survival: Who Lives, Who*

Dies, and Why : True Stories of Miraculous Endurance and Sudden Death (New York: W.W. Norton, 2004), Kindle edition, 24.

170 **"Survivors are attuned":** Ibid., 289.

170 **He cites the experience:** Ibid., 240–41.

170 **"Survivors take great joy":** Ibid., 289.

171 **The serenity prayer:** Reinhold Niebuhr, *Reinhold Niebuhr: Theologian of Public Life*, ed. Larry Rasmussen (Minneapolis: Fortress Press, 1991), 15.

Wonder

173 **"Men go forth":** St. Augustine, *The Confessions of St. Augustine, Bishop of Hippo*, trans. J. G. Pilkington (Edinburgh: T. & T. Clark, 1876), 248.

174 **Albert Huffstickler:** Albert Huffstickler, "Within and Without: Revelation," *Beneath Cherry Blossoms—The Lilliput Review Blog*, posted August 31, 2007, www.donw714.tripod.com/lilliputreviewblog.

175 **"Men were first led":** Aristotle, *Aristotle on His Predecessors: Being the First Book of His Metaphysics*, trans. A. E. Taylor (Chicago: Open Court Publishing, 1910), 75.

175 **Physicist James Clerk Maxwell's:** Arthur Koestler, *The Act of Creation* (London: Pan Books Ltd., 1964), 260.

175 **As Walt Whitman said:** Richard M. Bucke, *Walt Whitman* (Glasgow: Wilson & McCormick, 1884), 60.

176 **"Ten thousand flowers":** Wu-Men, *The Enlightened Heart: An Anthology of Sacred Poetry*, ed. Stephen Mitchell (New York: Harper Perennial, 1993), 37.

176 **As Goethe wrote:** George Henry Lewes, *The Life of Goethe*, ed. Nathan Haskell Dole (Boston: Francis A. Niccolls & Company, 1902), 129.

176 **"Atheist that I am":** Jesse Prinz, "How Wonder Works," *Aeon Magazine*, June 21, 2013, www.aeon.co.

176 **lacks the capacity to wonder:** Koestler, *The Act of Creation*, 260.

177 **"peeping Toms":** Arthur Koestler, *The Roots of Coincidence* (New York: Random House, 1972), 140.

177 **As Edgar Mitchell:** "Astronaut Quotes," The Overview Institute, accessed December 1, 2013, www.overviewinstitute.org.

177 **"What can we gain":** Thomas Merton, *The Wisdom of the Desert* (New York: New Directions, 1970), 11.

178 **Elon Musk:** Ashlee Vance, "Elon Musk, the 21st Century Industrialist," *Bloomberg Businessweek*, September 13, 2012, www.businessweek.com.

178 **Or, as Kurt Vonnegut:** Kurt Vonnegut, *The Sirens of Titan* (New York: RosettaBooks, 2010), Kindle edition, 320.

178 **As Professor George Vaillant:** George E. Vaillant, *Triumphs of Experience: The Men of the Harvard Grant Study* (Cambridge, MA: The Belknap Press, 2012), Kindle edition, 805–8.

178 **English poet Ted Hughes:** Ted Hughes, *Letters of Ted Hughes*, ed. Christopher Reid (London: Faber and Faber, 2007), 514.

178 **Essayist and philosopher Alain de Botton:** Alain de Botton, "Art for Life's Sake," *The Wall Street Journal*, November 3, 2013, www.online.wsj.com.

179 **Maxwell Anderson:** Maxwell L. Anderson, "Metrics of Success in Art Museums," The Getty Leadership Institute, 2004, www.cgu.edu.

179 **"catharsis":** Aristotle, *Poetics*, trans. Anthony Kenny (Oxford: Oxford University Press, 2013).

179 **"Every era has to":** Susan Sontag, *Styles of Radical Will* (New York: Picador, 2002), 3.

180 **What makes it harder:** *New York Times* critic Edward Rothstein said, "The artwork, document or fossil is a tourist site; the photograph is our souvenir. And the looking—for which museums were created—becomes a memory before it has even begun." Edward Rothstein, "From Picassos to Sarcophagi, Guided by Phone Apps," *The New York Times*, October 1, 2010, www.nytimes.com.

180 **Sherry Turkle, MIT professor:** Sherry Turkle, "The Documented Life," *The New York Times*, December 15, 2013, www.nytimes.com.

182 **In *The Shallows*:** Nicholas G. Carr, *The Shallows: What the Internet Is Doing to Our Brains* (New York: W.W. Norton, 2010), 168.

183 **Unframed:** *Unframed*, accessed December 1, 2013, www.lacma.wordpress.com/.

183 **It also launched:** "Reading Room," LACMA, accessed December 1, 2013, www.lacma.org.

183 **The Museum of Modern Art:** David Scott, "Museums, MOOCs and MoMA: The Future of Digital Education Realised?," *The Age*, December 9, 2013, www.theage.com.au.

183 **ArtBabble:** ArtBabble, accessed December 1, 2013, www.artbabble.org.

183 **Walker Art Center:** The Walker Channel, accessed December 1, 2013, www.walkerart.org.

183 **The Tate Modern:** "Apps," Tate, accessed December 1, 2013, www.tate.org.uk.

183 **the Rijksmuseum:** T. F. Foss, "Mash Up a Masterpiece, Courtesy of Amsterdam's Rijksmuseum," The Richard and Veryl Ivey Visual Resources Library, December 6, 2013, www.iveyvrl.wordpress.com.

184 **Inside this clay jug:** Kabir, *Kabir: Ecstatic Poems*, trans. Robert Bly (Boston: Beacon Press, 2011), Kindle edition, 530–32.

184 **When Socrates:** Mitchell Cohen and Nicole Fermon, eds., *Princeton Readings in Political Thought: Essential Texts Since Plato* (Princeton, NJ: Princeton University Press, 1996), 39.

186 **As philosopher Alan Watts:** Alan Watts, *This Is It: And Other Essays on Zen and Spiritual Experience* (New York: Pantheon Books, 1973), 32.

186 **the Beatles' classic:** Paul McCartney, "Let It Be," *Let It Be* (LP), Capitol Records, May 8, 1970.

187 **In the same way, a collection of poems:** Hana Volavková, ed., *I Never Saw Another Butterfly: Children's Drawings and Poems from Terezín Concentration Camp, 1942–1944* (New York: Schocken Books, 1994).

187 **Jung called the universal language of stories "archetypes":** Booker, *The Seven Basic Plots of Literature*, 240–42.

187 **Christopher Booker:** Ibid.

189 **"Ask your soul!":** Hermann Hesse, *My Belief: Essays on Life and Art*, trans. Denver Lindley (New York: Farrar, Straus and Giroux, 1974), 44.

190 **"What is success?":** Paulo Coelho, *Manuscript Found in Accra* (New York: Random House, 2013), 129.

191 **Geronda was not even that old:** Father Amfilochios, conversation with the author, 1996.

193 **according to a study by Fierce:** Randi Zuckerberg, *Dot Complicated: Untangling Our Wired Lives* (New York: HarperOne, 2013), 105.

193 **"No matter where you go":** Earl Mac Rauch, *The Adventures of Buckaroo Banzai* (New York: Pocket Books, 2001), 69.

193 **And as Dr. Rick Hanson:** Julie Beck, "How to Build a Happier Brain: A Neuropsychological Approach to Happiness, by Meeting Core Needs (Safety, Satisfaction, and Connection) and Training Neurons to Overcome a Negativity Bias," *The Atlantic*, October 23, 2013, www.theatlantic.com.

194 **philosopher Arthur Schopenhauer:** Martin Plimmer and Brian King, *Beyond Coincidence: Stories of Amazing Coincidence and the Mystery Behind Them* (New York: Thomas Dunne Books, 2013), Kindle edition, 903–04.

194 **To Carl Jung:** Ibid., 133–34.

194 **To author and journalist Arthur Koestler:** Ibid., 781–82.

195 **A woman named Mrs. Willard Lowell:** Ibid., 213–15.

195 **And then there is the man:** Sarah Koenig, "No Coincidence, No Story!," *This American Life*, Chicago Public Media, March 1, 2013, www .thisamericanlife.org.

195 **"Coincidences are kind of like shortcuts":** Ibid.

196 **In an episode on coincidences:** Ibid.

196 **Also on the show:** Ibid.

196 **Another example:** Ibid.

197 **As my sister, Agapi:** Agapi Stassinopoulos, *Unbinding the Heart: A Dose of Greek Wisdom, Generosity, and Unconditional Love* (Carlsbad, CA: Hay House, 2012), Kindle edition, 185–93.

198 **There are also plenty of uncanny historical coincidences:** Margaret P. Battin, "July 4, 1826: Explaining the Same-day Deaths of John Adams and Thomas Jefferson," *Historically Speaking: The Bulletin of the Historical Society* 6 (2005), www.bu.edu.

199 **Research has shown:** Plimmer and King, *Beyond Coincidence*, 82–84.

199 **And according to Ruma Falk:** Ruma Falk, "Judgment of Coincidences: Mine versus Yours," *The American Journal of Psychology* 102 (1989): 477–93.

199 **Plimmer and King note:** Plimmer and King, *Beyond Coincidence*, 136–41.

200 **As an old Chinese saying goes:** Koenig, "No Coincidence, No Story!"

200 **Carl Jung used the term:** Carl G. Jung, *Synchronicity: An Acausal Connecting Principle*, trans. R.F.C. Hull (Princeton: Princeton University Press, 2010), Kindle edition, 509–10.

200 **He concluded:** Ibid., 1942–43.

201 **That's perhaps why:** Plimmer and King, *Beyond Coincidence*, 223–26.

202 **as Yale scientist Pradeep Mutalik put it:** Pradeep Mutalik, "Numberplay: Rare Coincidences Are Very Common!," *The New York Times*, July 19, 2010, www.wordplay.blogs.nytimes.com.

203 **And as *The Onion*:** "World Death Rate Holding Steady at 100 Percent," *The Onion*, January 22, 1997, www.theonion.com.

205 **What made it harder for him:** Larry Witham, *Picasso and the Chess Player: Pablo Picasso, Marcel Duchamp, and the Battle for the Soul of Modern Art* (Lebanon, NH: University Press of New England, 2013), 256.

206 **His children:** Paul Johnson, *Creators: From Chaucer and Dürer to Picasso and Disney* (New York: Harper, 2006), 257.

206 **"The one aim":** Plato, *Plato: Complete Works*, eds. John M. Cooper and D. S. Hutchinson (Indianapolis: Hackett Publishing Company, 1997), 55–59.

206 **"memento mori":** Anthony W. Marx, "Address by President Anthony W. Marx," Amherst College Commencement, May 27, 2007, www.amherst.edu.

206 **Another Roman, Michelangelo:** Elisabeth Kübler-Ross, *Death: The Final Stage* (New York: Scribner, 2009), Kindle edition, 293–94.

206 **In Judiasm, mourning is divided:** "Jewish Funeral Traditions & Customs," Brighton Memorial Chapel, accessed December 1, 2013, www.brightonmemorialchapel.com.

207 **In Buddhism:** Joan Halifax, *Being with Dying: Cultivating Compassion and Fearlessness in the Presence of Death* (Boston: Shambhala, 2008), Kindle edition, 1111–13, 2980–83.

207 **As Dr. Ira Byock:** Ira Byock, *Dying Well: Peace and Possibilities at the End of Life* (New York: Riverhead Books, 1998), 86.

207 **Joan Halifax is a Zen Buddhist priest:** Halifax, *Being with Dying*, 197–99, 345–46.

208 **"Working so closely with death":** Ibid., 665–68.

208 **One particular lesson she learned:** Ibid., 1777–80.

208 **For Halifax this means:** Ibid., 355–56, 2845–46.

208 **Elisabeth Kübler-Ross writes:** Elisabeth Kübler-Ross, *Death*, 268–81, 2349–50.

209 **Kübler-Ross is:** Ibid., 267–68.

209 **Stan Goldberg:** Stan Goldberg, "The Hard Work of Dying," Stan Goldberg, Ph.D.: *Aging, Caregiving, Dying, and Recovering Joy*, 2009, stangoldbergwriter.com.

210 **In March 2010, Andy Whitfield:** Mike Fleeman, "Inside *Spartacus* Star Andy Whitfield's Brave Final Fight Against Cancer," *People*, June 26, 2012, www.people.com.

210 **In an extraordinary interview:** Tony Judt, interview with Terry Gross, "A Historian's Long View on Living with Lou Gehrig's," *This American Life*, Chicago Public Media, March 29, 2010, www.thisamericanlife.org.

211 **The idea has spread:** Jaweed Kaleem, "Death Over Dinner Convenes as Hundreds of Americans Coordinate End of Life Discussions Across U.S.," *The Huffington Post*, August 18, 2013, www.huffingtonpost.com.

211 **Like Death Over Dinner:** Paula Span, "Death Be Not Decaffeinated: Over Cup, Groups Face Taboo," *The New York Times*, June 16, 2013, www.newoldage.blogs.nytimes.com.

212 **As Pulitzer Prize–winning journalist Ellen Goodman:** Jaweed Kaleem, "Death Over Dinner, The Conversation Project Aim to Spark

Discussions about the End of Life," *The Huffington Post*, December 23, 2013, www.huffingtonpost.com.

212 **Goodman went "from covering":** Ellen Goodman, email to the author, December 27, 2013.

212 **Goodman has concluded:** Ellen Goodman, "The Most Important Conversation You'll Ever Have," *O, The Oprah Magazine*, September 17, 2012, www.oprah.com.

212 **And in most major cities:** Jaweed Kaleem, "Deathbed Singers, Threshold Choirs, Grow to Comfort Sick and Dying," *The Huffington Post*, May 2, 2013, www.huffingtonpost.com.

213 **In July 2013:** Jaweed Kaleem, "My Gift of Grace Card Game about Death Aims to Spark Conversations," *The Huffington Post*, July 29, 2013, www.huffingtonpost.com.

214 **NPR's Scott Simon:** Jaweed Kaleem, "Scott Simon's Tweets about Dying Mother Spur Conversation on Public Grief, Death on Social Media," *The Huffington Post*, August 9, 2013, www.huffingtonpost.com.

214 **"In journalism":** Ibid.

215 **Psychology professor Todd Kashdan:** Todd Kashdan, "Confronting Death with an Open, Mindful Attitude," *The Huffington Post*, March 2, 2011, www.huffingtonpost.com.

215 **Professor Kashdan goes on:** Ibid.

216 **The answer was a resounding yes:** Ibid.

216 **On October 27, 2013:** Prachi Gupta, "Laurie Anderson on Lou Reed's Death: 'We Had Prepared for This,'" *Salon*, November 6, 2013, www.salon.com.

217 **"As meditators":** Laurie Anderson, "Laurie Anderson's Farewell to Lou Reed: A Rolling Stone Exclusive," *Rolling Stone*, November 6, 2013, www.rollingstone.com.

217 **As Joan Halifax writes:** Halifax, *Being with Dying*, 1080–81.

Giving

223 **"I slept and dreamt that life":** David J. Skorton, "144th Cornell University Commencement Address," Cornell University, May 27, 2012, www.cornell.edu.

225 **more than sixteen million:** Carmen DeNavas-Walt, Bernadette Proctor, and Jessica Smith, "Income, Poverty, and Health Insurance Coverage in the United States: 2012," *Current Population Reports*, September 2013, www.census.gov.

226 **went from 37 percent in 2000:** Michelle Chau, Kalyani Thampi, and

Venessa R. Wight, "Basic Facts about Low-Income Children, 2009," National Center for Children in Poverty, October 2010, www.nccp.org.

226 **to 45 percent in 2011:** Sophia Addy, William Engelhardt, and Curtis Skinner, "Basic Facts about Low-Income Children," National Center for Children in Poverty, January 2013, www.nccp.org.

226 **a 2012 study at the University of Wisconsin:** Helen Y. Weng, Andrew S. Fox, Alexander J. Shackman, Diane E. Stodola, Jessica Z. K. Caldwell, Matthew C. Olson, Gregory M. Rogers, and Richard J. Davidson, "Compassion Training Alters Altruism and Neural Responses to Suffering," *Psychological Science* 24 (2013): 1171–80.

226 **"meditation enhances compassionate":** Paul Condon, Gaëlle Desbordes, Willa B. Miller, and David DeSteno, "Meditation Increases Compassionate Response to Suffering," *Psychological Science* Short Report (2013): 1–3.

227 **In Philadelphia, for example:** Sara Yin, "Laid-Off Lawyer Finds New Purpose in Pro Bono Foreclosure Work," *The Huffington Post*, September 22, 2010, www.huffingtonpost.com.

228 **"To feel the intimacy of brothers":** Pablo Neruda and Cesar Vallejo, *Neruda and Vallejo: Selected Poems*, trans. Robert Bly (Boston: Beacon Press, 1993), 12-13.

228 **Jacqueline Novogratz:** Jacqueline Novogratz, "How One Blue Sweater Started a Book Club and Changed Lives," *The Huffington Post*, February 16, 2010, www.huffingtonpost.com.

230 **Two thousand children:** "Children Dying Daily Because of Unsafe Water Supplies and Poor Sanitation and Hygiene, UNICEF Says," UNICEF press release, March 22, 2013, www.unicef.org.

230 **3 million children:** "Hunger Statistics," World Food Programme, accessed January 1, 2014, www.wfp.org.

230 **1.4 million from diseases:** "Seven Key Reasons Why Immunization Must Remain a Priority in the WHO European Region," European Immunization Week, accessed December 1, 2013, www.euro.who.int.

230 **A famous passage from Matthew:** Matt. 7:24–27, NIV.

231 **Watching Oprah Winfrey interview:** Diana Nyad, interview with Oprah Winfrey, *Super Soul Sunday*, Oprah Winfrey Network, October 13, 2013, www.oprah.com.

231 **John Burroughs put it:** John Burroughs, "The Divine Soil," *The Atlantic*, April 1908, www.theatlantic.com.

232 **"On the question":** Anthony de Mello, *One Minute Wisdom* (New York: Doubleday, 1986), 153.

232 **what David Foster Wallace called:** "David Foster Wallace, In His Own Words," *The Economist: Intelligent Life*, September 19, 2008, www .moreintelligentlife.com.

233 **"From everyone to whom":** Luke 12:48, NIV.

233 **The Bhagavad Gita:** Eknath Easwaran, trans., *The Bhagavad Gita* (Tomales, CA: Nilgiri, 2007), Kindle edition, 105.

234 **story by Rabbi David Wolpe:** David J. Wolpe, *Why Faith Matters* (New York: HarperCollins, 2008), Kindle edition, 1132–44.

235 **Bill Drayton coined the term:** Caroline Hsu, "Entrepreneur for Social Change," *U.S. News and World Report*, October 31, 2005, www .usnews.com.

235 **Sally Osberg, CEO of the Skoll Foundation:** Sally Osberg, "Social Entrepreneurship: Why It Matters," *The Huffington Post*, March 28, 2012, www.huffingtonpost.com.

236 **As author and entrepreneur Seth Godin:** Seth Godin, "Quid Pro Quo (You Can't Play Ping Pong by Yourself)," *Seth's Blog*, www .sethgodin.typepad.com.

236 **"No one can live happily":** Lucius Annaeus Seneca, *Ad Lucilium Epistulae Morales, vol. 1*, trans. Richard M. Gummere (London: William Heineman, 1917), 315.

237 **David Letterman:** Dave Itzkoff, "A Traitor to His Class? Such Good Fun," *The New York Times*, November 4, 2013, www.nytimes.com.

237 **as Einstein put it:** "Einstein Is Terse in Rule for Success," *The New York Times*, June 20, 1932, www.query.nytimes.com.

237 **the hormone oxytocin:** Navneet Magon and Sanjay Kalra, "The Orgasmic History of Oxytocin," *Indian Journal of Endocrinology and Metabolism* 15 (2011): 156–61.

237 **Researchers have found:** M. J. Stephey, "Can Oxytocin Ease Shyness?," *Time*, July 21, 2008, www.content.time.com.

237 **In a study by neuroscientist Paul Zak:** Wynne Parry, "Naughty or Nice? A Brain Chemical May Tell," *Live Science*, December 17, 2012, www.livescience.com.

238 **Oxytocin, the "love hormone":** Magon and Kalra, "The Orgasmic History of Oxytocin: Love, Lust, and Labor," 156–61.

238 **As professor of psychiatry Richard Davidson:** Richard Davidson, email to the author, January 1, 2014.

238 **psychologist Paul Ekman:** Daniel Goleman, "Hot to Help: When Can Empathy Move Us to Action?," *Greater Good*, March 1, 2008, www .greatergood.berkeley.edu.

239 **One study demonstrated:** Matthew D. Lieberman, *Social: Why Our*

Brains Are Wired to Connect (New York: Crown Publishers, 2013), Kindle edition, 3489–93.

239 **Harvard Business School:** Lara B. Aknin, Christopher P. Barrington-Leigh, Elizabeth W. Dunn, John F. Helliwell, Robert Biswas-Diener, Imelda Kemeza, Paul Nyende, Claire Ashton-James, and Michael I. Norton, "Prosocial Spending and Well-Being: Cross-Cultural Evidence for a Psychological Universal," Harvard Business School working paper, 2010, www.hbs.edu.

239 **A study led by scientists:** Mark Wheeler, "Be Happy: Your Genes May Thank You for It," UCLA Cousins Center for Psychoneuroimmunology press release, July 29, 2013, UCLA Newsroom website, www.newsroom.ucla.edu.

240 **"If you bring forth":** The Gospel of Thomas, 76.

240 **study led by Dr. Suzanne Richards:** Caroline E. Jenkinson, Andy P. Dickens, Kerry Jones, Jo Thompson-Coon, Rod S. Taylor, Morwenna Rogers, Clare L. Bambra, Iain Lang, and Suzanne H Richards, "Is Volunteering a Public Health Intervention? A Systematic Review and Meta-Analysis of the Health and Survival of Volunteers," *BMC Public Health* 13 (2013).

240 **2005 Stanford study:** Alex H. Harris and Carl E. Thoresen, "Volunteering is Associated with Delayed Mortality in Older People: Analysis of the Longitudinal Study of Aging," *Journal of Health Psychology* 10 (2005): 739–52.

240 **A study from Duke University:** John Wilson and Marc Musick, "The Effects of Volunteering on the Volunteer," *Law and Contemporary Problems* 62 (1999): 141–68.

240 **Johns Hopkins study:** Camille Noe Pagan, "How Volunteering Boosts Your Brain," *Prevention*, November 2011, www.prevention.com.

241 **A 2013 study by UnitedHealth Group:** "Doing Good Is Good for You: 2013 Health and Volunteering Study," UnitedHealth Group, accessed December 1, 2013, www.unitedhealthgroup.com.

241 **Another 2013 study:** "Virtue Rewarded: Helping Others at Work Makes People Happier," University of Wisconsin-Madison press release, July 29, 2013, on the University of Wisconsin-Madison News website, www.news.wisc.edu.

242 **"If you want to live a longer":** Sara Konrath, "How Volunteering Can Lessen Depression and Extend Your Life," *Everyday Health*, August 22, 2013, www.everydayhealth.com.

242 **Salespeople with the highest:** Adam Grant, *Give and Take: A Revolutionary Approach to Success* (New York: Viking, 2013), 7.

242 **The highest achieving negotiators:** Ibid., 252.

242 **Grant also cites research:** Ibid., 31.

242 **Starbucks, under the leadership:** Joe Nocera, "We Can All Become Job Creators," *The New York Times*, October 17, 2011, www.nytimes .com.

242 **raised over $15 million:** "Create Jobs for USA Fund: Overview," Opportunity Finance Network, accessed December 1, 2013, www.ofn.org.

242 **more than five thousand jobs:** Ibid.

242 **Schultz explained:** Lee Brodie, "Invest in America," *Mad Money with Jim Cramer*, CNBC, July 27, 2013, www.cnbc.com.

243 **In 2013:** Howard Schultz, "Message from Howard to Partners: Come Together," Starbucks Newsroom, October 8, 2013, www.news .starbucks.com.

243 **A 2010 San Diego State University study:** "Study: Students more stressed now than during Depression?," Associated Press, January 12, 2010, www.usatoday30.usatoday.com.

243 **To teach children about emotional literacy:** Mary Gordon (Roots of Empathy founder), conversation with the author, August 30, 2013.

244 **In her program:** "Mary Gordon," *Ashoka: Innovators for the Public*, accessed December 1, 2013, www.ashoka.org.

244 **Parents teach empathy:** Maia Szalavitz and Bruce D. Perry, "Born for Love: Welcome," *Psychology Today*, February 11, 2010, www.psychology today.com.

244 **Bill Drayton emphasizes:** Bill Drayton (Ashoka CEO), conversation with the author, August 30, 2013.

245 **As Laura Arrillaga-Andreessen put it:** Laura Arrillaga-Andreessen, *Giving 2.0: Transform Your Giving and Our World* (San Francisco: Jossey-Bass, 2012), Kindle edition, 879–81.

245 **"all donors equal in the eyes":** Dennis Whittle, "Online Giving Challenge with $500,000 in Prizes," *Pulling for the Underdog: A Blog from Dennis Whittle*, December 13, 2007, www.denniswhittle.com.

245 **In 2013, Giving Tuesday:** Henry Timms (Giving Tuesday founder), email to author, December 4, 2013.

246 **And though Giving Tuesday:** "Global Giving," Giving Tuesday, accessed January 1, 2014, www.community.givingtuesday.org.

246 **Improv Everywhere:** The Carnegie Hall Orchestra, "Improv Everywhere's 'Conduct Us' Lets Random People Lead the Orchestra," *The Huffington Post*, September 25, 2013, www.huffingtonpost.com.

246 **Monica Yunus and Camille Zamora:** Joe Van Brussel, "Monica Yunus, Camille Zamora of Sing for Hope Share Why They Placed 88

Pianos throughout New York City (VIDEO)," *The Huffington Post*, July 6, 2013, www.huffingtonpost.com.

247 **Robert Egger:** Robert Egger, *Everyday Heroes: 50 Americans Changing the World One Nonprofit at a Time*, ed. Katrina Fried (New York: Welcome Books, 2012), 61.

247 **We tend to identify creativity:** David Kelley and Tom Kelley, *Creative Confidence: Unleashing the Creative Potential within Us All* (New York: Crown Publishers, 2013), 2–3.

247 **As David and Tom Kelley:** Ibid., 55.

248 **"Every man":** Henry Miller, *Henry Miller on Writing* (New York: New Directions, 1964), 25.

248 **In her book *Unbinding the Heart*:** Stassinopoulos, *Unbinding the Heart*, 45–47.

250 **The phrase "To know":** While this is commonly attributed to Ralph Waldo Emerson, the authorship is unknown: "Success," The Ralph Waldo Emerson Society, accessed December 1, 2013, www.emerson.tamu.edu.

250 **The day before she died:** Katherine Fung, "NPR's Scott Simon Live Tweeting His Mother's Final Days," *The Huffington Post*, July 29, 2013, www.huffingtonpost.com.

250 **John Bridgeland:** Ron Fournier, "The Outsiders: How Can Millennials Change Washington if They Hate It?," *The Atlantic*, August 26, 2013, www.theatlantic.com.

250 **Millennials lead the way:** "America's Civic Health Index," The National Conference on Citizenship, Executive Summary, August 27, 2009, www.ncoc.net.

251 **The numbers are even higher:** Fournier, "The Outsiders."

251 **That's the goal of the Franklin Project:** "Franklin Project: About Us," The Aspen Institute, accessed December 16, 2013, www.aspeninstitute.org.

252 **Points of Light Foundation:** "Our History," Points of Light Foundation, accessed December 1, 2013, www.pointsoflight.org.

252 **After achieving success:** "Secretary General's MDG Advocacy Group," UN News Center, accessed December 31, 2013, www.un.org.

253 **"Our generation wants":** Amanda Terkel, "National Service Ignored in 2012 Candidates' Discussion of Jobs Crisis," *The Huffington Post*, May 30, 2012, www.huffingtonpost.com.

253 **As Dr. Ervin Staub:** "Choosing to Rescue," *Facing History and Ourselves*, accessed December 1, 2013, www.facinghistory.org.

257 **The Reverend Henry Delaney:** Henry Delaney, conversation with the author, 1993.

Epilogue

259 **David Foster Wallace:** "David Foster Wallace, in His Own Words."

Appendix A

263 **"focusing is about":** Ben Popper, "Steve Jobs and the Value of Saying No," *The New York Observer*, August 25, 2011, www.betabeat.com.

263 **Third Metric features editor:** Carolyn Gregoire, "In a World of Constant Digital Distractions, These Tools Can Help You Stay Focused and Be More Present," *The Huffington Post*, December 20, 2013, www.huffingtonpost.com.

263 **In 2012, Harvard researchers:** Belinda Luscombe, "Why We Talk about Ourselves: The Brain Likes It," *Time*, May 8, 2012, www .healthland.time.com.

265 **David E. Meyer:** Steve Lohr, "Smartphone Rises Fast from Gadget to Necessity," *The New York Times*, June 9, 2009, www.nytimes.com.

267 **Taking breaks:** Diana Yates, "Brief Diversions Vastly Improve Focus, Researchers Find," University of Illinois News Bureau, February 8, 2011, www.news.illinois.edu.

269 **Higby's creators wrote:** "About This Project," Higby, accessed December 30, 2013, wolffolins.com/higby.

Appendix B

269 **compiled by Carolyn Gregoire:** Carolyn Gregoire, "These Digital Meditation Tools Can Be Your Gateway to a Calmer, More Effective Life," *The Huffington Post*, December 30, 2013.

270 **"We must get out":** Mark Williams, John Teasdale, Zindel Segal, and Jon Kabat-Zinn, *The Mindful Way Through Depression: Freeing Yourself From Chronic Unhappiness* (New York: Guilford Press, 2007), 46.

270 **"urban meditation app":** Stephen Fortune, "Rohan Gunatillake," Protein, accessed December 20, 2013, www.prote.in.

271 **Buddhify "actually changes":** "What People Think of Buddhify," Buddhify, accessed December 1, 2013, buddhify.com.

271 **MSIA's teachings consist of:** "Meditation and Spiritual Exercises," Movement of Spiritual Inner Awareness, accessed December 30, 2013, www.msiaonlineclasses.com.

272 **Chopra joined forces:** "Oprah Winfrey and Deepak Chopra Launch 21-Day Meditation Experience on Desire and Destiny," OWN: Oprah Winfrey Network press release.

274 **"power of now":** Eckhart Tolle, *The Power of Now: A Guide to Spiritual Enlightenment* (Novato, CA: New World Library, 2004).

Index